T0236248

Creating Business Applications with Microsoft 365

Techniques in Power Apps, Power BI, SharePoint, and Power Automate

Second Edition

Jeffrey M. Rhodes

Apress®

Creating Business Applications with Microsoft 365: Techniques in Power Apps, Power BI, SharePoint, and Power Automate

Jeffrey M. Rhodes
Colorado Springs, CO, USA

ISBN-13 (pbk): 978-1-4842-8822-1   ISBN-13 (electronic): 978-1-4842-8823-8
https://doi.org/10.1007/978-1-4842-8823-8

Copyright © 2022 by Jeffrey M. Rhodes

This work is subject to copyright. All rights are reserved by the Publisher, whether the whole or part of the material is concerned, specifically the rights of translation, reprinting, reuse of illustrations, recitation, broadcasting, reproduction on microfilms or in any other physical way, and transmission or information storage and retrieval, electronic adaptation, computer software, or by similar or dissimilar methodology now known or hereafter developed.

Trademarked names, logos, and images may appear in this book. Rather than use a trademark symbol with every occurrence of a trademarked name, logo, or image we use the names, logos, and images only in an editorial fashion and to the benefit of the trademark owner, with no intention of infringement of the trademark.

The use in this publication of trade names, trademarks, service marks, and similar terms, even if they are not identified as such, is not to be taken as an expression of opinion as to whether or not they are subject to proprietary rights.

While the advice and information in this book are believed to be true and accurate at the date of publication, neither the authors nor the editors nor the publisher can accept any legal responsibility for any errors or omissions that may be made. The publisher makes no warranty, express or implied, with respect to the material contained herein.

Managing Director, Apress Media LLC: Welmoed Spahr
Acquisitions Editor: Smriti Srivastava
Development Editor: Laura Berendson
Coordinating Editor: Shrikant Vishwakarma

Cover designed by eStudioCalamar

Cover image by Philip Oroni on Unsplash (www.unsplash.com)

Distributed to the book trade worldwide by Apress Media, LLC, 1 New York Plaza, New York, NY 10004, U.S.A. Phone 1-800-SPRINGER, fax (201) 348-4505, e-mail orders-ny@springer-sbm.com, or visit www. springeronline.com. Apress Media, LLC is a California LLC and the sole member (owner) is Springer Science + Business Media Finance Inc (SSBM Finance Inc). SSBM Finance Inc is a **Delaware** corporation.

For information on translations, please e-mail booktranslations@springernature.com; for reprint, paperback, or audio rights, please e-mail bookpermissions@springernature.com.

Apress titles may be purchased in bulk for academic, corporate, or promotional use. eBook versions and licenses are also available for most titles. For more information, reference our Print and eBook Bulk Sales web page at http://www.apress.com/bulk-sales.

Any source code or other supplementary material referenced by the author in this book is available to readers on GitHub (https://github.com/Apress). For more detailed information, please visit http://www. apress.com/source-code.

Printed on acid-free paper

This book is dedicated to my late parents, who steadfastly supported me my whole life: Brigadier General (ret.) James M. Rhodes, Jr., Catherine Harrington Rhodes (mother), and Sylvia Dunlevy Rhodes (stepmother).

Table of Contents

About the Author

 **Jeffrey Rhodes** is a founder and Chief Technical Officer of Platte Canyon Multimedia Software Corporation, a leader in developing commercial e-learning software. He graduated at the top of his class at the Air Force Academy, where he earned a bachelor's degree in electrical engineering. Jeff received a master's degree in economics from the London School of Economics, which he attended under a British Marshall Scholarship. He is the author of *Creating Business Applications with Office 365: Techniques in SharePoint, PowerApps, Power BI, and More*; *Programming for e-Learning Developers: ToolBook, Flash, JavaScript, and Silverlight*; and *VBTrain.Net: Creating Computer and Web Based Training with Visual Basic .NET*. He also co-wrote *The ToolBook Companion*. He lives in Colorado Springs with his wife Sue and is the proud father of his sons Derek and Michael.

About the Technical Reviewers

Fabio Claudio Ferracchiati is a senior consultant and a senior analyst/developer using Microsoft technologies. He works for BluArancio (`www.bluarancio.com`). He is a Microsoft Certified Solution Developer for .NET, a Microsoft Certified Application Developer for .NET, a Microsoft Certified Professional, and a prolific author and technical reviewer. Over the past ten years, he's written articles for Italian and international magazines and coauthored more than ten books on a variety of computer topics.

Arun Sharma is a techno-strategic leader and carries deep experience in development consulting, cloud, AI, and the IoT space. He is currently associated with Fresh & Pure, an agritech startup, in the position of Director Program Management–Automation and AI. He has expertise in various technologies (Microsoft Azure, AWS, Ali Cloud), IoT, ML, microservices, bots, Dynamics 365, PowerPlatform, SAP Crystal Reports, DevOps, Docker, and containerization. He has more than 20 years of experience in a wide range of roles such as GM–Paytm, Delivery Manager at Microsoft, Product Manager at Icertis, Lead and Architect Associate at Infosys, Executive Trainer at Aptech, and Development Consultant at CMC. He has managed CXO-level relationships on strategic levels, sales, cloud consumption, consulting services, and adoption with medium- and large-size global customers.

Acknowledgments

As I finish this, my fifth book, my mind is on my awesome family. My mom, dad, and stepmother are unfortunately no longer with us. But I still think of them often. My older brother Jim inspires me every day with how he tackles numerous health challenges, while still keeping a positive outlook and DJ'ing a weekly music program. My sister Joni is the leader of our family and has a heart of gold. She hosts every big event and is always there when you need her. She and my brother-in-law Sean are our travel buddies as well. Figure 1 is one of my favorite family pictures from when we were young.

Figure 1. *My sister Joni, my dad, my brother Jim, my mom, and me*

ACKNOWLEDGMENTS

I spent most of my teenage years with my stepmother, Sylvia, and we became very close. We lost her too early. Figure 2 is from my high school graduation, which was extra special because my dad handed out the diplomas as the Wing Commander of the Air Force Base, which is kind of like being the mayor when stationed overseas.

Figure 2. *My dad, myself, and my stepmother Sylvia at my high school graduation*

My wife Sue is my best friend and biggest supporter. I feel so fortunate that I met her at the Air Force Academy, and we've been happily married for over 34 years. Our sons Derek and Michael have made our lives infinitely richer. We are very proud of the honest and caring men they have become. We are equally proud of our daughter-in-law, Alexis. Her kindness and fun-loving nature are contagious.

Thank you all for the love and support. My life would be empty without you!

Introduction

This book is geared toward power users and what I call business developers. While some of the applications and techniques require a degree of understanding programming, my objective is to make the solutions accessible to the non-computer scientist.[1] The joy of writing an application or visualization that makes your and/or a co-worker's life better is something I hope you all can experience. Sometimes, the solutions can help hundreds or thousands of users, and other times, like the example later where I first used Access and then Power BI to help my wife detect errors in spreadsheets, just have a single user. Either way, I hope these techniques help you and your organization with these powerful tools.

Changes in This Edition

Well over half of this edition is brand new. With the huge expansion of Teams, SharePoint – in my view – has largely faded into the background. Its primary purpose now is a file storage location for Teams and as data storage via lists for Power Apps and Power Automate. In addition, Microsoft 365 is now most often deployed in the Azure cloud rather than being hosted on-premise. With that security model, it is much less common to allow custom scripting in SharePoint pages, not to mention that SharePoint pages themselves are less used compared to Teams posts, tabs in Teams channels, etc. So I have removed all the JavaScript and jQuery custom scripting examples. SharePoint Designer workflows and InfoPath forms are deprecated as well, so those are gone. Microsoft Flow has been renamed Power Automate, and I've greatly expanded its coverage and added numerous new examples of how to effectively use Power Apps and Power BI. I've also added Teams content, such as sending chats/posts and scheduling Teams Meetings via Power Automate. I've thoroughly updated the remaining content as well.

---

[1] Which I am as well. My undergraduate degree is in electrical engineering while my master's is in economics. While I took some Pascal and FORTRAN in college, I discovered my love of programming using a language called *OpenScript* in a now-defunct e-Learning authoring environment called *ToolBook*.

Audience Level

While some programming expertise will be helpful in understanding the code in Power Apps, the actions in Power Automate, and the custom columns in Power BI, I do not assume that you are a programmer. I start the book with a new *"Programming in the Power Platform"* chapter that introduces these tools and compares them to more traditional programming in .NET and HTML/JavaScript. Anyone who is willing to learn and feels at home in front of a keyboard can truly benefit.

CHAPTER 1

Programming in the Power Platform

The Power Platform is a great environment but does things a bit differently than traditional development tools. This chapter[1] illustrates this as we take on the challenge of a simple form to compose and send an email in .NET, HTML/JavaScript, Power Apps on its own, and Power Automate and Power Apps in combination. That will allow us to examine core programming concepts and explain how the Power Platform implements them, often in ways different than those of you familiar with other environments might expect. If you are not familiar with these other environments, however, feel free to jump ahead to the Power Apps section.

Core Programming Concepts

The basic idea of programming is that it is made of objects that have Properties, Methods, and Events. *Properties* are things that an object *has*. These are attributes like height, width, color, visible, and text. *Methods* are things that an object can *do*. They are actions or capabilities available in the object. A *media player* object, for example, would have events like play, rewind, pause, fast forward, and stop. *Events* are actions recognized by an object that your code can respond to. A button object has a *Click* event. A *media player* object fires an event when the media it is playing reaches its end, allowing you to jump to the next item in the playlist or prompt the user for what to do next.

---

[1] I wrote a whole book years ago with an e-Learning programming challenge implemented in ToolBook, Flash, JavaScript, and Silverlight. All of these except JavaScript are now defunct.

© Jeffrey M. Rhodes 2022
J. M. Rhodes, *Creating Business Applications with Microsoft 365*,
https://doi.org/10.1007/978-1-4842-8823-8_1

In most of our examples, we will have *Textbox* objects that contain the *To* email address and *Subject* of the email and a *RichTextBox* object that contains the *Body* of the email. These values will be *Properties* of their corresponding objects. We will then handle the *Click* event of the *Send Email* button and write code to set the properties of the appropriate *Mail* object, finally calling a *Send Email* method of that object to actually send our email. When we get to Power Apps, we will see that the event is called *OnSelect* instead of *Click*. Power Automate doesn't actually have an interface, so we will use a modified version of our Power Apps example to let Power Automate do the heavy lifting.

.NET

We will start with a standard .NET Windows Forms application using Visual Basic[2] with Visual Studio as a development environment. Figure 1-1 shows Visual Studio with the *Toolbox* on the left for dragging on controls and the design surface in the middle (with separate design and code files as discussed shortly). The *Solution Explorer* at the upper right shows all the files, while the *Properties* window below it gives an interface for setting properties for whatever object is selected. In this case, I've selected the *Send Email* button and am setting its *BackColor* property.

---

[2] I like Windows Forms for this purpose as opposed to *Windows Presentation Foundation* since its relationship between methods, properties, and events is more straightforward. As for Visual Basic, its syntax is closer to the syntax in the Power Platform. Plus, I am an old-time VB rather than C# guy.

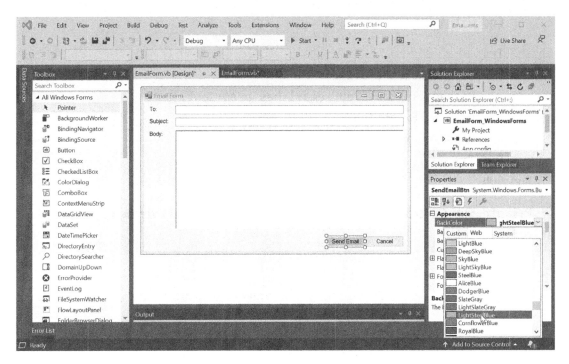

Figure 1-1. *Windows Forms Application in Visual Studio Showing the Setting of a Property*

The code is contained in the EmailForm.vb file and is shown in Listing 1-1.

Listing 1-1. Sending an Email in Windows Forms and Visual Basic.Net

```vb
Imports System.Net.Mail

Public Class EmailForm
    Private Sub SendEmailBtn_Click(sender As Object, e As EventArgs)
Handles SendEmailBtn.Click
        Dim mailId As New MailMessage()
        Dim clientId As New SmtpClient("localhost")

        With mailId
            .From = New MailAddress("info@plattecanyon.com")
            .To.Add(New MailAddress(ToBox.Text))
            .Subject = SubjectBox.Text
            .Body = BodyBox.Text
```

```
        End With

        Try
            clientId.Send(mailId)
            Message.Text = "Your email has been sent."
        Catch ex As Exception
            MessageBox.Show(ex.Message)
        End Try
    End Sub

    Private Sub CancelBtn_Click(sender As Object, e As EventArgs) Handles
CancelBtn.Click
        Me.Close()
    End Sub
End Class
```

The *Imports System.Net.Mail* line tells the code that we want to use functions within that *Namespace*. It allows us to use a shorter *MailMessage()* syntax rather than repeat the whole *System.Net.Mail.MailMessage()* part every time. All the action happens in our *Click* handler. Visual Studio automatically names our subroutine *SendEmailBtn_Click*. The important part is the *Handles SendEmailBtn.Click*. This means that this code gets called in response to the *Click* event for the button. We then create two objects: *MailMessage* and *SmtpClient*. The latter is what sends the actual email. For more elaborate implementations, we would pass it the name of the mail server and some credentials, but here, we just tell it to use our local web server (*localhost*). With our mail message, we then set its *From, To, Subject,* and *Body* properties. Notice how we read from the *ToBox, SubjectBox,* and *BodyBox* objects on the form and specifically read their *Text* properties. Notice also how naming the objects (as opposed to leaving them TextBox1, TextBox2, etc.) makes our code much more readable and easier to maintain. This will carry over to Power Apps and Power Automate as well. The *Try - Catch* syntax is used when we think our code may generate an error. Since sending an email can easily generate an error, this is appropriate. It allows us to display a message to the user instead of just crashing upon any failure. We call the *Send* method and pass our *mailId* object as a parameter. If this succeeds, we make it to the next line and we set the *Text* property of our *Message* label to "Your email has been sent."[3] If *Send* fails, the *Catch* line give us an *Exception* object. We display the *Message* property of that object. If the user clicks the *Cancel* button, we call the *Close* method of the form.

HTML/JavaScript

Our next example won't actually send the email since that can't be done directly from JavaScript,[4] Instead, we will launch our default email program, as shown in Figure 1-2.

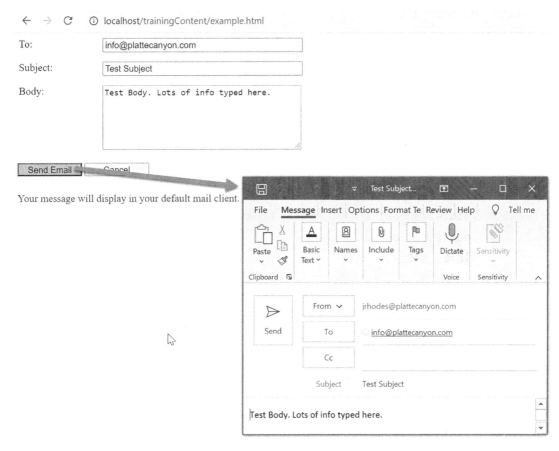

Figure 1-2. *Generating an email from an HTML and JavaScript page*

---

[3] Note how we can set the *Text* of the label directly. We will see that when we get to Power Apps, this is not possible in that environment. We will use variables instead.

[4] We could call code like Listing 1-1 from JavaScript or by "posting" to a web server if desired.

The gist of the solution is that we build a link like this: *mailto:info@plattecanyon. com?subject=Test Subject&body=Test Body. Lots of info typed here.* We then launch the link to bring up the default mail client like Outlook. Listing 1-2 shows the implementation.

Listing 1-2. HTML, styles, and JavaScript for generating an email

```
<!DOCTYPE html>

<html lang="en" xmlns="http://www.w3.org/1999/xhtml">
<head>
    <meta charset="utf-8" />
    <title>Send Email</title>
    <style>
        label {
            width: 100px;
            position: absolute;
            left: 10px;
        }

        input {
            width: 300px;
            position: absolute;
            left: 140px;
        }

        textarea {
            width: 300px;
            position: absolute;
            left: 140px;
        }

        button {
            width: 100px;
            height: 20px;
            position: relative;
            top: 100px;
        }
```

```
        span{
            position: relative;
            top: 125px;
            color: maroon;
        }

        #SendEmailBtn {
            background-color: lightsteelblue;
        }
    </style>
    <script>
        function SendEmail() {
            var toValue = document.getElementById("ToBox").value;
            var subjectValue = document.getElementById("SubjectBox").value;
            var bodyValue = document.getElementById("BodyBox").value;
            var mailString = "mailto:" + toValue + "?subject=" +
subjectValue + "&body=" + bodyValue;

            window.open(mailString, "emailWindow");
            document.getElementById("message").innerHTML = "Your message
will display in your default mail client."
        }

        function CloseWindow() {
            window.close();
        }
    </script>
</head>
<body>
    <label>To:</label><input id="ToBox" type="text" />
    <br />
    <br />
    <label>Subject:</label><input id="SubjectBox" type="text" />
    <br />
    <br />
    <label>Body:</label><textarea id="BodyBox" rows="6" cols="20">
</textarea>
    <br />
```

```
    <button id="SendEmailBtn" type="button" onclick="SendEmail()">Send
Email</button> <button id="CancelBtn" type="button"
onclick="CloseWindow()">Cancel</button>
    <br />
    <span id="message"></span>
</body>
</html>
```

Let's start with the HTML at the bottom. HTML *input* objects are for a single line, so we use that for the *To* and *Subject* information. For the *Body*, we use a *textarea* object. As you might expect, we use *button* objects to send the email or cancel. We use a *span* to display our message after the user clicks the button. To get all the objects to line up correctly, we use the styles near the top of the listing.[5] When we list just the name of the object as in *input*, that applies to all the objects of that type on the page. Note the *width*, *position*, *left*, *top*, etc. are all *properties* of the corresponding objects. When we include the # sign as in *#SendEmailBtn*, that limits it to just an object with that *id*. So the *lightsteelblue* background color only applies to the *Send Email* button.

Now let's talk code. We handle the *onclick* event by listing the function we will call in response: *onclick="SendEmail()"*. We look in the script section[6] for the corresponding code. In it, we build variables to hold info we need: *toValue*, *subjectValue*, and *bodyValue*. This introduces us to a common challenge in programming (and one we will tackle later in a later chapter in Power Apps): how to get from the *name* of an object to the *reference* for the object. To read the *value* property of the *ToBox* object, we need to get from the string "ToBox" to the object *ToBox*. That is the purpose of the *document.getElementById("ToBox")* syntax.[7] Once we have our three variables, we concatenate them into our *mailString* variable. We then call the *open* method of the *window* object to launch our mail client. For our cancel functionality, we call its *close* method instead.

---

[5] We would normally put the styles in a Cascading Style Sheet (CSS) file that we could share among multiple pages.

[6] Like the CSS file, we would typically put the JavaScript in a separate .js file.

[7] The recurring need for "selectors" to go from *id*, *class*, or other information to object references is one reason for the popularity of the jQuery JavaScript library. For example, our code would be *$("#ToBox").value* if we were using jQuery. I covered jQuery in depth in the previous edition of this book in the context of adding functionality to SharePoint pages with JavaScript. Since that is much less common in SharePoint Online, I have removed those examples from this edition.

To display our message, we get the object reference to our *span* object and then set its *innerHTML* property to be the text we want.

Power Apps

Now that we've seen a couple of standard environments, let's tackle this task in Power Apps. We start by selecting a Canvas app from blank, as shown in Figure 1-3.

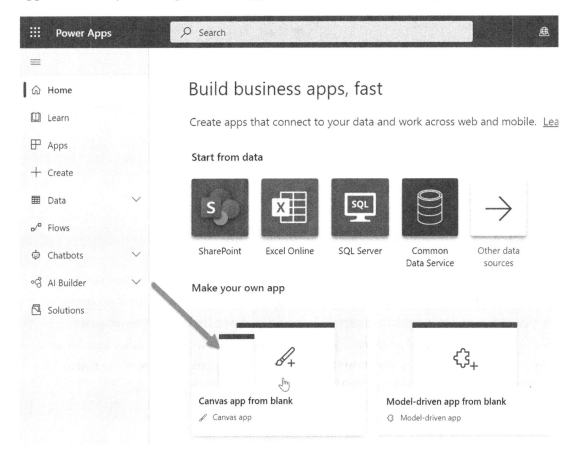

Figure 1-3. *Building a Canvas app from blank*

We choose Tablet as our format and then start adding objects. We use *labels* and *text input* controls in a similar way to our previous examples. To allow a formatted body, we use a *Rich text editor*, as shown in Figure 1-4. We choose it instead of the *HTML text control* since the latter only allows the display but not the entry of text. We continue by adding two buttons and arranging our objects on the screen.

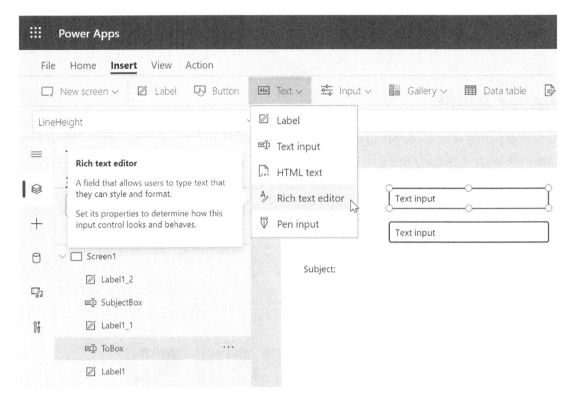

Figure 1-4. *Adding a Rich text editor in Power Apps*

One of the most interesting and powerful aspects of Power Apps is how the entire development is accomplished in the browser, as opposed to a specialized program like Visual Studio. As we see in Figure 1-5, the drop-down list of choices when we select an object is a mix of *properties* we can set and *events* we can handle. In addition, there is typically a property sheet on the right-side of the screen where we can also set properties. In Figure 1-5, we can set the *Text* of the button in either location.

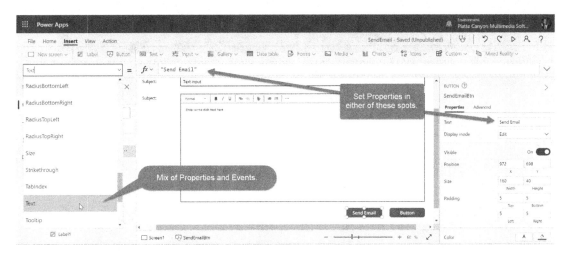

Figure 1-5. *Setting a property in Power Apps*

As we lay out the rest of the screen, we see that Power Apps controls have a *Default* property, as shown in Figure 1-6. This is what shows up when the user first enters the screen. If it is blank, then the *HintText* property displays to give an indication to the user as to what to do with that control.

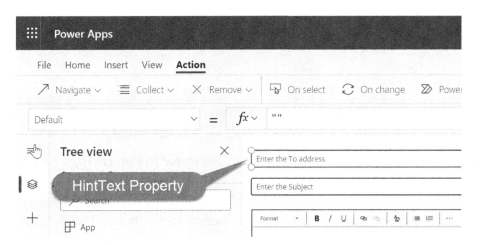

Figure 1-6. *Default and HintText properties of a Text Input control*

Our next task is to add the Office 365 Outlook connector so we can send email. Figure 1-7 shows us the steps: go to *Data*, *Add data*, and then search for *Outlook*.

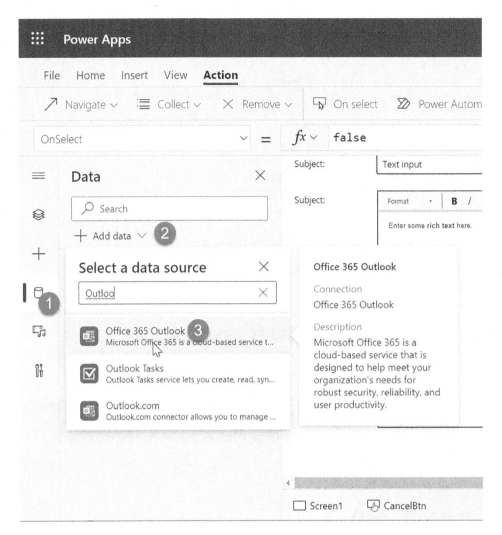

Figure 1-7. *Adding the Office 365 Outlook Connector to Power Apps*

We are now ready to implement the rest of the solution. We select our *SendEmailBtn* object and choose its *OnSelect* event (which is analogous to *Click* and *onclick* that we saw in our previous examples). Figure 1-8 shows how Power Apps gives us both the parameters of the *SendEmailV2* method but also Intellisense where it displays a list of the available properties and methods upon typing the "." after the object name. Notice how we enter the code directly in the entry box (rather than in another file) so that code goes side-by-side with property values. You can drag down the box to make it bigger to see all your code.

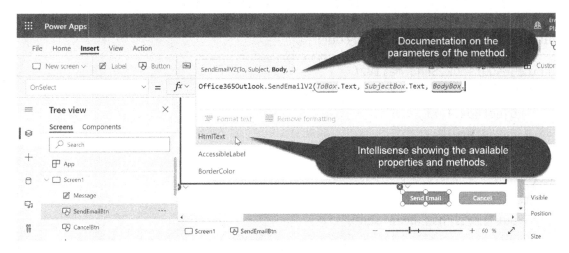

Figure 1-8. *Method documentation and Intellisense inside Power Apps*

Let's look at the message we want to send after the email is sent. Unlike .NET and JavaScript, we can't directly set a property of one object from another. Instead, we set the *Text* property to be a variable, as shown in Figure 1-9.

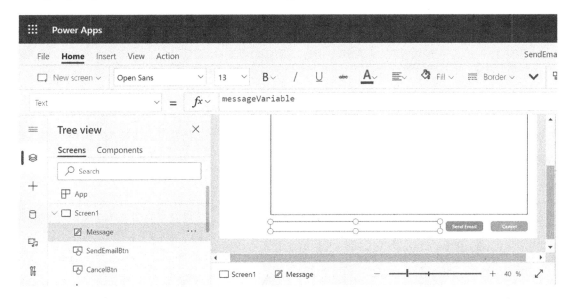

Figure 1-9. *Setting the Text property to a variable in Power Apps*

13

We then can change the value of that variable when the user clicks the *Send Email* button. Here is the entire *OnSelect* code:

```
Office365Outlook.SendEmailV2(
    ToBox.Text,
    SubjectBox.Text,
    BodyBox.HtmlText
);
Set(
    messageVariable,
    "Your email has been sent."
)
```

Notice how the ability to use the *Office365Outlook* connector makes it easy to send email. Our .NET example needed a mail server and associated credentials, while sending email was not even possible with our HTML and JavaScript solution. With PowerApps, it was just one line of code. We then use the *Set* command[8] to give our *messageVariable* the value of "Your email has been sent." This makes that text display, as shown in Figure 1-10.

---

[8] This is an example of a *global* variable, meaning its value will be available on another screen within Power Apps. I could have used a *context* variable instead by using this syntax: *UpdateConte xt({messageVariable: "Your email has been sent."})*. A context variable can only be referenced from the screen where it was created.

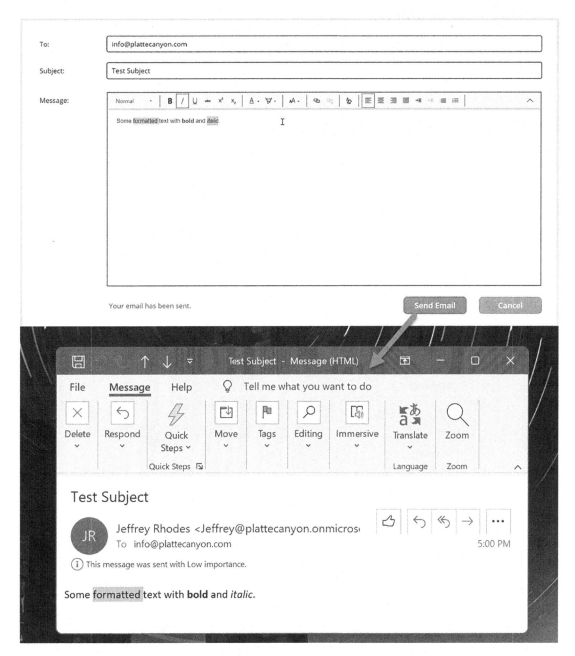

Figure 1-10. *Power Apps Email Form and Resulting Email*

Our last task is the implementation of the *Cancel* button. Its *OnSelect* code is simply the *Exit()* method, which exits the user out of PowerApps. Figure 1-10 shows the form in action with the resulting email. We could do a little clean-up, such as making the email

15

normal importance (it defaults to low importance) and adding some error checking to prevent an email with a blank *To*, *Subject*, or *Body*, but this is pretty good I think for our opening application.

Power Automate/Power Apps

Rather than using Power Apps itself to send the email, we could have used Power Automate. For that, we start in Power Automate by creating an *Automated cloud flow*, as shown in Figure 1-11.

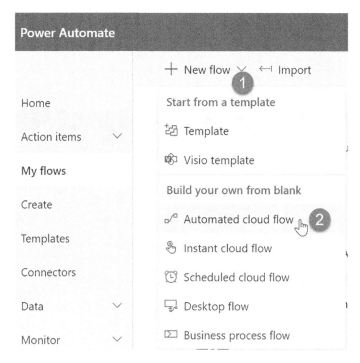

Figure 1-11. *Creating an Automated cloud flow in Power Automate*

Name your flow and then click the Skip button rather than selecting a trigger.[9] Instead, select *Power Apps* from the various trigger icons and then *Power Apps (V2)*[10], as shown in Figure 1-12.

---

[9] I would expect Power Apps to be a trigger, but it does not show up at the time of this writing.
[10] As a general rule, pick the latest version of any trigger or method. This will have the most functionality.

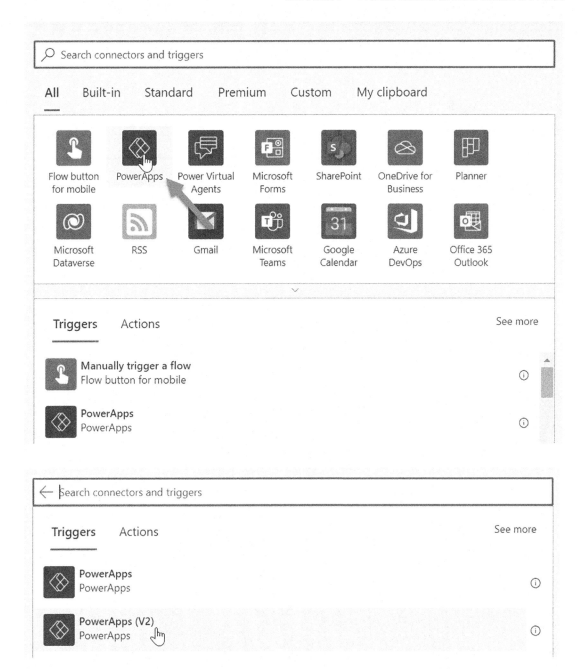

Figure 1-12. *Selecting the Power Apps trigger*

From there, we add an input for each parameter we want to pass in from Power Apps. These are the *Email*, *Subject*, and *Message*, as shown in Figure 1-13.

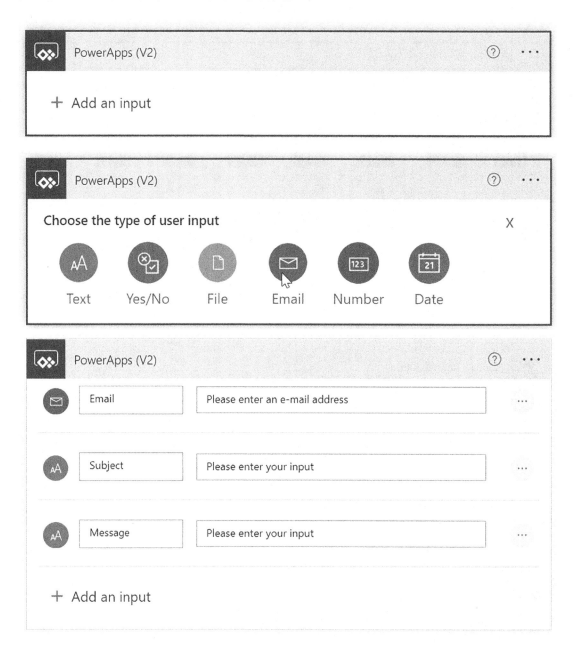

Figure 1-13. *Creating the Parameters to be sent from Power Apps*

We click *New step* search for *Outlook* and then *Send* so we can select *Send an email (V2)*, as shown in Figure 1-14.

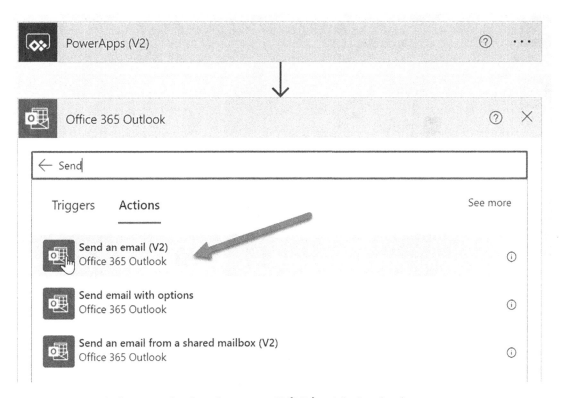

Figure 1-14. *Selecting the Send an email (V2) with Outlook*

The last step on the Power Automate side is to click on each option (To, Subject, Body) and then *Add dynamic content.* The beauty of Power Automate is that it gives whatever values are available, in this case the *Email, Subject,* and *Message* parameters we will get from Power Apps. This is shown in Figure 1-15.

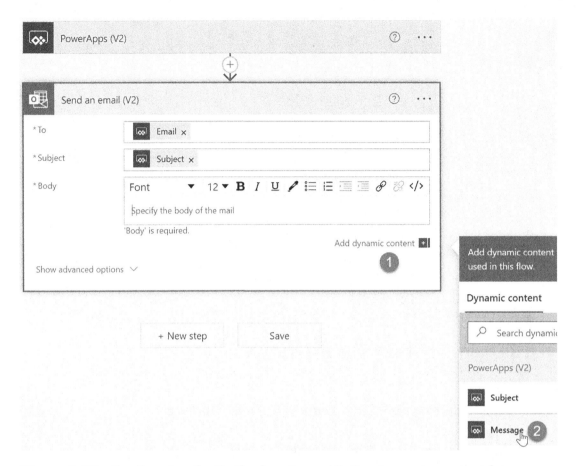

Figure 1-15. *Configuring the Outlook action with the dynamic content from Power Apps*

Back in Power Apps, we save our app as a new name, select the Send Email button, go to the Action tab, and select Power Automate. This gives us a list of our flows that have Power Apps as a trigger, as shown in Figure 1-16. Note that this will replace the entire *OnSelect* code. So you may want to create a new button first and then copy your code over once you are ready.

Figure 1-16. *Connecting to Power Automate from Power Apps*

You then pass in the parameters, as shown in Figure 1-17. Notice how Power Apps gives information on the name of each parameter to help you keep things straight.

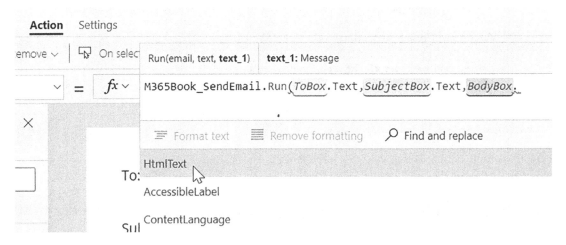

Figure 1-17. *Calling the Power Automate flow from Power Apps and setting each parameter*

Here is the complete *OnSelect* code:

```
M365Book_SendEmail.Run(
    ToBox.Text,
    SubjectBox.Text,
    BodyBox.HtmlText
);
Set(
    messageVariable,
    "Your email has been sent."
)
```

We test in Power Apps, see the result in our email program, and can even inspect the results of each call to the flow in Power Apps, as shown in Figures 1-18 and 1-19. This ability to debug in Power Automate is very helpful and something we will use later in the book.

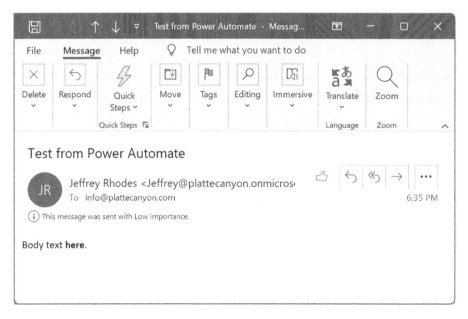

Figure 1-18. *The resulting email sent from Power Automate*

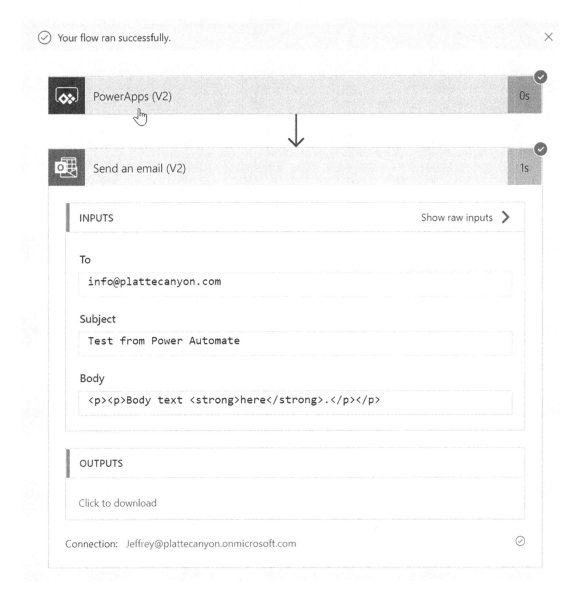

Figure 1-19. *The corresponding output results in Power Automate*

Summary

In this chapter, we learned the ways the Power Platform is similar to traditional development environments like .NET and HTML/JavaScript AND the important ways it is different. We built our two Power Apps. In the first, we did all the logic within Power Apps. In the second, we saw how we could pass parameters from Power Apps and then use Power Automate to do much of the work.

CHAPTER 2

Updating a SharePoint List Using Power Apps

Power Apps[1] is a powerful forms tool in Microsoft 365. It is not a direct replacement of InfoPath (which I covered in the previous edition of this book but is now largely obsolete) as it does things differently (and often better). I particularly like that Power Apps can be created completely in the browser, are optimized for mobile devices, can connect to a multitude of data sources, and have a familiar Visual Basic-like syntax.[2]

In this chapter, we will build a simple application to view and update a SharePoint list. Our overall objective is to create a help ticketing system with these requirements:

- Users will fill out a form when they arrive in person at the help desk. It will only include information they know such as issue, description, who they are, and their department.

- Technicians see new items by default but can search for existing items. They can set additional information such as the status, issue category, assigned technician, and notes. Technicians can also add items for situations like phone and email support.

We will build the data source (SharePoint list), make relatively minor changes to the default form, and then create another form to add to or update the list. We will then continue the development in later chapters.

---

[1] I have found Shane Young of PowerApps911 YouTube channel helpful for learning about Power Apps: www.youtube.com/channel/UC7_OGRP8BYvtGB8eZdPG6Ng. Check out my YouTube channel as well at www.youtube.com/channel/UCadnfEVO8PD48xbsE2GhxEg.

[2] By using the & to concatenate values, for example. I'm a big Visual Basic fan and actually wrote a previous book called *VBTrain.Net: Creating Computer and Web Based Training with Visual Basic .NET*.

© Jeffrey M. Rhodes 2022
J. M. Rhodes, *Creating Business Applications with Microsoft 365*,
https://doi.org/10.1007/978-1-4842-8823-8_2

SharePoint List

Figure 2-1 shows our SharePoint list along with the default form. Notice that clicking the *Customize with Power Apps* link launches Power Apps.

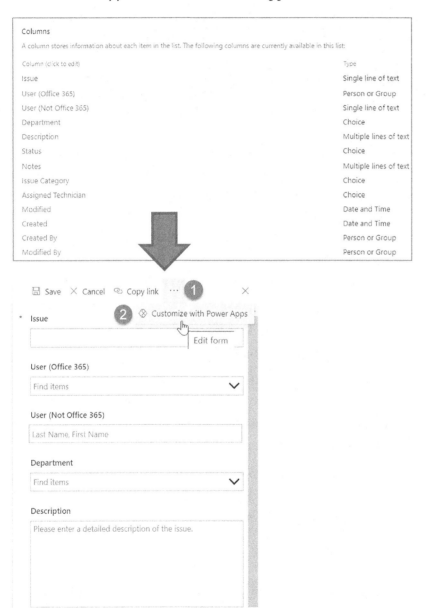

Figure 2-1. *Help Tickets SharePoint list with corresponding SharePoint form. Clicking Customize with Power Apps launches Power Apps*

Customizing the form won't meet all our requirements since it will be there can only be one form that is launched when the user clicks New (we want separate forms for users and technicians). Plus, we don't to want to have to go to the SharePoint site at all. We want to make all edits via Power Apps. The SharePoint site will instead mainly be a *Power BI* data source for visualizations showing our ticket information.[3]

There is still some value in customizing the form as it gives us nice new capabilities and helps us learn Power Apps. One of the first things you will notice in our customized form is that the *Description* is now only a single line. Figure 2-2 shows how we drag the *Height* to give more space and then set the *Mode* property to be *TextMode.MultiLine*. While we are at it, we set the *HintText* property to give the user more instructions on what to do.

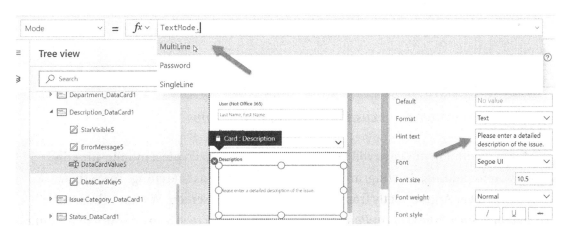

Figure 2-2. *Updating the Height, HintText, and Mode properties of the Description input*

Figure 2-3 shows the resulting form in SharePoint.

---

[3] We will dig deep into Power BI in later chapters. Another use of Power BI would be to have a "New Tickets" report that could be sorted by date and time. Technicians could use to determine who has been waiting longest and call that person next. We hope to build this into the Power Apps technician application as well.

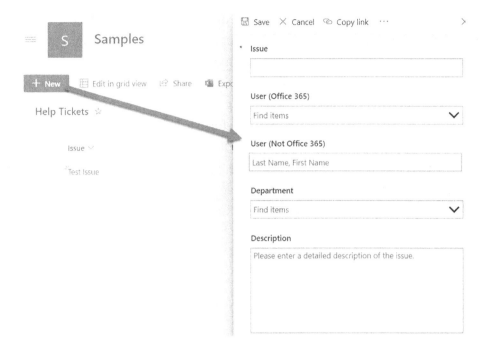

Figure 2-3. *New Item form customized with Power Apps*

More powerful in our case will be to use Power Apps to create a mobile-friendly application for adding, deleting, and editing items as well as searching. To do that, we launch Power Apps directly from our Office 365 home screen. We then choose the *SharePoint – Start from a SharePoint list to create a three-screen app* option. This default to the phone size (the other choice we can do from a blank app is tablet). From there, we select SharePoint as our connection and either enter the URL of our site (just include the site and not the list) or choose from our *Recent sites*. We then choose from the available SharePoint lists. Figure 2-4 shows the result. Notice how Power Apps created the screens for browsing the data, viewing the details, and editing the data. We update the *App Name* and *Description* properties and then set the application to *Confirm exit* and then set a corresponding message.

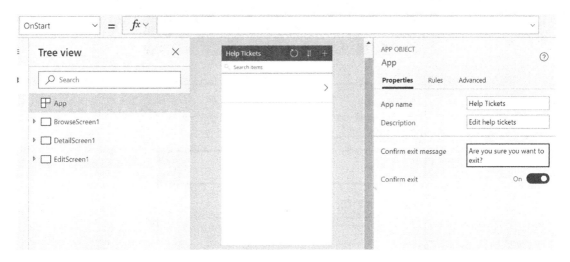

Figure 2-4. *Power Apps application with Browse, Details, and Edit screens*

We could do extensive edits as needed within Power Apps, but we will save this for a more customized solution in a later chapter. For now, we will save[4] and then share it with other users. Figure 2-5 shows the resulting *New Item* screen. Notice that we could access this with the Power Apps mobile application as well.

---

[4] Be sure to save immediately as automatic saving does not kick in until you save the application the first time.

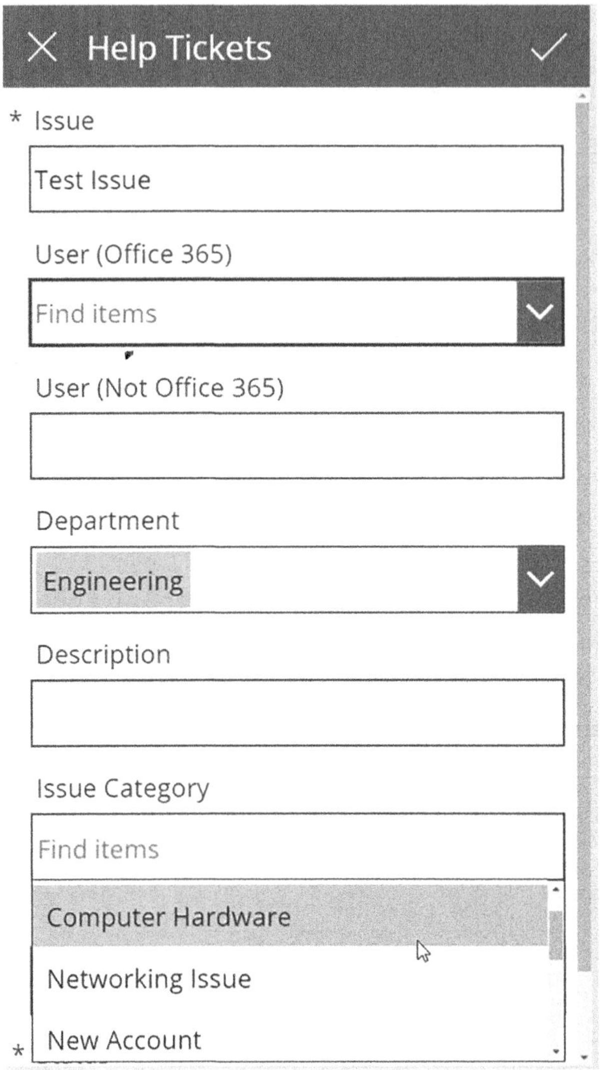

Figure 2-5. *New Item screen for Help Tickets list*

Summary

This chapter introduced us to Power Apps as the replacement for InfoPath as a way to customize and extend SharePoint's built-in editors. Since I typically like to use Power Apps directly and not send users to the back-end SharePoint site, we won't customize in this way going forward. But this gives us a good foundation and gives us an early indication of Power App's capabilities.

CHAPTER 3

Creating an Approval Process with Power Automate

A great addition to Microsoft 365 was Power Automate, previously known as Microsoft Flow. It goes way beyond the old workflows in SharePoint, allowing you to connect and act on all kinds of "triggers" as well as schedule your own flows. We will have lots of examples in later chapters, but we will start with an approval workflow triggered from a SharePoint. We will also use the Outlook 365 action to send a notification email.

Building the SharePoint List

For our example, we will create an Equipment Request list, as shown in Figure 3-1. We add columns for the submission date, required date, manager,[1] estimated cost, etc. We also add a Status column that we default to *Submitted* and then set via Power Automate to either *Approved* or *Rejected* based on the approval results.

---

[1] We add Manager as a *Person* column so that we can use it for email, a Teams post, etc. As you will see, we can get access to Display Name, Department, and other properties as needed.

© Jeffrey M. Rhodes 2022
J. M. Rhodes, *Creating Business Applications with Microsoft 365*,
https://doi.org/10.1007/978-1-4842-8823-8_3

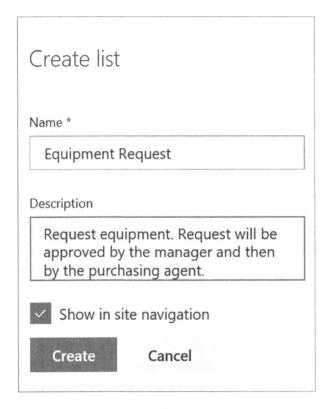

Figure 3-1. *Custom Equipment Request list*

Creating the Power Automate Flow

We create an *Automated cloud flow,* as shown in Figure 3-2. We will look at other types of flows, particularly *Scheduled cloud flows,* later in the book.

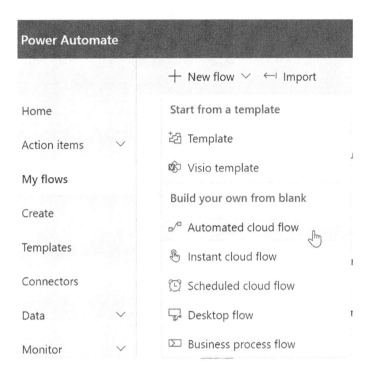

Figure 3-2. *Creating an Automated Cloud Flow*

We name the flow, choose the trigger to be when an item is created in our SharePoint list, and then click the *Create* button, as shown in Figure 3-3.

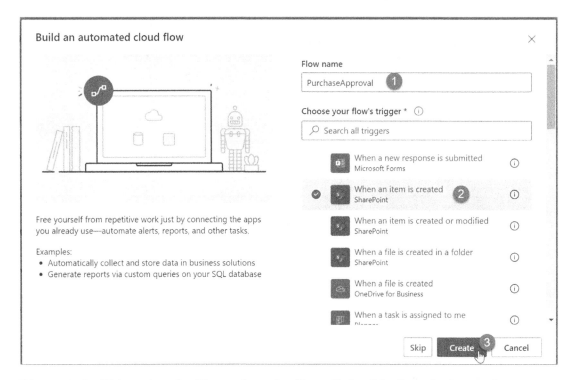

Figure 3-3. *Triggering the Flow when the SharePoint List Item Is Created*

We select our SharePoint site and then select the name of the list. Our next step is to select Approvals (you can search to find it) and then choose *Start and wait for an approval* (Figure 3-4).

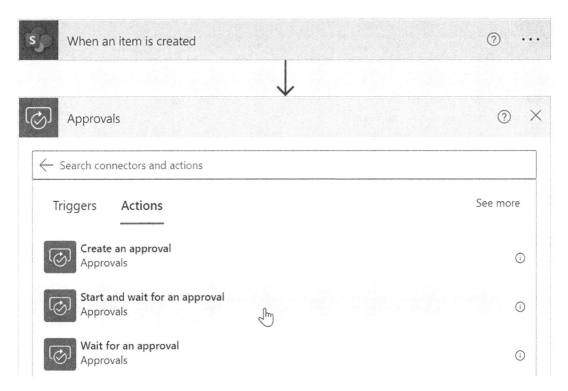

Figure 3-4. *Choosing to Start and Wait for an Approval*

Since we are only doing a single approval for the manager, we can choose to select the *First to Respond* or *Everyone Must Respond*. One of the great things about Power Automate is that it offers up what information is available when you select *Add dynamic content*. As shown in Figure 3-5, we include the list item *Title* column as part of the approval title and then choose the *Manager Email*[2] for the *Assigned to* value.

---

[2] Notice how the Manager DisplayName, Email, Picture, Department, etc. are available since we used the Person type for the Manager SharePoint column.

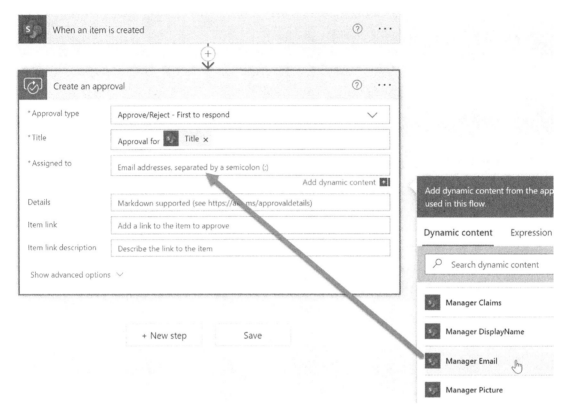

Figure 3-5. *Populating Approval Values with SharePoint List Content*

Figure 3-6 shows the fully populated approval request. Notice all the information that we include in the *Details.* This avoids the need for the approver to go back to the original SharePoint list item unless they need still more data, though the link to the list item makes the original request just a click away.

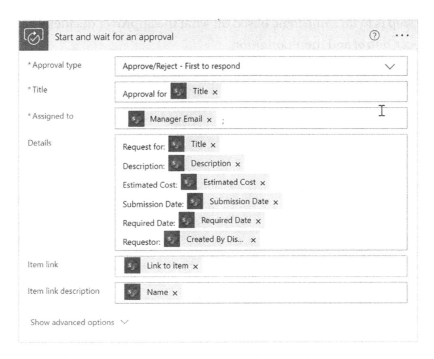

Figure 3-6. *Fully Populated Approval Request*

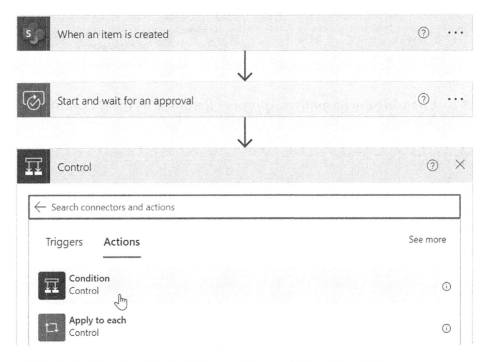

Figure 3-7. *Selecting the Control Connector and then Condition*

Our next step is to do some logic based on what the approver decides. We add a new step and select *Control* and then *Condition*.

As we see in Figure 3-8, we then select *Responses Approver response*.

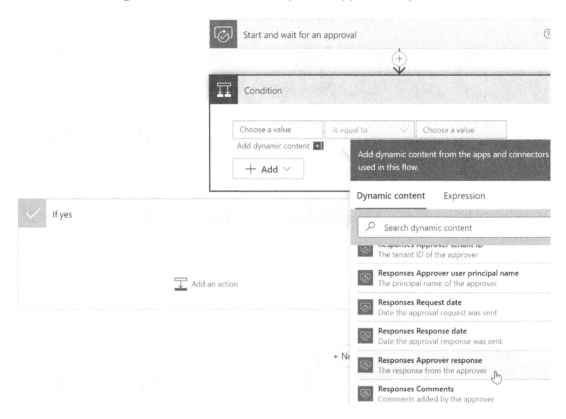

Figure 3-8. *Choosing the Responses Approver Response as the If Condition*

Power Automate realizes that there could be multiple response and thus embeds our logic in an *Apply to each* loop, as shown Figure 3-9. We check if to see if the response is *Approve.*

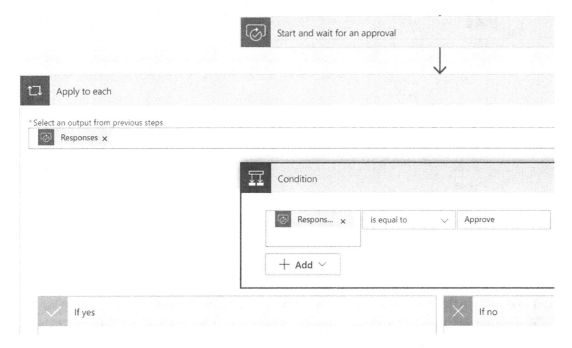

Figure 3-9. *Power Automate Switches to Apply to Each and then Control*

Why want to send an email based on the approval result. We use Office 365 Outlook and then the Send an email (V2) method,[3] as shown in Figure 3-10.

___

[3] As a general rule, pick the latest version (V2, V3, etc.) since that has the most functionality. Microsoft leaves previous versions when parameters change so as to not break old flows.

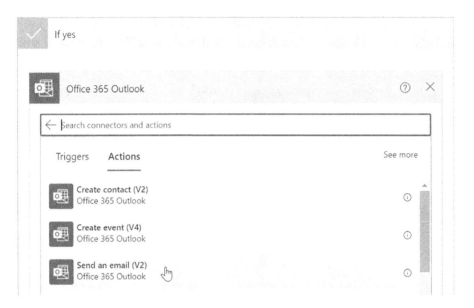

Figure 3-10. *Using Office 365 Outlook to Send a Notification Email*

As with the preceding approval request, we use information from the SharePoint list item to populate the emails.[4] We also use data from the approval such as the name and the *Response Comments*. Figure 3-11 shows the Approved results, while Figure 3-12 show the email sent when the request is disapproved.

---

[4] I could have used our approval status variable explained as follows to only send a single email, but in the real world, there may be different copied users, extra info, etc. on rejections. So I decided to have a separate email action for Yes and No.

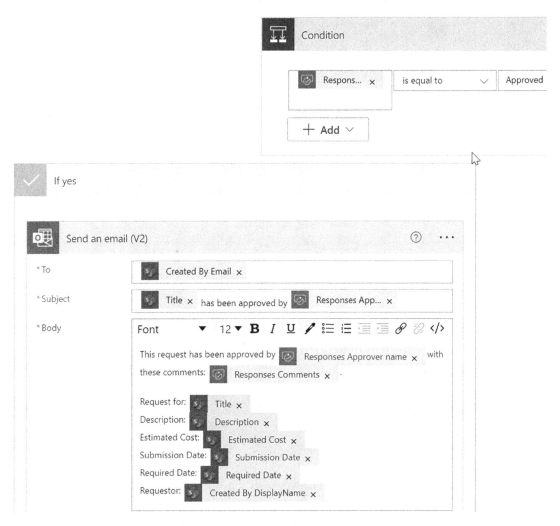

Figure 3-11. *Approved Email*

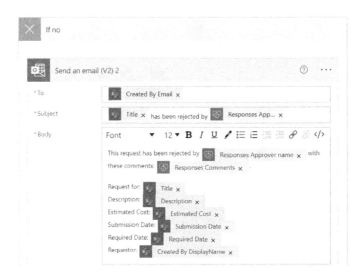

Figure 3-12. *Rejected Email*

Once we send the email, our last task is to update the *Status* column in our SharePoint list item. While we could do this twice (like we did for the preceding emails), this is pretty inefficient. Instead, we modify our logic to initialize an *ApprovalStatus* variable to *Approved* and then change it to *Rejected* when the request is not approved. This is shown in Figure 3-13.

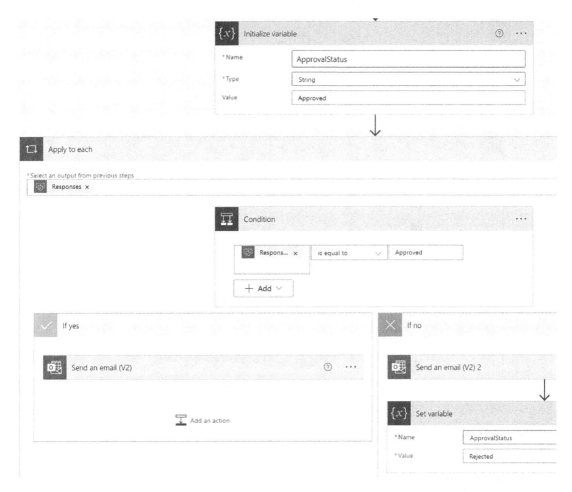

Figure 3-13. *Initializing and Setting the ApprovalStatus Variable*

We are now ready to update our list item with the value of the *ApprovalStatus* variable, as shown in Figure 3-14. We use the *Update item* method, select our site and list name, and then choose the associated *ID* and *Title*.[5]

---

[5] ID is important here as it tells SharePoint which list item to update. Recall there could be many approvals out for review simultaneously. *Title* is required just because it is a required column. Requiring this, since there is already a value, is more a weakness of the interface.

Figure 3-14. *Updating the SharePoint List Item with the Approval Status*

Whew. We are now finished with the flow and ready to test.

Testing the Flow

We add a new item in SharePoint[6] and wait for the fun to begin. We quickly get a notification in Teams, as shown in Figure 3-15. We get both a popup notification and an entry in our Activity Feed.

---

[6] We could do this in the standard SharePoint form or via Power Apps.

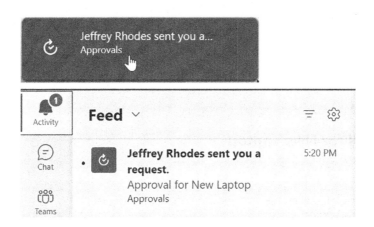

Figure 3-15. *Approval Notifications in Teams*

Click on the notification or going to the Approvals app in Teams, we see the form shown in Figure 3-16. Notice how all the elements shown back in Figure 3-6 are displayed: Request, Description, Estimated Cost, etc. The link to the SharePoint list item is listed as the attachment. It gives the approver a spot to enter comments and then the ability to either *Approve* or *Reject*.

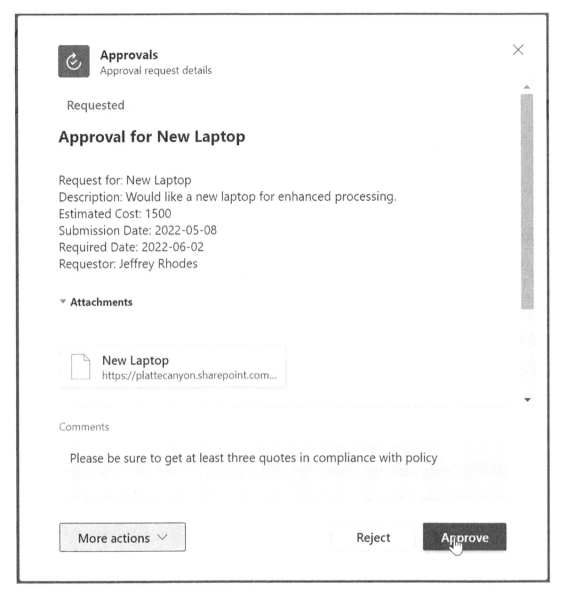

Figure 3-16. *Approval Form in Teams*

Power Automate also sends an email allowing approval or rejection that way, as shown in Figure 3-17. This is how all approvals worked before Microsoft created the *Approvals* app.[7]

---

[7] You can tell that less attention has been devoted so far to the email notification process since the email is from the older *Microsoft Flow* name rather than being from *Power Automate*.

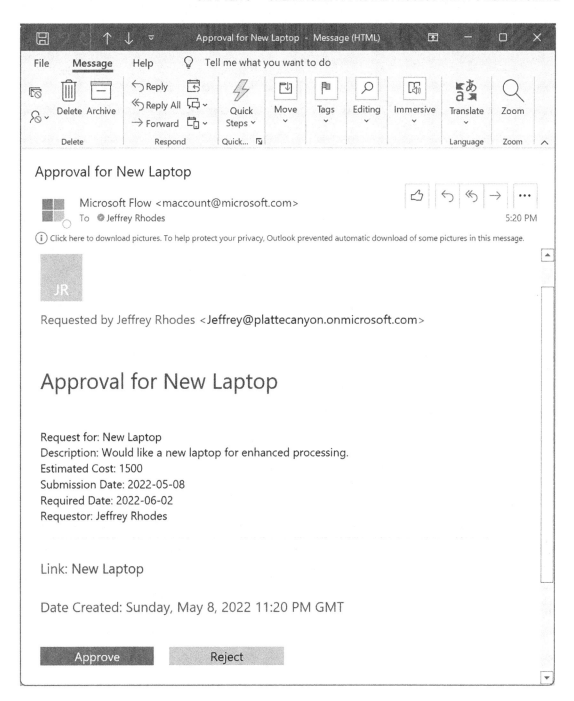

Figure 3-17. *Approval via Email.w*

Whichever way we processed the approval or rejection, our flow logic kicks in (Figure 3-11) and sends the corresponding email, as shown in Figure 3-18.

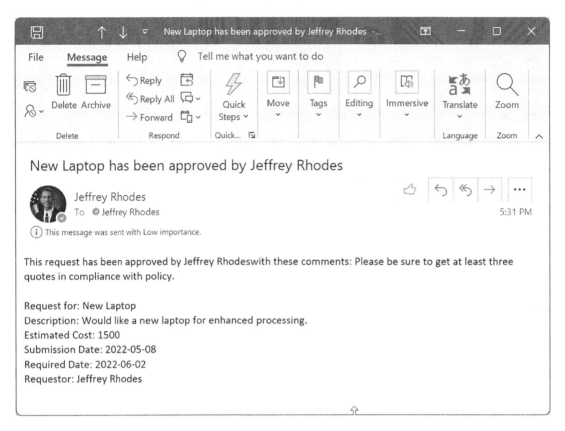

Figure 3-18. *Approval Status Email*

Although all seemed to work, it is still a good idea to go back to Power Automate, see if the run was successful, and then click on it to view its status (Figure 3-19). This is even more important if Flow shows an error or if the logic was incorrect.[8] A green circle with a white check mark shows the successful logic path. Everything was fast (0 seconds) except for the *Start and wait for an approval* (49 seconds), since this included the time waiting for me to approve via Teams or Email. Our condition was *true* and thus we went down the *if yes* path.

---

[8] For example, I had originally used *Approved* instead of *Approve* in the condition statement and got a rejected email instead of an approved one.

Figure 3-19. *Debugging the Flow Run and Seeing Its Logic*

Summary

In this chapter, we triggered an approval workflow whenever a SharePoint list item was created. We sent the approval to the manager listed in the SharePoint list item/entry form and included the relevant information about the request. We then sent either an approval or rejection email to the submitter of the request.

CHAPTER 4

Creating a Survey Response Dashboard with Power BI

Power BI is a powerful tool for visualizing data. Of particular relevance for this book is its ability to use SharePoint lists as a data source. In this chapter, we will demonstrate how to use Power BI to display SharePoint survey data. This is particularly useful for a long-running survey such as for a help desk. The ability of Power BI to slice the data and separate out more recent submissions is crucial to spotting trends and addressing any issues.

SharePoint's Default Visualization

As shown in Figure 4-1, SharePoint's built-in graphical summary displays all results. If the survey has been in place for the past five years, seeing recent trends are impossible. In addition, there is no way to click on the *Very Dissatisfied* responses, for example, and drill down into their comments or other information.

We will use the free *Power BI Desktop* application to build these visualizations. Those with the appropriate licenses can then publish the visualizations to the Power BI Service, which is much more convenient as viewing can be in the browser directly, via Teams, via SharePoint, or even within Power Apps. Another advantage of the Power BI service is the scheduled refreshes of the data. Still another is the fact that the viewer of the report doesn't have to have their own credentials to the data source, in this case the SharePoint list.

© Jeffrey M. Rhodes 2022
J. M. Rhodes, *Creating Business Applications with Microsoft 365*,
https://doi.org/10.1007/978-1-4842-8823-8_4

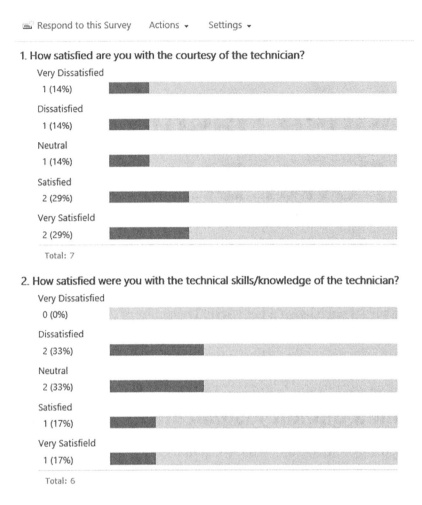

Figure 4-1. *SharePoint's graphical survey summary*

Connecting to Our SharePoint Results

To get started, we select *Get Data* in Power BI Desktop and choose *SharePoint List* or *SharePoint Online List,* as shown in Figure 4-2. You normally want to select the newer (2.0) implementation. This limits the need to rename columns that have been truncated, for example. However, for survey data, you want the 1.0 version so you get important information such as the date for the response.

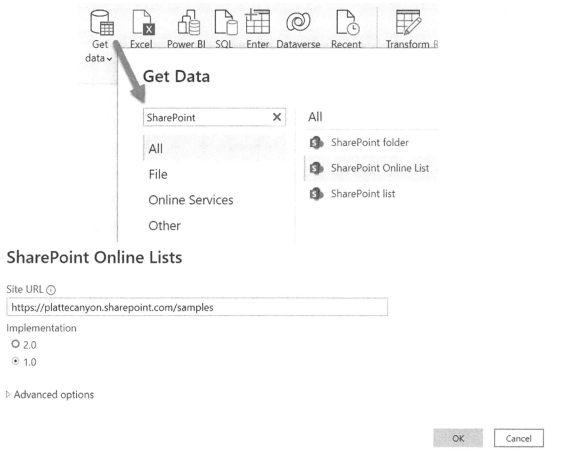

Figure 4-2. *Getting Data from a SharePoint List*

We put in the path to our site (not including the survey itself). Power BI will prompt us to either use our current credentials or to log into our Microsoft account, as appropriate. It then allows us to select one or more lists, as shown in Figure 4-3.

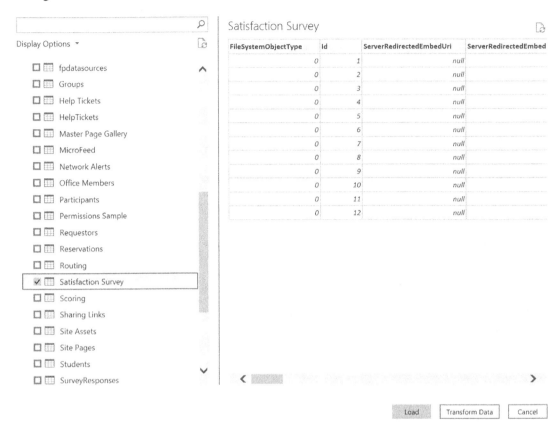

Figure 4-3. *Selecting a SharePoint Survey List in Power BI Desktop*

Our next step is to *Transform data,* as shown in Figure 4-4.

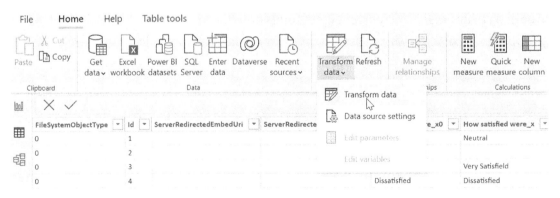

Figure 4-4. *Transform Data in Power BI Desktop*

Power BI gives us a nice interface to filter our data, rename columns, and much more. It shows all the actions in APPLIED STEPS so we can view, edit, or remove them later (see Figure 4-6). Better yet, these steps are re-accomplished on the live data each time we refresh the data. You might notice in Figure 4-4 that the column names are truncated as in *How satisfied are_x0*. It will be most convenient to rename them to the full text of the associated question. To do that, we right-click on the column and select *Rename.* We then copy in the full question from SharePoint.

Some of the columns are displayed as *Record* or *Table.* In that case, we click the button on the right side of the column, as shown in Figure 4-5. We choose to include the *Title* column, which has the first name and last name. We then rename it to *Submitter.*

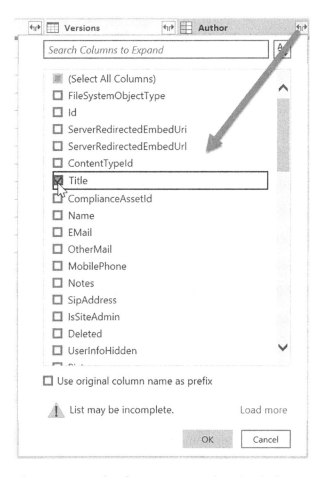

Figure 4-5. *Expanding a Record column into individual elements*

To display responses that are within a specific range, it will be useful to create a column that shows the number of days between today's date and the data of the response. To do this, we go to the *Add Column* tab and then select *Custom Column*. We will name the column *DaysPassed* and use this formula:

```
DateTime.From(DateTime.LocalNow()) - [Modified] + #duration(0, 6, 0, 0)
```

This gives the number of days since the survey was modified. We add six hours since, in my case, the Office 365 server is six hours later than my local time. Since we don't care about decimals, we *Change Type* of the column to a whole number. Figure 4-6 shows the results.

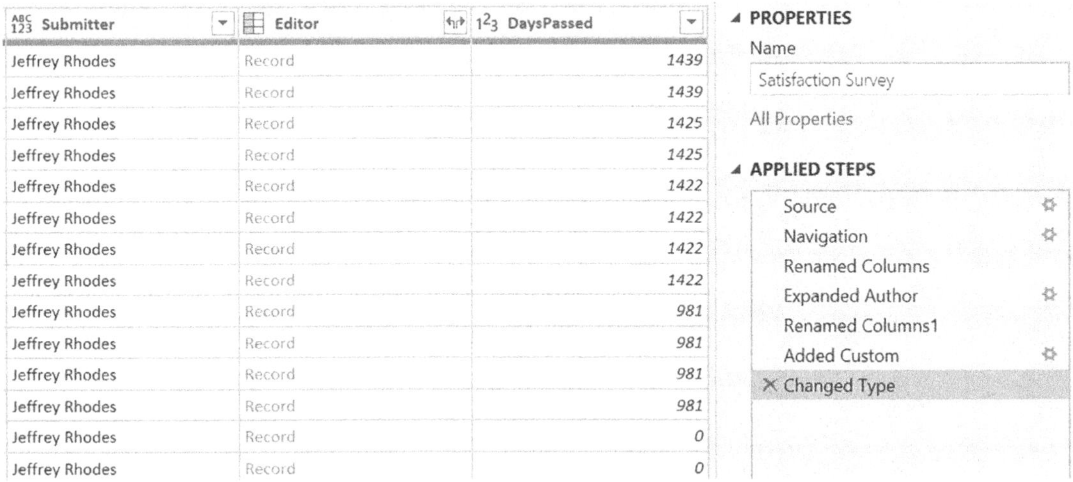

Figure 4-6. *Expanded and custom columns in Power BI Query Editor*

Visualizing Our Data

Now that we have the data like we want it, we are ready to make some visualizations. We go to the *Report* view and create a *Pie Chart* visualization. We drag the question into *Details* and then the *Id* column as the *Values,* as shown in Figure 4-7. Power BI defaults to the *count* of the ID, which we then rename as # *of Responses*. This then shows us the number of responses of each type (Satisfied, Dissatisfied, etc.).

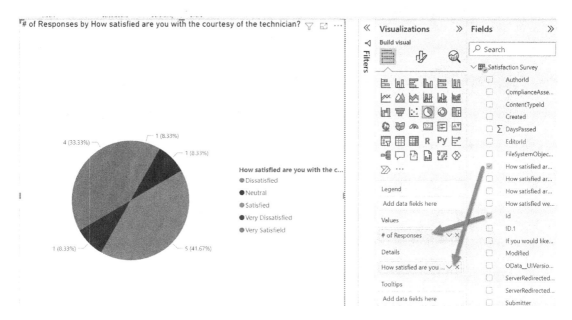

Figure 4-7. *Pie Chart Visualization in Power BI*

Rather than letting Power BI define the colors, we next go to *Format – Visuals – Slices – Colors* to give our own colors for each of the response types.[1] Figure 4-8 shows the results. We use a *Slicer* and connect it to the *Created* date[2] (which we rename Survey Date). We use the *Table* visualization to display detailed information such as the name of the person who filled out the survey.

---

[1] I prefer to go to Photoshop to find the color I want, grab that color in hexadecimal format (such as 073f05 for *Very Satisfied*), and then paste that into Power BI.

[2] Power BI interprets the data type as *String*. You need to change it to *Date/Time* in order for the slicer to display as slider, as shown in Figure 4-8.

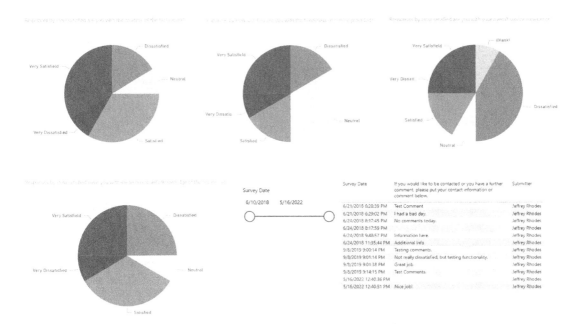

Figure 4-8. *Completed visualizations showing pie chart per question, slicer of the survey date, and table of additional information*

One of the most powerful features of Power BI is the ability to drill down into specific data. In Figure 4-9, we see the results of clicking on the *Dissatisfied* result in the first question. The other questions adjust to how they were answered for the survey(s) that were dissatisfied for the first question. The table adjusts as well. The manager can then contact the customer to get more details and ensure the problem does not happen again.

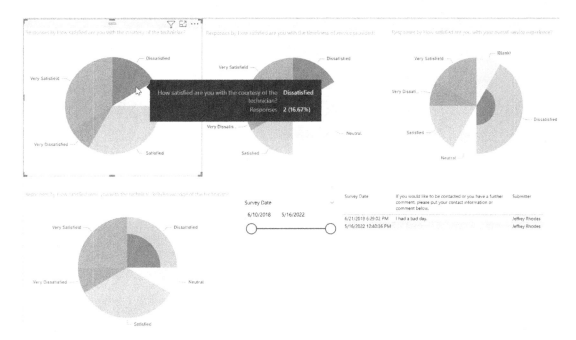

Figure 4-9. *Drilling down on a Dissatisfied result in Power BI*

If you have Power BI Pro, you can publish to the Power BI Service via Power BI Desktop. It then displays in the browser, as shown in Figure 4-10. This has the huge advantage of not requiring the installation of Power BI Desktop on each client machine.

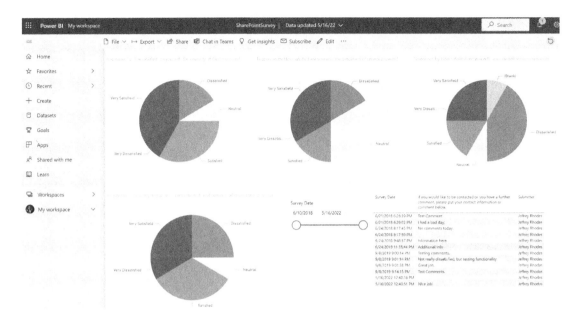

Figure 4-10. *Published Power BI Report*

You can then embed the report into a Teams channel (Figure 4-11) and/or SharePoint page (Figure 4-12).

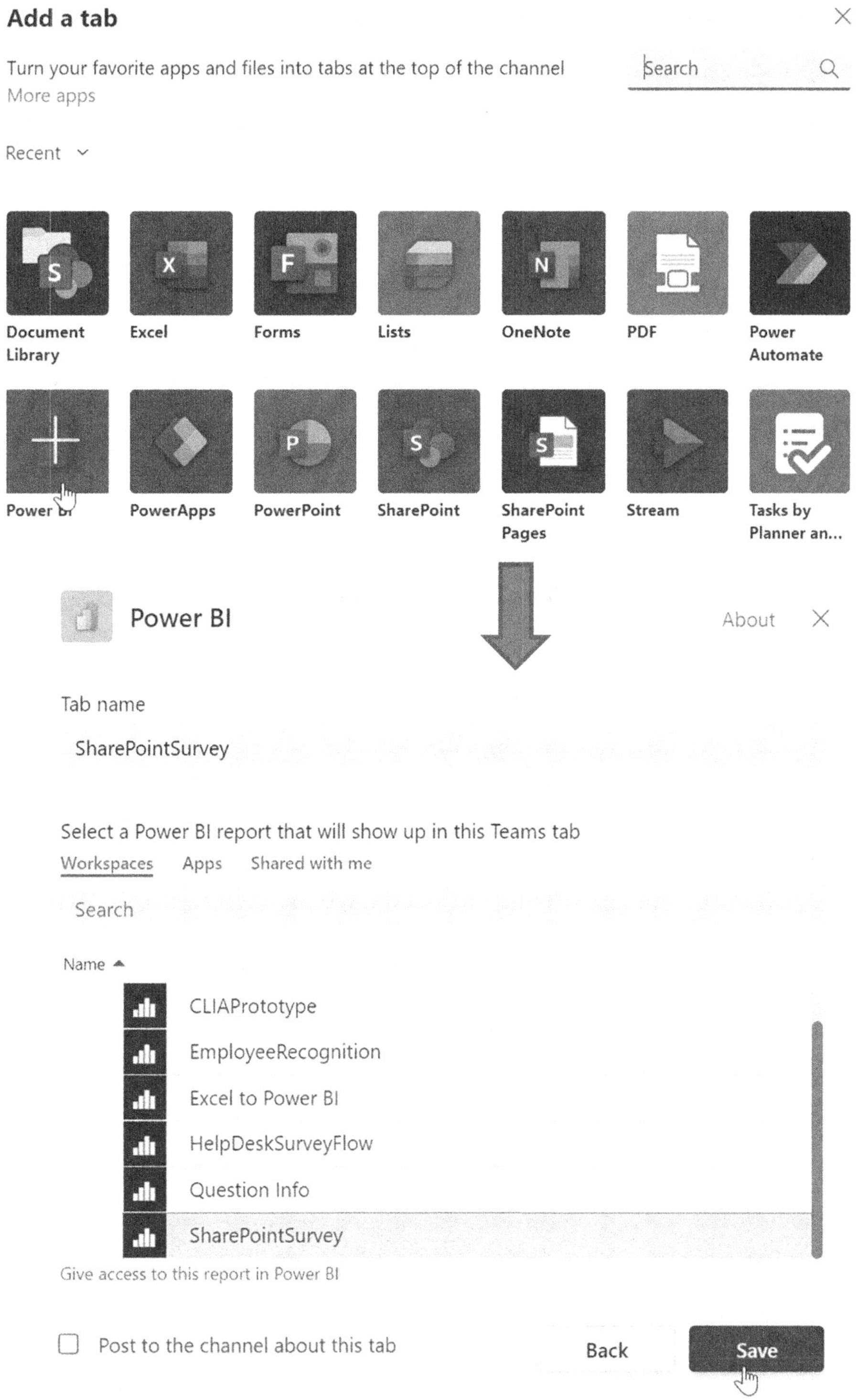

Figure 4-11. *Adding Power BI as a Tab in a Teams Channel*

Figure 4-12. *Adding Power BI to a SharePoint Page*

Summary

In this chapter, we used SharePoint survey responses as our data source within Power BI. We transformed our data and added a *Days Passed* custom column that allowed us to easily create filters to show the most current week, month, quarter, and year if desired. We also saw how to customize the colors of our data to match up with our expectations that green is good, red is bad, and yellow is in-between. Finally, we learned how to display our reports in Teams or SharePoint.

CHAPTER 5

Creating a Survey Solution with Forms, Power Automate, SharePoint, and Power BI

An exciting feature of Microsoft 365 is Microsoft Forms, which makes it very easy to create forms and surveys. In this example, we will show create a survey for our help desk in Forms (similar to what we did with a built-in SharePoint survey in the last chapter). Since Forms tend to wait until requested to create an Excel spreadsheet of the responses, I like to use Power Automate to copy each survey response to a SharePoint[1] list. We then use this SharePoint list as our Power BI data source.

Configuring the Form

One big advantage of Forms over SharePoint's built-in survey capabilities is the ability to allow anyone to respond. This is configured on the *Share* tab, as shown in Figure 5-1.

---

[1] This has the added benefit of keeping a permanent record of the response. If someone inadvertently or intentionally deleted a survey response, the record of the response is still in SharePoint.

© Jeffrey M. Rhodes 2022
J. M. Rhodes, *Creating Business Applications with Microsoft 365*,
https://doi.org/10.1007/978-1-4842-8823-8_5

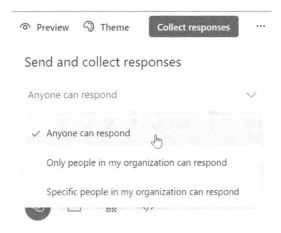

Figure 5-1. *Sharing a form to allow anyone to respond*

Figure 5-2 shows a section of a survey.

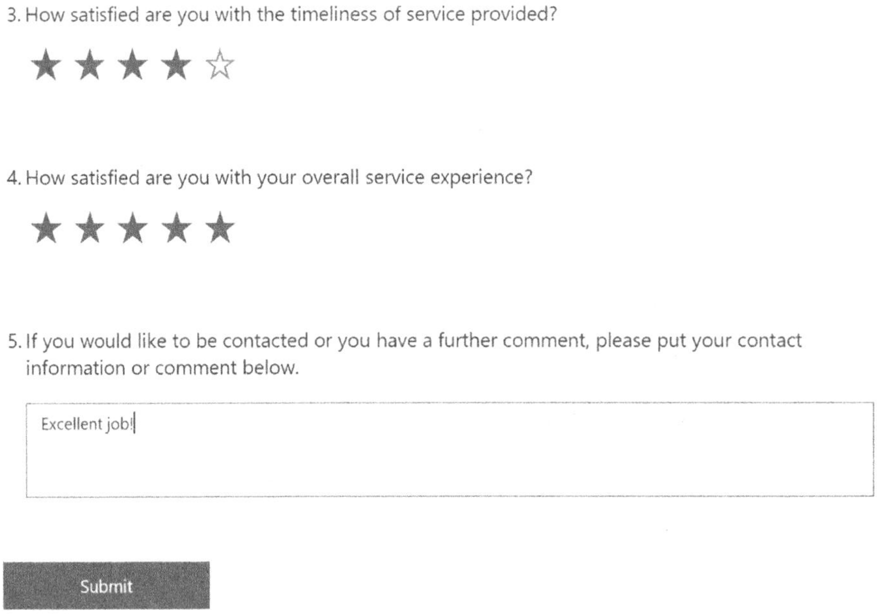

3. How satisfied are you with the timeliness of service provided?

★ ★ ★ ★ ☆

4. How satisfied are you with your overall service experience?

★ ★ ★ ★ ★

5. If you would like to be contacted or you have a further comment, please put your contact information or comment below.

Excellent job!

Submit

Figure 5-2. *Microsoft Forms Survey*

Figure 5-3 shows the resulting form in SharePoint.

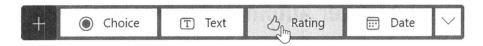

Figure 5-3. *Microsoft Forms question type: Choice, Text, Rating, and Date*

Notice that there is a built-in *Rating* question type where you can set the number of levels (the preceding has five). Figure 5-3 shows the interface when you click the *Add new* button. You can also choose to include a subtitle, make the question required, allow a "long answer" (for the *Text* question type), limit to a number or range (again for *Text*), allow multiple answers, the "shuffling" of answers, and/or an *Other* option (*Choice* type). Since we will automatically get the date when we add the response to SharePoint, I don't normally include a *Date* type unless I am looking for them to enter a date in the future such as the "required by" date.

Adding the SharePoint List

Our next step is to create a list (Figure 5-4) in SharePoint for holding the data. I typically make all the columns *Single line of text* or *Multiple lines of text*.[2] This avoids data type problems when being transferred from Power Automate. We can fix the data types once we get to Power BI.

Issue Summary	Issue Resolved?	Issue Elevated?	Technician Respons...	Technician Knowled...	Customer Satisfacti...	Turnaround Time	Technician Courteous	Recommend CFAM	Comments
Computer problem	Yes	No	5	5	5	5	Yes	Yes	n/a now
Reset local admin password; install printer drivers	Yes	No	5	5	5	5	Yes	Yes	
WiFi Connection	Yes	No	5	5	5	5	Yes	Yes	
New LAC certificates	Yes	No	4	4	4	5	Yes	Yes	Most of the certificate issues were solved, but not all. This may be beyond the expertise of the CFAM people. But I did have to go down a second time as the first person didn't do all the...

Figure 5-4. *SharePoint list for holding the Forms survey data*

---

[2] Be sure to use *Multiple lines of text* if more than 255 characters are possible, such as for a multiple response question.

Creating the Power Automate Flow

Within Power Automate, we create a new flow from a template and search for *SharePoint,* as shown in Figure 5-5. We choose the one to *Record form responses in SharePoint.*

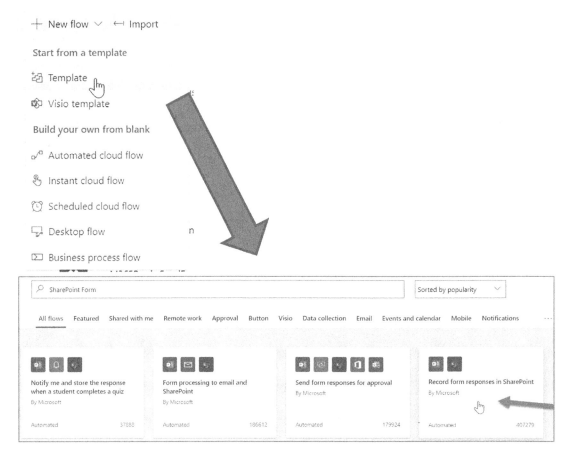

Figure 5-5. *Creating a flow from a SharePoint/Forms template to record responses*

From there, we pick the form and fill in each field in turn (Figure 5-6). Notice that the template includes the *Apply to each* action. If you were building this flow from scratch, you would need to add this action. We get the *List of Responses* in each case.

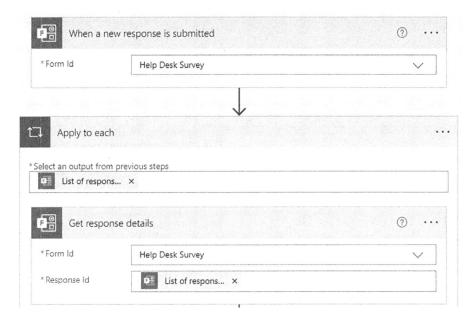

Figure 5-6. *Filling out the Power Automate template*

We then select the SharePoint site and list that we want to populate. From there, we go to each list column and select the corresponding form entry. The beauty of Power Automate is that it presents you with the relevant information you need. In this case, it is the list of questions from the form that need answers to be copied to SharePoint. All this is shown in Figure 5-7. Note that the form questions are labeled by the text of the question. As many of these start with *How satisfied were you ...*, it is helpful to have the form open when doing this step.

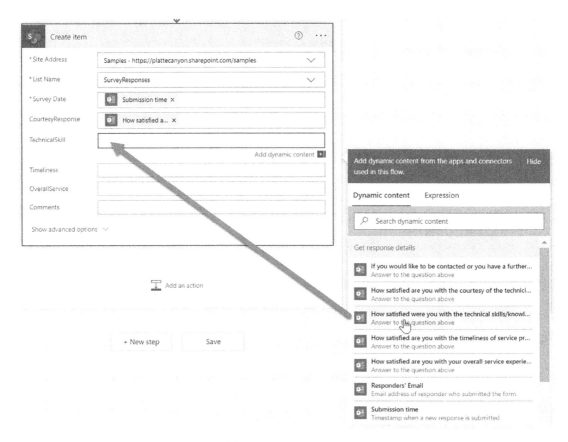

Figure 5-7. *Matching Form answers to SharePoint columns*

Once you save the flow, fill out the form and then go to both Power Automate and SharePoint to see the results. If there are errors, click on the *Run history* to see the details.

Visualize in Power BI

From here, the task is very similar to the previous chapter, where we connected Power BI to a SharePoint survey. We rename the columns as needed and update the data types. In particular, we update the *Survey Date* column to be *DateTime* and the various rating columns to be *Whole Numbers*. We create a *DaysPassed* column with this formula:

```
=DateTime.From(DateTime.LocalNow()) - [Created]
```

This allows us to segregate responses into the most recent week, month, quarter, etc. as needed. This type of data also lends itself to *Measures* as well. I like to distinguish between custom columns and measures this way: custom columns are good for manipulation of data that depends on a single row while measures are good for data across rows. Our DaysPassed column from earlier depends on the single value of the Created column (together with figuring out today's date) and thus should be a custom column. But if we want the average over multiple rows, that will be a good measure. Figure 5-8 shows how we add a measure. We select *New measure,* enter the name (Average Courtesy in this case), and then the formula using the Data Analysis Expressions (DAX) language. In this case, we use the *AVERAGE* function and then select our *[Technician Courteous]* column.

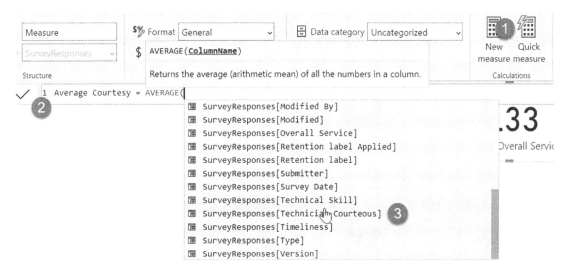

Figure 5-8. *Adding a Power BI Measure*

Figure 5-9 shows how the measure shows up with other *Fields* on the far right and how to use it just like another data element. In this case, we show it in a card visualization. The nice thing is that the measure takes its values from the current context. So if the user slices or drills down on the data (by editing the *Survey Date* slicer or drilling down on *Technical Skill,* for example), the measure values automatically update.

Figure 5-9. *Configuring the Average Courtesy Measure*

Figure 5-10. *Power BI showing survey results with pie chart visualization, slicers, and measures*

We also update the Data colors again so that low score (1) is red, a high score (5) is green, and the ones in between transition from orange to yellow to light green.

Summary

This chapter introduces what I find to be a very powerful use case: collecting data via Microsoft Forms, using Power Automate to copy it to SharePoint, and then visualizing it via Power BI. This protects the data and allows improved drill-down and slicing of data by response date and other metrics.

CHAPTER 6

Power BI Challenges with JSON, XML, and Yes/No Data

Adding in multiple answers, multiple lines of text, and Yes/No responses leads to some additional challenges in visualizing data. This chapter looks at some of these challenges and how to address them.

JSON and HTML Data Formats

Our first example comes from an *IT Demographic Survey* of all our personnel. Figure 6-1 shows a section of the survey that reveals problematic data.

© Jeffrey M. Rhodes 2022
J. M. Rhodes, *Creating Business Applications with Microsoft 365*,
https://doi.org/10.1007/978-1-4842-8823-8_6

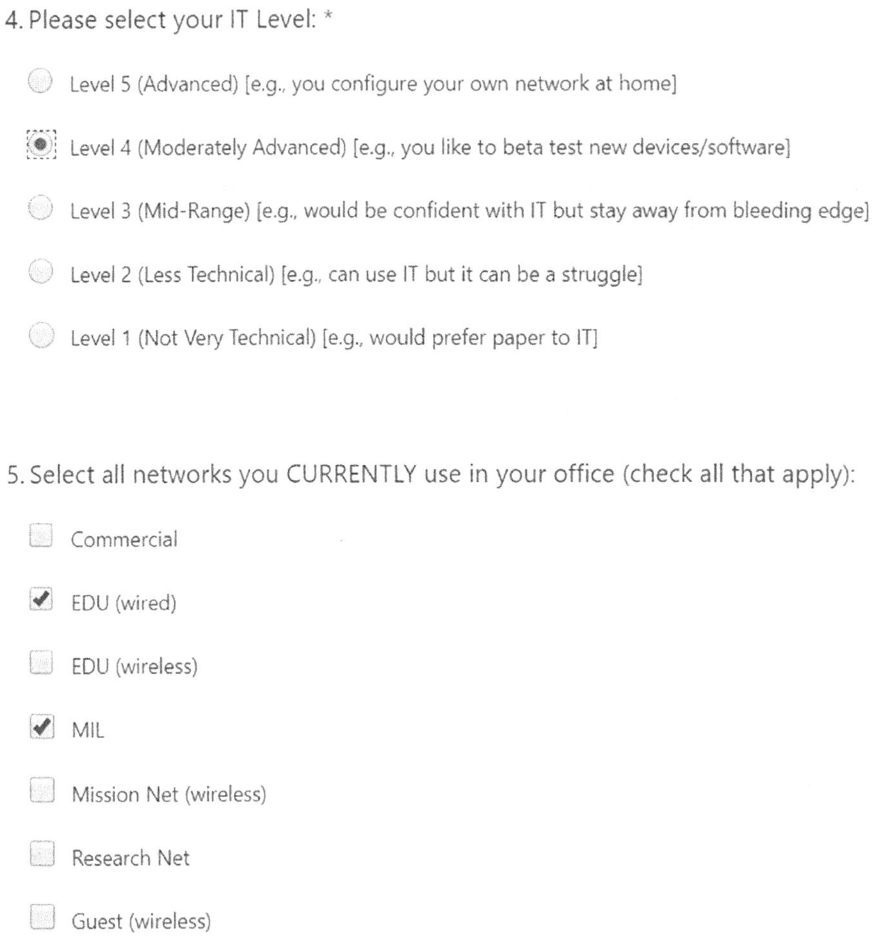

4. Please select your IT Level: *

○ Level 5 (Advanced) [e.g., you configure your own network at home]

◉ Level 4 (Moderately Advanced) [e.g., you like to beta test new devices/software]

○ Level 3 (Mid-Range) [e.g., would be confident with IT but stay away from bleeding edge]

○ Level 2 (Less Technical) [e.g., can use IT but it can be a struggle]

○ Level 1 (Not Very Technical) [e.g., would prefer paper to IT]

5. Select all networks you CURRENTLY use in your office (check all that apply):

☐ Commercial

☑ EDU (wired)

☐ EDU (wireless)

☑ MIL

☐ Mission Net (wireless)

☐ Research Net

☐ Guest (wireless)

Figure 6-1. *Form questions that generate JSON and HTML*

I used the same technique as the previous chapter to copy each response to a SharePoint list using Power Automate. We see the first inkling of an issue when we look at the data in SharePoint, as shown in Figure 6-2. The extra explanatory text after Level 4 gets copied (since it was part of the answer).

ITLevel ∨	CurrentNetworks_Office ∨
Level 4 (Moderately Advanced) [e.g., you like to beta test new devices/software]	["EDU (wired)","MIL"]

Figure 6-2. *SharePoint display of the data showing the complete answer text and JSON format*

More significantly, the multiple answers get represented as:

```
["EDU (wired)","MIL"]
```

Those with some web programming experience might recognize this as *JavaScript Object Notation* (JSON). When we connect to the data in Power BI, we see an additional issue in that the data is displayed as HTML,[1] as shown in Figure 6-3.

A^BC Visual Projection Capability	A^BC Current LMS
<div class="ExternalClass3865B7F1AB4142DEAD4A4F35924E022B">N/A</div>	["N/A"]
<div class="ExternalClassE89BC5E188494C92998F948FB46F942E">Yes. The current vi...	["Blackboard"]
<div class="ExternalClassF86B0F8FAD5E44D987841E3D6CE3E78C">Yes. The current v...	["Blackboard","Moodle"]
<div class="ExternalClassEE4439EDB7E043AAA92224E8C186DE20">No. The current vi...	["Canvas","Blackboard","Infinit...

Figure 6-3. *HTML Format in Power BI for multiline text in SharePoint*

The value looks like this:

```
<div class="ExternalClassE89BC5E188494C92998F948FB46F942E">Yes. The current
visual projection capability in my classroom is sufficient.</div>
```

Working with the Data in Power BI

As in the previous chapter, we connect to the SharePoint list as our data source and then *Transform data* to begin manipulating the data. Our first task is to deal with the HTML format. While we could extract the values as XML (like we will with JSON as follows),

---

[1] This might not have happened if I had selected *Plain Text* in the SharePoint column properties, but users had already started responding to the survey by then. However, we will see that using *FieldValuesAsText* gets us back to plain text.

that is subject to error if there are stray brackets in the data AND it is more problematic for *null* data. Instead, we want to use a similar technique as a previous chapter where we connect to the SharePoint list in the 1.0 implementation, as shown in Figure 6-4.

Figure 6-4. Connecting to a SharePoint list with the 1.0 implementation

This gives us additional options when transforming our data. In particular, it exposes the *FieldValuesAsText* column, which allows us to extract the plain text version of any of our column values. This is shown in Figure 6-5.

Figure 6-5. *Retrieving Field Values as Text*

Our first task is to deal with *null* data. We initially sent out the survey requiring answers, but we updated it later for the stragglers with a request to just fill out the first four questions with the option to skip the rest. For those columns that were JSON, this meant we needed put in *[]* for that data. This is shown in Figure 6-6. Note that we used to enter *null* for the *Value to Find* but now we just leave it blank.

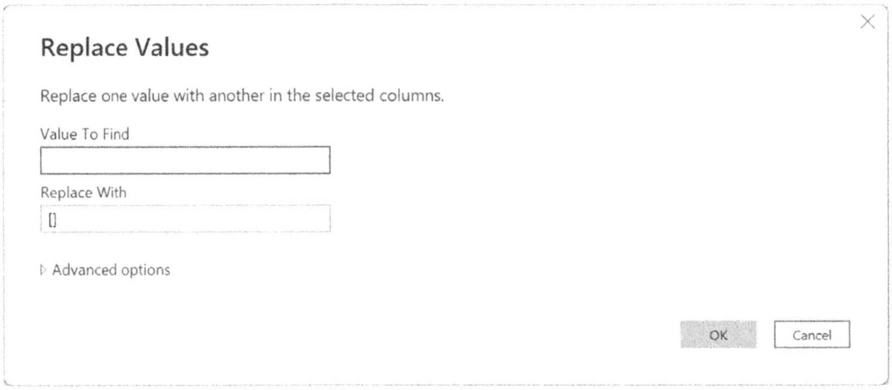

Figure 6-6. *Replacing null JSON values in Power BI*

Our next task is to remove all the extraneous text from our *IT Level* and instead have it show *Level 1* through *Level 4*. As shown in Figure 6-7, we use the *Extract* option and then use *First Characters*, which turns out to be seven. This will make our visualizations much cleaner.

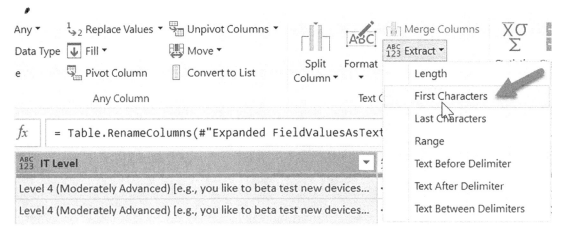

Figure 6-7. *Extracting the first seven characters of the IT Level column*

We have two tasks when working with the JSON data. The first is to eliminate the brackets and the quotes. We do this by going to *Extract – JSON*, as shown in Figure 6-8.

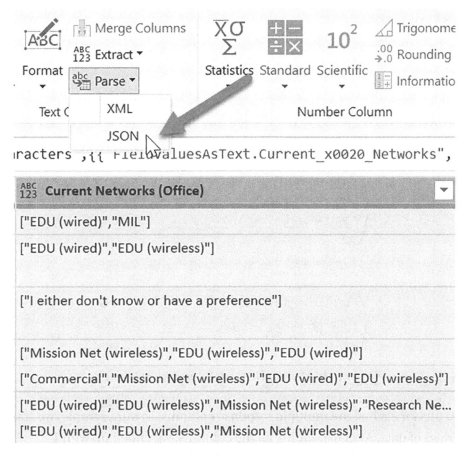

Figure 6-8. *Parsing JSON data in a multiple response column*

The second task is more difficult. Notice how the first row contains *EDU (wired), MIL* while the second contains *EDU (wired), EDU (wireless)*. If we do a visualization "as is," one "pie slice" will be the *EDU (wired), MIL* combination and the other will be the *EDU (wired), EDU (wireless)* combination. What we actually want is to show two *EDU (wired)* answers and one each for *MIL* and *EDU (wireless)*. To make this happen, we need to split each response into its own row. As shown in Figure 6-9, we click on the "Expand" button at the top of the column.[2] We then select *Expand to New Rows*.[3] Each entry gets its own row. Notice the circled *Id* values in Figure 6-9. These are duplicated and are how we will match up these extra rows to the original responses.

---

[2] Note how the previous step of parsing the JSON turned the values to *List* instead of text.

[3] We could also choose *Extract Values*. In that case, we would pick the delimiter (comma in this case) and then we could tell it whether to make rows or columns.

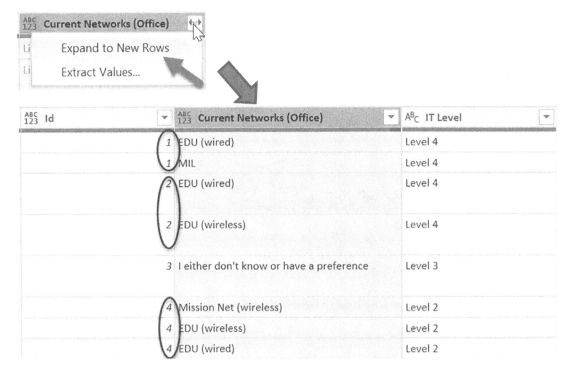

Figure 6-9. *Expanding multiple responses into separate rows*

We do this for each of the multiple response columns. In our example, we started with 270 rows of data. After expanding all the columns, we ended up with 1,227,676 rows! Luckily, Power BI can handle this extra data just fine.

Visualizing the Data in Power BI

After performing these steps on all our JSON columns,[4] we are ready to visualize the data. As we have seen in previous examples, we put the desired column (*Current Networks (Office)* in this case) as the *Details* and then find a unique value like *Id* for the *Count*. Figure 6-10 shows the results. When we look at the tooltip showing the # *of Responses* for *EDU (wired)*, we see the problem. 308,753 responses reflect all the expanded rows described earlier in this chapter and does not reflect the true data.

---

[4] We also created a *DaysPassed* column as in past examples using the formula *=DateTime. From(DateTime.LocalNow()) - [Created]*. We can use this in future years to compare survey results over time.

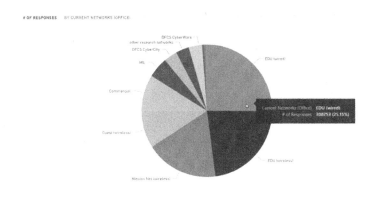

Figure 6-10. *Erroneous results when using Count*

We can now take advantage of the fact we noticed in Figure 6-9 that the *Id* values were duplicated when we expanded the rows. We use *Count (Distinct)* instead as shown in Figure 6-11. The *# of Responses* is now reasonable at 261. Notice how the percentage is much different as well.

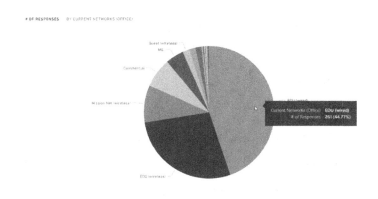

Figure 6-11. *Correct results when using Count (Distinct)*

Another implication of the expanded rows becomes apparent when we want to view the actual data. I normally use a Table for this purpose. If we do that here, however, we see all the duplicate data (name, department, IT Level, etc.). Instead, we can use a *Matrix,* as shown in Figure 6-12. We add each desired element to *Rows* and then click the *Expand all down one level in the hierarchy* button (see arrow in Figure 6-12) until it is disabled. We then go to the *Format your visual* tab and turn off *Stepped Layout* under *Row headers* ➤ *Options*.

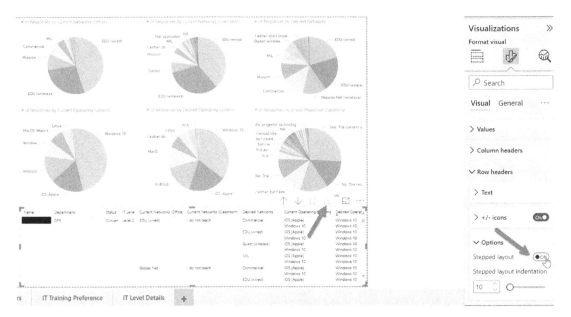

Figure 6-12. *Using a Matrix without stepped layout instead of a Table*

Working with Yes/No Data

Our final task for this chapter is to effectively display Yes/No (or Boolean) data. Figure 6-13 shows a portion of a daily status check form. It is largely a series of Yes/No/ Other questions on whether various systems and networks are operational.

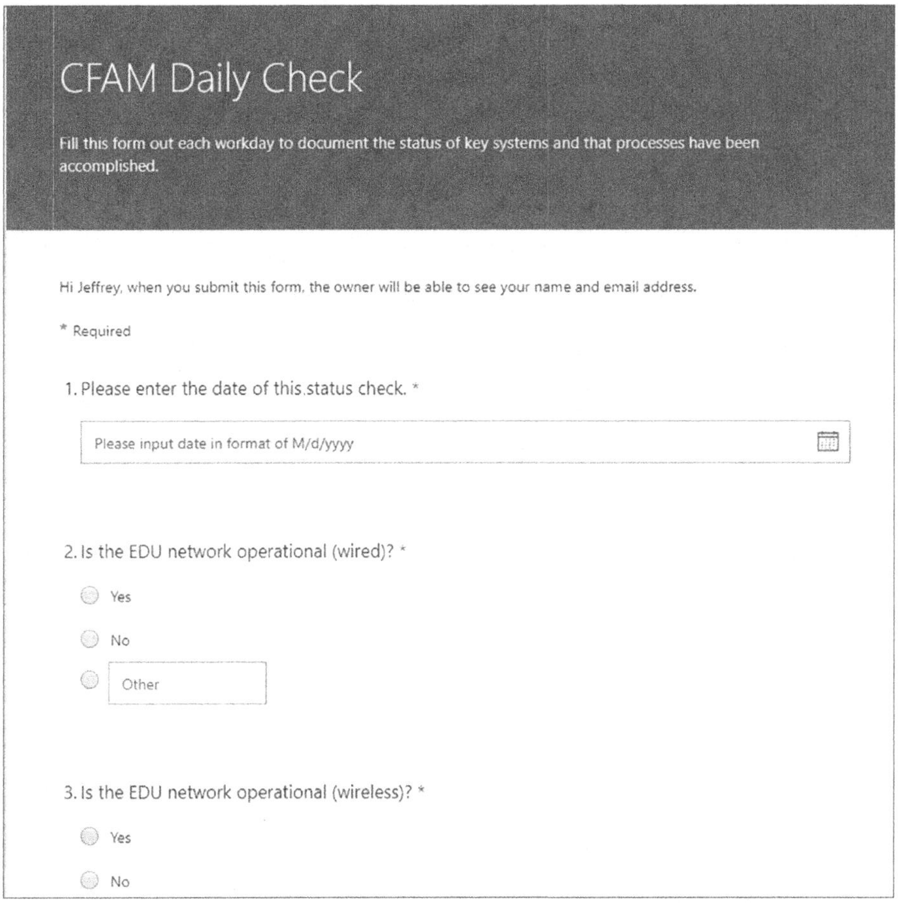

Figure 6-13. *Daily Check form showing Yes/No data*

While we could easily make a standard pie chart for each question showing the numbers of *Yes* and *No* responses, this doesn't give us the desired "dashboard" of both the most recent date (Figure 6-14) and the results over a given time frame (Figure 6-15). To do this, we need to make some adjustments to the data.

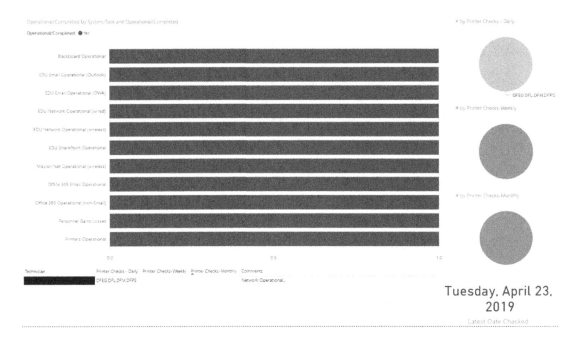

Figure 6-14. *Dashboard showing most recent Daily Check data*

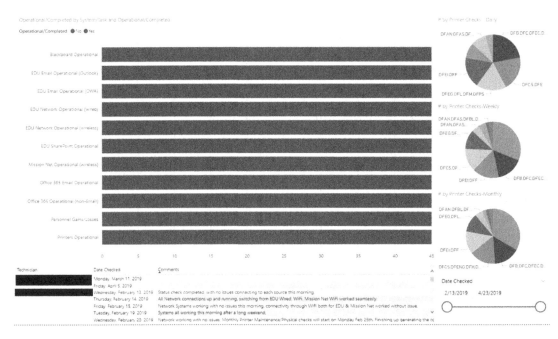

Figure 6-15. *Dashboard showing Daily Check data over time*

As with previous examples, we go to *Transform data*. Before we get into the Yes/No data, let's look at how we come up with the "Most Recent Date." We don't want to limit this to "today" since the daily check may not have occurred yet and we want to use yesterday's (or Friday's if this a Monday) data. For this, I found the easiest way was to first create a *MostRecentSubmissionDate* column using this formula:

```
=List.Max(#"Changed Type"[Created])
```

But where does the *#"Changed Type"* bit come from? That is actually referencing a prior step. To see that, we need to look at the Advanced Editor, as shown in Figure 6-16. With some study, you will see that each step is named and then the next or other later rows refer to that name (#"Changed Type", #"Added Custom", etc.).

Figure 6-16. *Using the Advanced Editor to reference a previous step*

This gives us a column that has the same value in every row, for example *8/23/2022 1:34:33 PM*. We then add a *Conditional Column* that we name *isMostRecentDate*. We put *1* in this column if the *Created* column equals the *MostRecentSubmissionDate* and *0* if not, as shown in Figure 6-17.

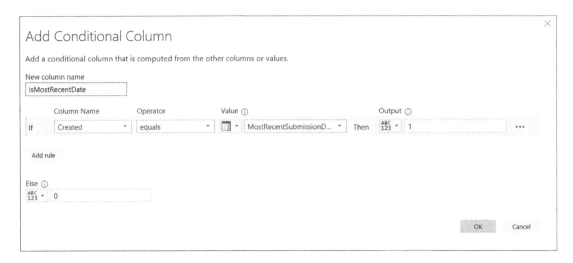

Figure 6-17. *isMostRecentDate conditional column*

We change its type to *True/False* and then use it as the *Page Level Filter,* as shown in Figure 6-18. This limits all data on the page/tab to only the most recent.

Figure 6-18. *isMostRecentDate page-level filter*

Getting back to our Yes/No data, we remove all the unneeded columns (*Author, Editor,* etc. that came over from SharePoint). We then select all the Yes/No columns and choose to *Unpivot Only Selected Columns,* as shown in Figure 6-19. This gives us a new *Attribute* column (that was the previous column name) and a new *Value* column (which is Yes/No/Other). We rename these to *System/Task* and *Operational/Completed,* respectively.

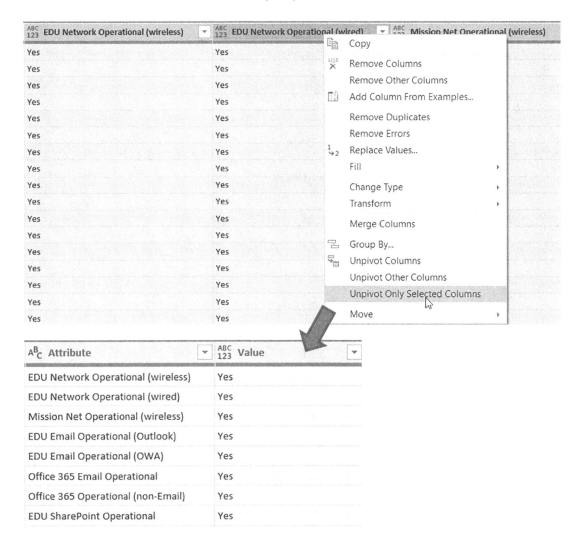

Figure 6-19. *Unpivoting Yes/No columns leading to Attribute and Value columns*

We are now ready to make our visualization. We choose *Stacked Bar Chart* and use *System/Task* for the Axis, *Operational/Completed* as the Legend and the *Count of Operational/Completed* as the Value. This is shown in Figure 6-20.

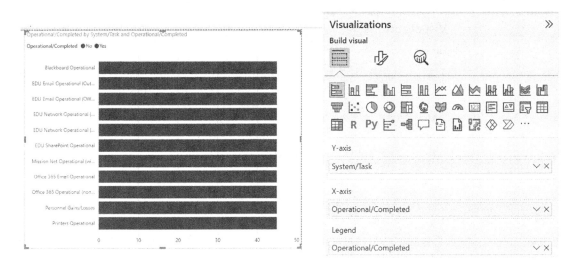

Figure 6-20. *Configuring the stacked bar chart*

Since *Yes* is good and *No* is bad in our context, we set the Data Colors so that *Yes* is green and *No* is red. This is shown in Figure 6-21.

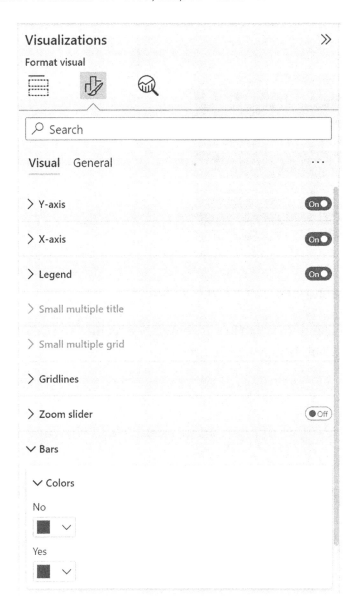

Figure 6-21. *Configuring custom data colors*

Summary

This chapter introduced us to several tools and techniques that help us work with some of the more complicated data types and still accurately and effectively display our data and get the insights that we need.

CHAPTER 7

Power BI Case Study: Monitoring BMC Remedy Help Tickets

Power BI can also be used for non-Microsoft 365 content. This chapter is a case study on using Power BI to visualize data directly from a back-end database. While it takes some work in finding and massaging the data, the payoff can be huge.

A Remedy Dashboard

Remedy is an IT Service Management software that manages incidents, work orders, and other "Help Desk" items. An important task is monitoring ticket status, how long they have been open, whether they have been assigned, and other tasks. Before Power BI, this had been accomplished by exporting data from Remedy to Excel and then creating charts. Not only was this labor-intensive, but the data was stale by the time it was presented at a staff meeting. Figure 7-1 shows a sample of using Power BI instead. It covers data from the previous 90 days and shows the number of tickets by support group (section), the status, the organization (Mission Element) with the issue, who submitted the ticket,[1] who the ticket was assigned to, etc.

---

[1] As we will discuss later in the chapter, finding out the submitter for a ticket was a major issue. This was because technicians used their *Common Access Card* to log into the system. This in turn meant that the "login" info in Remedy was a number associated with this card. Going into the Remedy to view a ticket only showed this number. We fixed this with Power BI.

© Jeffrey M. Rhodes 2022
J. M. Rhodes, *Creating Business Applications with Microsoft 365*,
https://doi.org/10.1007/978-1-4842-8823-8_7

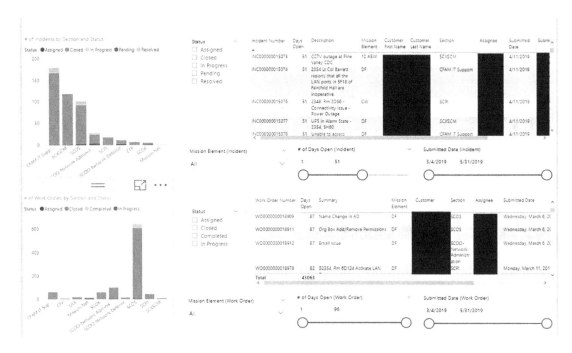

Figure 7-1. *Power BI dashboard showing Remedy ticket data*

Configuring the Power BI Data Source

Remedy did not expose a data source that could be used by Power BI, so I went straight to its database (Microsoft SQL Server in our case). It took some effort to find the right data, but eventually discovered the BMC developers had created views to match the names of the relevant Remedy forms: *CTM_People*, *HPD_HelpDesk*, and *WOI_WorkOrder*.[2] Looking at the data, one immediate issue was that the dates were all numbers. A quick search found these were being stored in Unix or POSIX time, which the number of seconds since January 1, 1970. This is one of the many things we can address once we get to Power BI.

---

[2] This approach is not documented. After mentioning it to BMC personnel, I did a webinar for one of their support executives, who was excited about the possibilities and planned to show it to other customers.

Within Power BI, we choose *SQL Server* database as the data source and then enter the *Server, Database,* and *Credentials*.[3] We add a query for each of our desired views.

The only reason we need *CTM_People* is to look up the first and last name of the support staff. As explained in a previous footnote, the mechanics of "Single Sign-On" via a Common Access Card (CAC) meant the *login ID* displayed within Remedy was a bunch of numbers. Remedy forms take care of this for the *assignee* of the ticket but not for the *submitter* of the ticket. We can use this *CTM_People* view to fix the issue. As shown in Figure 7-2, we set up a relationship between these tables and link the *Submitter* and *Remedy_Login_ID* columns. When it comes time to display who submitted the ticket, we grab the name from *CTM_People* in order to display the actual name.

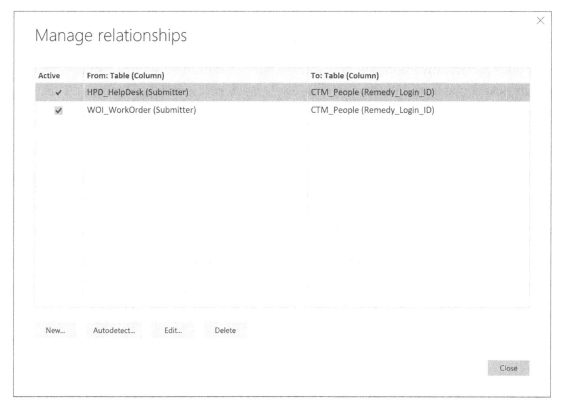

Figure 7-2. Relationships between the CTM_People and HPD_HelpDesk/WOI_Workgroups views

---

[3] One problem was that Power BI has a limit of 10,000 tables/views and the Remedy database exceeded that limit. So, you can't pick the view you want. Instead, pick any table and then go into the *Advanced Editor* and put the correct view name in there. Rename the query to match the correct view name.

For both *HPD_HelpDesk* (which contains incidents) and *WOI_WorkOrders* (which contains work orders[4]), we create a custom *SubmitDateCustom* column using this formula:

```
SubmitDateCustom = #datetime(1970, 1, 1, 0, 0, 0) + #duration(0, -6, 0, [Submit_Date])
```

This converts from the Unix date discussed earlier. The *duration* function takes account of the time zone so the time is Mountain rather than Coordinated Universal Time (UTC), previously known as Greenwich Mean Time. As with previous examples, we create a *DaysPassed* column that shows the number of days since the *SubmitDateCustom*:

```
DaysPassed - DateTime.From(DateTime.LocalNow()) - [SubmitDateCustom]
```

This is particularly important here as we want to flag (and do special visualizations) for any ticket open longer than our *service level agreement* (such as seven days). The main other challenge was that the *Status* was stored as a numeric value. We duplicated the *Status* column and then *Replaced Values* with the corresponding text values (Assigned, In Progress, Completed, Resolved, etc.).[5]

One of my later tasks was to manage a particular support team that used this same system. This often involved submitting tickets to other support teams. It was useful to follow up on these tickets. Figure 7-3 shows an example of how this approach can be customized. We used the same queries as before but then filtered the data to ONLY show tickets submitted by the members of my particular support team. The report then showed exactly who is assigned to that ticket as well as its current status.

---

[4] In a nutshell, incidents are things that are broken (like being unable to send an email) while work orders are new tasks (like creating an account).

[5] Since these were not documented, figuring out what each number represented meant looking in the database for the numeric status value and then looking that ticket up in Remedy to see the actual text value.

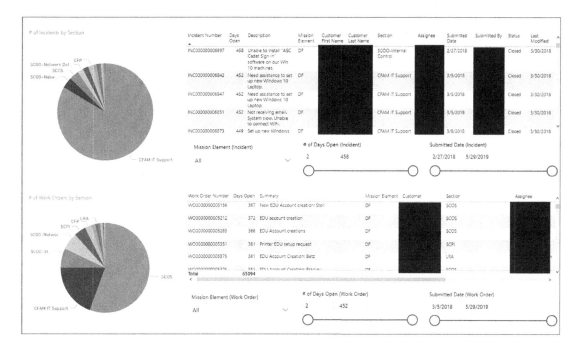

Figure 7-3. *Power BI dashboard showing the status of tickets submitted by a particular support team*

This just scratches the surface of what this kind of approach can do. We can look at which organizations and users submit the most/least tickets and which support groups and technicians handle them. We could even integrate our survey data from previous chapters show that data and flag any correlations.

Summary

In this chapter, we connected to BMC Remedy to visualize Help Ticket data directly from the back-end data source. It illustrates one of the most powerful aspects of the product, which is to transform raw data and skip the traditional process of spreadsheets, pivot tables, and the like.

CHAPTER 8

Building a Help Ticketing System in PowerApps and SharePoint: New Ticket Form

This chapter continues our case study of using the Power Platform to create a Help Desk ticketing system and then visualize and track its data. These types of systems can very effectively fill the gaps between spreadsheets and paper forms on the low end and elaborate and expensive systems like Remedy and ServiceNow.

The new help desk group for our area initially only had paper forms for in-person visits, which was certainly not optimal. With the advent of Microsoft 365, I wanted to see what its new capabilities could do. I introduced the SharePoint list data source for a new solution in an earlier chapter.

New Ticket Form

At that time, all our users did not yet have Microsoft 365 accounts.[1] But that wasn't a problem because a "kiosk" computer[2] would itself have a M365 account and would be "signed in." Figure 8-1 shows my initial look for a *New Ticket* form.

---

[1] Email, SharePoint, and other services were on-premise and not tied to Microsoft 365.

[2] Originally an extra Windows laptop but later we used an iPad.

© Jeffrey M. Rhodes 2022
J. M. Rhodes, *Creating Business Applications with Microsoft 365*,
https://doi.org/10.1007/978-1-4842-8823-8_8

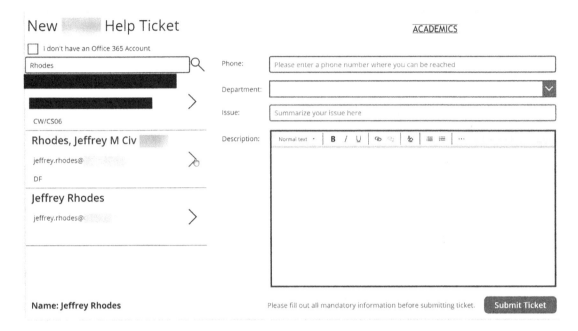

Figure 8-1. *New Ticket form showing the lookup of users in Microsoft 365 as well as cues for proper entry*

Setting Up in Power Apps

For this form, we choose to create a *Blank canvas app* in Power Apps and choose the *Tablet format.*[3] Our next task is to add a *SharePoint* data source and point it to our *Help Tickets* list. We also add an *Office365Users* data source we will use to look up users (for those who have Microsoft 365 accounts). Finally, we add an *Office365 Outlook* data source for sending email. These data connections are shown in Figure 8-2.

---

[3] *Tablet* since it was primarily for the kiosk computer. Once we let users create their own tickets, then the *Phone* format made more sense.

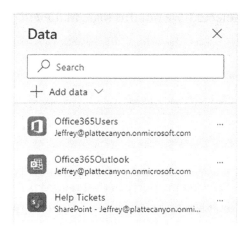

Figure 8-2. *Office 365 Users, Outlook, and SharePoint data sources*

Our first big task is to allow the user to find himself or herself in Office 365. We add a *Text Input* for the search and an icon for the magnifying glass. We use a *Gallery* control to display the results so users can type in their name and find their record. To make that work, we set the Gallery's *Items* property to:

```
Office365Users.SearchUserV2({searchTerm:searchUser.Text, top: 10}).value
```

This gives us a *Table* that we then "bind" to the Gallery control with each record displaying in a separate cell. As we discussed in our opening chapter, I like how Power App's web-based editor uses a single interface for both setting properties and programming. In traditional editors like Visual Studio and languages like C#, you set properties in one window and then put the programming into a separate "code behind" file. In Power Apps, we can add programming right into the same place where we set the property values.[4] In the preceding code, we set the *Items* property of the control by calling the *SearchUserV2* method of the *Office365Users* data connection. We set the *searchTerm* parameter to be the *Text* property of our *searchUser* Text Input control. We limit our values to the top 10.

We set the *Gallery* to be a *Title* layout and associate the controls with the *DisplayName, Mail,* and *Department* attributes from Office 365. To make it easier

---

[4] As we have discussed, programming is largely a matter of reading/setting properties, responding to events, and calling methods. Events are listed right along with properties in the editor, making it as easy to handle them as it is to set properties.

to tell which user we have selected, we put this logic in the *Fill* property of the *DisplayName* label:

```
If(
    ThisItem.IsSelected,
    Color.Yellow,
    RGBA(0, 0, 0, 0)
)
```

This means that if the *IsSelected* property of that record is true, then the background fill color is yellow. Otherwise, it is white.

Similarly, we set the *Text* property of the *UserName* label at the bottom left of Figure 8-1 to be:

```
"Name: " & If(
    NoO365Account.Value,
    FirstNameInput.Text & " " & LastNameInput.Text,
    If(
        UsersGallery.Visible,
        UsersGallery.Selected.GivenName & " " & UsersGallery.Selected.
Surname,
        ""
    )
)
```

This code makes more sense if we refer to Figure 8-3, which shows the form when the user checks the *I don't have an Office 365 Account* box. When that box is true, we concatenate the first name and last name the user enters. If not, we see if the *UsersGallery* is visible (we hide it until the user starts searching since it otherwise defaults to the first user) and, if so, concatenate the *GivenName* and *Surname* properties. Otherwise, we leave the name part blank.

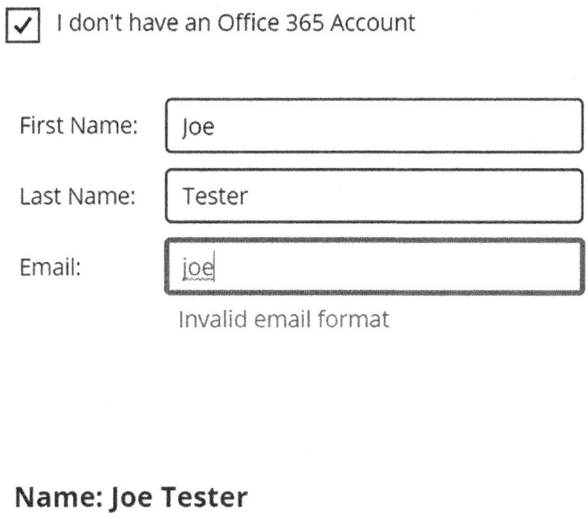

☑ I don't have an Office 365 Account

First Name: | Joe |

Last Name: | Tester |

Email: | joe |

Invalid email format

Name: Joe Tester

Figure 8-3. *Entering name and email when the user does not have an Office 365 account*

Here is the code for the *UsersGallery Visible* property:

```
(!NoO365Account.Value && (searchUser.Text <> "" &&
!IsBlank(searchUser.Text)))
```

In words, this says to show the Gallery when the *I don't have an Office 365 Account* box is unchecked AND when search text is not an empty string AND is not blank.

Note how there is a label showing that the email format is invalid. We make this work by setting its *Visible* value to be:

```
If(
    NoO365Account.Value,
    If(
        IsMatch(
            EmailInput.Text,
            Match.Email
        ) || IsBlank(EmailInput.Text),
        false,
        true
    ),
    False
)
```

This demonstrates a "nested" If condition. If the *NoO365Account* box is checked, then we see if we have a valid email format (the second If). If not, the *Visible* is false. To check the valid format, we use the *IsMatch* method, passing it what the user entered and telling it to match it to an *Email* format. Since email is not required, we also allow it to be blank. In those cases, *Visible* is false. Otherwise (not blank and invalid), it is true. We use similar logic to set the *BorderColor* to maroon[5] when the format is invalid:

```
If(
    NoO365Account.Value,
    If(
        IsMatch(
            EmailInput.Text,
            Match.Email
        ) || IsBlank(EmailInput.Text),
        RGBA(0, 18, 107, 1),
        RGBA(184, 0, 0, 1)
    ),
    RGBA(0, 18, 107, 1)
)
```

Let's look at the right side of Figure 8-1. We set the *HintText* property for the Phone and Issue to give users more information on what to enter. For Department, we could have linked it to the choices within SharePoint (see later chapters for examples), but we don't want there to be a default that the user just accepts in this case. Instead, we set the values explicitly with the initial choice being blank. We then make sure there is a selection before allowing the form to be submitted. To do this, we set the Items property to be:

```
["","DF","DFAN","DFAS","DFB","DFBL","DFC","DFCE","DFCS","DFEC","DFEG","DFEI
","DFEM","DFENG","DFF","DFH","DFK","DFL","DFLIB","DFM","DFMI","DFMS","DFP",
"DFPS","DFPY","DFR","DFRO","DFRO (UAS)","DFS","Other"]
```

---

[5] RGBA stands for Red-Green-Blue-Alpha, where each value goes from 0 to 255. Alpha gives the amount of transparency. A tool like Photoshop is good from coming up with these values. Note as in other examples that you can also use named colors like *Color.Yellow.*

Issue is the single-most important field, so we give it a maroon highlight until the user enters information. We do that by setting the *BorderColor* property to be:

```
If(
    IssueInput.Text = "",
    RGBA(184, 0, 0, 1),
    RGBA(0, 18, 107, 1)
)
```

The last task before we write the ticket data to SharePoint is to ensure we have all the required information. For that, we make the *RequiredValuesLabel* and give it the text of "Please fill out all mandatory data before submitting ticket." We set its *Visible* property to be:

```
If(
    (DepartmentDropDown.SelectedText.Value = Blank() || DepartmentDropDown.
SelectedText.Value = "" || IssueInput.Text = "" || InvalidFormatLabel.
Visible),
    true,
    false
)
```

The || represents an OR condition. So if there is no department selected, no issue entered, or if the invalid email format warning is showing (see preceding discussion), we show this label.

Writing Data Back to SharePoint

We are now ready to write the ticket back to our SharePoint data source.[6] We handle the *OnSelect* event, as shown in Figure 8-4. Notice how you can drag down the entry space in the browser to give more space for typing.

---

[6] Note that this would work for Excel or other data source as well.

Figure 8-4. *Handling the OnSelect event and writing ticket data to the SharePoint data source*

Listing 8-1 shows the code after clicking the *Format text* link shown in Figure 8-4. We will go through each section in turn.

Listing 8-1. OnSelect code for writing ticket information to a SharePoint list

```
If(
    RequiredValuesLabel.Visible,
    false,
    If(
        NoO365Account.Value,
        Patch(
            'Help Tickets',
            Defaults('Help Tickets'),
            {
                Issue: IssueInput.Text,
                'Phone Number': PhoneInput.Text,
                Department: DepartmentDropDown.SelectedText,
                Description: DescriptionInput.HtmlText,
                'User (Not Office 365)': LastNameInput.Text & ", " &
                FirstNameInput.Text,
                'Email (Not Office 365)': EmailInput.Text
            }
        ),
        Patch(
            'Help Tickets',
            Defaults('Help Tickets'),
            {
```

```
            Issue: IssueInput.Text,
            'Phone Number': PhoneInput.Text,
            Department: DepartmentDropDown.SelectedText,
            Description: DescriptionInput.HtmlText,
            'User (Office 365)': {
                '@odata.type': "#Microsoft.Azure.Connectors.SharePoint.
                SPListExpandedUser",
                ODataType: Blank(),
                Claims: Concatenate(
                    "i:0#.f|membership|",
                    UsersGallery.Selected.Mail
                ),
                DisplayName: UsersGallery.Selected.DisplayName,
                Email: UsersGallery.Selected.Mail,
                Department: "",
                JobTitle: "",
                Picture: ""
            }
        }
    )
)
);
If(
    !RequiredValuesLabel.Visible,
    Office365Outlook.SendEmailV2(
        "notificationEmail@test.com",
        "New Ticket - " & IssueInput.Text & " (" & UserName.Text & ")",
        "User: " & UserName.Text & "<br/><br/>Issue: " & IssueInput.Text &
        "<br/><br/>Description: " & DescriptionInput.HtmlText,
        {
            IsHtml: true,
            Importance: Normal
        }
    );
    Reset(IssueInput);
```

```
    Reset(DescriptionInput);
    Reset(DepartmentDropDown);
    Reset(EmailInput);
    Reset(LastNameInput);
    Reset(FirstNameInput);
    Reset(searchUser);
    Reset(NoO365Account);
    Reset(PhoneInput);
    Reset(UsersGallery);
    UpdateContext({popupVisible: true}),
    false
)
```

We first check to see if our *RequiredValuesLabel* is visible. If so, we know we have
an error (and don't have to repeat all our earlier error-checking logic) and return *false*
(which means nothing else will happen). Next, we check to see if the user has an Office
365 account. If so, we send the *User (Office 365)* info. Otherwise, we send the *User (Not
Office 365)* information. Note that we added the non-365 email as a separate SharePoint
column so we could use that to send an email when the technician resolves the ticket.
To write the information to SharePoint, we call the *Patch* method.[7] The first parameter is
the data source (*Help Tickets* list). The second parameter is the *record* we want to modify.
We call the *Defaults* method to create a record.[8] This also puts any default values into
the columns. For example, the *Status* column defaults to *New* and thus we don't have to
write it here. Finally, for complex columns like *Person* or *Lookups*, we pass in an object
(defined with {}) with properties corresponding to the column name in the SharePoint
list. Note how column names with spaces need to be in single quotes. The "no Office
365" case is simpler because we just pass in the first name, last name, and email. When
we have a 365 user, however, we need to pass in an object. Here it is again:

---

[7] I prefer using *Patch* instead of the built-in method (e.g., from creating from a template) of
submitting the form since it gives more control over what is happening. You will see lots of
examples of Patch through the rest of the book.

[8] We will see later that we can reference the record/list item we want to update if we are doing that
instead.

```
{
  '@odata.type': "#Microsoft.Azure.Connectors.SharePoint.
SPListExpandedUser",
  ODataType: Blank(),
  Claims: Concatenate(
      "i:0#.f|membership|",
      UsersGallery.Selected.Mail
  ),
  DisplayName: UsersGallery.Selected.DisplayName,
  Email: UsersGallery.Selected.Mail,
  Department: "",
  JobTitle: "",
  Picture: ""
}
```

We start with an OData (Open Data Protocol) type to tell Power Apps that this is a SharePoint *person*. We take advantage of the fact that the Claims (credentials) are in the format *i:0#.f|membership|<email address>*. We need that, the *DisplayName* and the *Email* in order to present the proper user to SharePoint.

Returning to Listing 8-1, we use the *Office365Outlook* data connection and call its *SendEmailV2* function,[9] passing in the address, the subject (note how we put the issue and the user in there), and the body (showing the user, issue, and description). Notice how to use the HTML break (<br />) tag to put in hard returns. That goes along with setting the *IsHtml* property to true. Power Apps defaults to a low importance email, so we set it to *Normal*. From there, we now want to *Reset* all the entries so this kiosk form is ready for the next user. Notice how we can separate commands with semicolons (;). That's it except for the *UpdateContext* line, which we will cover next.

In testing this form, users weren't sure if their ticket got submitted correctly. So I decided to add a popup confirmation. For that, we use a local variable we will call *popupVisible*. It defaults to false, but we use the *UpdateContext* command to set it to true. Figure 8-5 shows how we implement this as a group of a button, icon (the X at the upper right), and a label. We set the *Visible* property of the group to be *popupVisible*. Clicking either the button or the X sets the *popupVisible* variable back to false, which closes the popup and makes the form ready for the next user.

---

[9] We found that this email notification was not necessary once the technician app was deployed and users could see the ticket queue there instead. We then removed this email altogether.

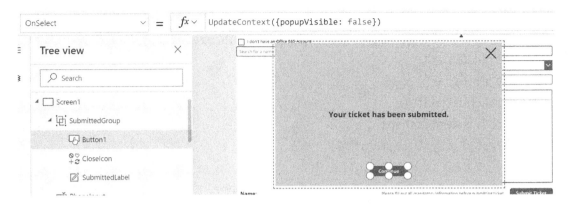

Figure 8-5. *Popup confirmation group with its Visible property controlled by the popupVisible local variable*

By design, this initial form is fairly simple. Users identify themselves, say what their problem is, and provide some optional identity details. The app updates our data source (SharePoint list) and sends out an email notification of the new ticket. We will pick up this story in later chapters.

Summary

In this chapter, we continued our extended example of building a help ticketing system in the Power Platform. We created a kiosk form for adding a ticket. Since not all users had Microsoft 365 accounts at that time, the form has some logic to account for that. It saves the ticket data back to a SharePoint list and notifies the technicians there is a new ticket to be handled.

CHAPTER 9

Continuing the Help Ticketing System: Technician Form

This chapter continues with our example of building a Help Ticketing solution with the Power Platform. We look at what technicians need. Since they need to look up tickets and interact with them over time, there is more functionality than the user submission form we examined in the last chapter.

Now that we have our tickets in the SharePoint list, we can significantly improve the productivity of our help desk technicians by letting them manage tickets on their mobile devices (as well as their computer if desired). We let Power Apps build the basic plumbing of the form and then customize from there.

In Power Apps, we choose to *Start from SharePoint*, which defaults to a Canvas app with a Phone layout. We then tell it to use our SharePoint list as the data source. Power Apps makes us three screens: *Browse*, *Detail*, and *Edit*. We will go through the edits to each of these screens in turn.

Browse Screen

On the *Browse* screen, we want to add a *Status* drop-down box so a technician can filter the tickets by status. We default it to *New* so that new tickets will show up by default. We also want to change the Search from the default of searching by Title (*Issue* in our case) to search by Technician. Finally, we want to edit what information is displayed in *BrowseGallery1*. All of these are shown in Figure 9-1.

© Jeffrey M. Rhodes 2022
J. M. Rhodes, *Creating Business Applications with Microsoft 365*,
https://doi.org/10.1007/978-1-4842-8823-8_9

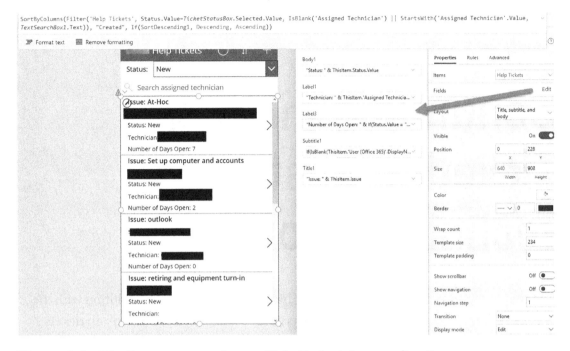

Figure 9-1. *The Browse screen in our Help Technician application*

We insert a label and drop-down box for our status. We move the gallery down a bit to make room. We set the *Items* property of the drop-down box to be *Choices('Help Tickets'.Status)*. This ties it to the *Choice* column in SharePoint and makes sure the choices on the form are updated when the SharePoint column is edited. For the *Search* functionality, we change the *HintText* to give an indication that the search is for the assigned technician. The next step is to change the Items property for the gallery to be:

```
SortByColumns(Filter('Help Tickets', Status.Value=TicketStatusBox.Selected.
Value, IsBlank('Assigned Technician') || StartsWith('Assigned Technician'.
Value, TextSearchBox1.Text)), "Created", If(SortDescending1, Descending,
Ascending))
```

We take advantage of the fact that the *Filter* method can take multiple parameters. So in addition to the default *StartsWith* parameter, which we adjust by making it applicable to the *Assigned Technician* column,[1] we add the matching of the *Status* to what we

---

[1] Notice how we use an OR condition (||) and *IsBlank()* to account for the fact that there won't be a technician assigned at first. Without this, only tickets with an assigned technician would be displayed (and we couldn't then see the tickets to assign them to someone).

select in the *Status* drop-down box. The last parameter sets the order of searching. *SortDescending1* is a context variable that is toggled by the up and down arrows at the top of the screen. The arrows' *OnSelect* events have this value: *UpdateContext({SortDesc ending1: !SortDescending1})*. This means to make *SortDescending1* true if it was false and vice-versa. We list *Descending* first since *SortDescending1* defaults to false and we want an *Ascending* sort initially so the oldest tickets are at the top.

One complication that took me hours to debug[2] later is the minute we use the *Filter* command on a "complex" column like *Status* (since it is a SharePoint choice column), Power Apps limits us to 500 records by default. This is a big problem since our newest tickets are at the end of the SharePoint list. You can raise this limit to 2000 but needs some significant work to go above that (as we will show in a later chapter). To be fair, the Power Apps editor warned me about the filter limit; I just ignored it:). You can see the warning icon in Figure 9-1. Fixing this turned out to be non-trivial. Before coming up with the more general solution covered later, I made *Single Line Text* columns called *Ticket Status* and *Ticket Assigned Technician* and used a workflow[3] to automatically update these columns when either the *Status* or *Assigned Technician* values changed. The updated Items value then looks like this:

```
SortByColumns(Filter('Help Tickets', 'Ticket Status'=TicketStatusBox.
Selected.Value, 'Ticket Assigned Technician'="" || StartsWith('Ticket
Assigned Technician', TextSearchBox1.Text)), "Created", If(SortDescending1,
Descending, Ascending))
```

Notice how we needed to get rid of the *IsBlank()* function as well. The good news is these changes fixed the issue.

Our last task on this screen is the edit the information shown in the gallery control. Referring again to Figure 9-1, we add two extra labels to the card so we can show the *Issue, User, Status, Assigned Technician*, and *Number of Days Open*. Since it not obvious what the data represents, we add a description before the value as in *"Status: " & ThisItem.Status.Value*. As you might recall, we can have either an *Office 365 user* or a

---

[2] I was making other edits to the form and couldn't get any of the new tickets I created for testing to show up. I eventually figured out that only the first 500 records were being retrieved from the list (e.g., including all our resolved and currently being worked tickets).

[3] A SharePoint 2013 workflow at the time, but this can be done Power Automate instead. We show this technique as well as the better process of using collections to avoid delegation issues later in the book.

non-Office 365 user. To avoid having to confuse our screen with two values (one of which would be blank), we use this logic for our user display:

```
If(IsBlank(
    ThisItem.'User (Office 365)'.DisplayName),
    ThisItem.'User (Not Office 365)',
    ThisItem.'User (Office 365)'.DisplayName
)
```

The *Number of Days* functionality takes advantage of the useful *DateDiff* function to give us the number of days between two dates:

```
"Number of Days Open: " & If(
    Status.Value = "Resolved",
    DateDiff(Created,'Resolved Date'),
    DateDiff(Created,Now())
)
```

If the ticket has been resolved, we stop the clock and use the difference between *Resolved Date* and *Created*. Otherwise, we use the *Now()* function to get the difference between the current date and time and *Created*.

Details Screen

On the *Details* screen (Figure 9-2), we click *Edit fields* to display the desired data and to add or delete fields (columns). We display the *ID* primary key value from SharePoint, but rename it as the *Ticket Number*. We also show the *Created* date so the technician can see when the ticket was first entered. The *(custom)* identifier means that we have unlocked the data card to change the controls and/or the formulas. We customized User as well to put in the same formula described earlier. The renaming of ID is a customization as was including our *Number of Days Open* information below the *Created* value. We also unlocked *Description* and *Notes* to use an *HTML Text* control so the HTML/Rich Text that we input in the form in the last chapter as well as the notes that the technicians add will be displayed correctly.[4]

---

[4] We could have used the *Rich text editor* control as well and, in fact, that works better when it comes time to edit the *Description*.

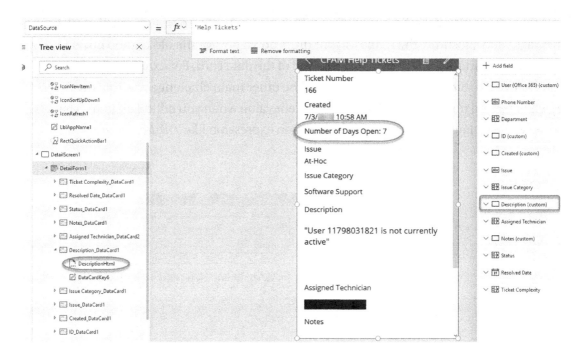

Figure 9-2.   *The Details screen in our Help Technician application*

New/Edit Screen

The *Edit* form (also used for new records) is similar to the one for users to create a ticket discussed in the previous chapter. However, we need to include all the fields rather than just the issue, user, etc. This is because a technician may use this form to open and close a ticket all in one action, for example, when they help a customer over the phone and then document the ticket afterwards. Figure 9-3 shows the form in the development environment. As with other screens, we use *Edit fields* to add or delete what fields/ columns we want to include. Many of these are customized. The biggest reason is because Power Apps uses combo boxes rather than drop-down boxes for choices like *Department, Issue Category, Assigned Technician,* and *Status.* Changing this[5] involves unlocking the data card, adding a *Drop-down* control and making it the same size and position as the combo box, changing its *Items* property (to something like *Choices('Help Tickets'.Status))*,

---

[5] I didn't notice the problem with the default combo box control when testing on a computer. However, when I published a version to the help desk and a technician tested on his iPad, each combo box displayed the iPad's virtual keyboard and that got in the way of filling in the form. Switching to drop-down boxes fixed that problem.

and then deleting the combo box. This results in a couple of error messages. You click the messages and substitute the name of your drop-down box for the old combo box name. The most important is for the *Update* method of the data card. For example, for *Status* you change it to *StatusDropDown.Selected*. The other main challenge was that the drop-down boxes did not correctly display the current value when you edited an item. That was because the Default value needed to be set to an expression like *ThisItem.Status.Value*.

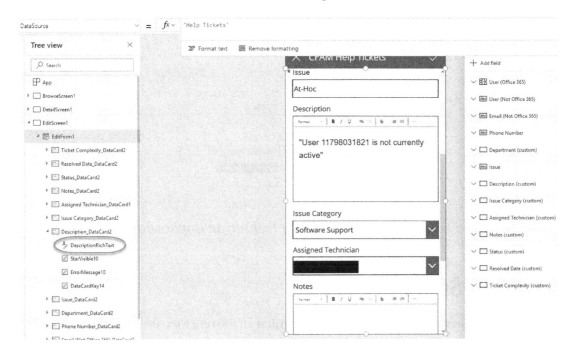

Figure 9-3. *The New/Edit screen in our Help Technician application*

The other main change was to enable the entry of HTML/Rich Text into the *Description*. You might think we would use the *HTML Text* control again, but that displays HTML but does not allow the user to edit or enter it. Instead, we need to use the *Rich text editor* control.

A time-saving feature is to set the *Resolved Date* value to the current date when the technician changes the *Status* to Resolved. To do that, we unlock the *Resolved Date Data Card* and set the *DefaultDate* to:

```
If(
    StatusDropDown.Selected.Value = "Resolved",
    Today(),
    Parent.Default
)
```

We check the value of the *StatusDropDown* and, if it is Resolved, we set it to the built-in *Today()* function. Otherwise, we use the original value, which is *Parent.Default*.

A disconcerting problem surfaced when using the application to change a ticket status. Since we are filtering on *Status* (see Figure 9-1), this meant our ticket disappeared once we saved it. For example, we open the application, change the *Status* filter to *Assigned/In Progress* and select the ticket we want. This takes us to the *Details* screen. We edit the ticket and change its status to *Resolved*. We are returned to the Details screen, but now a different ticket is displayed. That's because our current item now doesn't meet the filter. To fix that, the most logical solution (to me at least) was to change the filter to our new status (Resolved in this example). To make this work, we need to know our current filter value and, if the new status is different, change the filter.

Another related requirement is to send the user an email when the ticket is resolved. For that logic, we need to know our current ticket status and then send the email if the status has changed to *Resolved*.[6] For both of these requirements, we need to share values between different screens and thus need global variables. We set them when we create a new ticket (*OnSelect* event for the *IconNewItem1* button):

```
Set(
    CurrentFilterStatus,
    TicketStatusBox.Selected.Value
);
Set(
    CurrentTicketStatus,
    "New"
);
NewForm(EditForm1);
Navigate(
    EditScreen1,
    ScreenTransition.None
)
```

---

[6] We don't just want to send an email any time the ticket is saved with the status of *Resolved* since the user could get duplicate emails such as in the situation where a technician edits a ticket to add additional notes. Instead, we only want to send the email the one time the status is changed to *Resolved*.

Notice the syntax for setting a global variable: *Set(<variable name>: <variable value>)*. As we have seen before, we separate statements with semicolons. The *NewForm* and *Navigate* methods were already in place from the wizard that built the form. We have similar logic when we edit an item:

```
Set(
    CurrentFilterStatus,
    TicketStatusBox.Selected.Value
);
Set(
    CurrentTicketStatus,
    DataCardValue7.Selected.Value
);
EditForm(EditForm1);
Navigate(
    EditScreen1,
    ScreenTransition.None
)
```

We read the *DataCardValue7* to get the current status of the ticket in this case.

Now that we have what we need to determine if the status is different from the current filter, we need to allow our status filter to be set programmatically (instead of just by the user selecting an option). We need another global variable (since *TicketStatusBox* is on a different screen). We set its *Default* value to this variable, which we will name *ticketStatusDefault*. We don't need to initialize it, since when it is blank the value will use the first one in the list, which is the *New* value we want.

We take care of both these requirements (updating the filter and sending a resolution email) by handling the *OnSuccess* event[7] for the form, as shown in Listing 9-1.

---

[7] We could do this in the *OnSelect* event for the Save button (*IconAccept1* control), but we then have a problem if there is an error. The filter would have changed and now our form would potentially disappear. Instead, we wait until we know our changes were successful.

Listing 9-1. OnSuccess code for updating the filter and send a resolution email

```
If(
    CurrentFilterStatus<>StatusDropDown.Selected.Value,
    Set(
        ticketStatusDefault,
        StatusDropDown.Selected.Value
    ),
    false)
If(
    (StatusDropDown.Selected.Value = "Resolved" && CurrentTicketStatus <>
"Resolved"),
    Office365.SendEmail(
        If(
            IsBlank('User (Office 365)_DataCard1'.Default),
            DataCardValue16.Text,
            DataCardValue10.SelectedItems).Email
        ),
        "Your Ticket Has Been Resolved - " & DataCardValue9.Text,
        "Dear " & If(
            IsBlank('User (Office 365)_DataCard1'.Default),
            DataCardValue11.Text,
            First(DataCardValue10.SelectedItems).DisplayName
        ) & "<br /><br />We are pleased to inform you that your ticket has
been resolved. Here are the details: <br /><br />Issue: " & DataCardValue9.
Text & "<br /><br />Description: " & DescriptionRichText.HtmlText & "<br
/><br />Assigned Technician: " & AssignedTechnicianDropDown.Selected.Value
& "<br /><br />Notes: " & NotesRichText.HtmlText & "<br /><br />If you
have any questions or would like to address this or another issue, please
call us at 555-1212 or email us at <a href='mailTo:emailhidden@test.com'>
emailhidden@test.com</a>. <br /><br /><b><a href='https://forms.office.com/
Pages/ResponsePage.aspx?id=hiddenIdentifier'>Please take our survey</a>
</b>.<br /><br /><br />Thanks, <br /><br />The Help Desk",
```

```
        {
            IsHtml: true,
            Importance: Normal
        }
    ),
    false
);
;Back()
```

We compare our *CurrentFilterStatus* global variable to what we just set on
the Edit form (*StatusDropDown.Selected.Value*). If those are different, we set the
ticketStatusDefault variable to be the new status. This is enough to change the filter.

We then compare the status from the form to our *CurrentTicketStatus* global variable.
If the status just changed to *Resolved*, we send the user an email. We do some logic to
figure out whether they have an Office 365 account or whether to use the email they
entered (*DataCardValue16* represents that value on the Edit form). If they have an
Office 365 account, we need to take account of the fact that the combo box holding
the user information *could* have multiple items selected. So we use the syntax *First
(DataCardValue10.SelectedItems)* to get our hands on the user. We then read the *Email*
property. The next parameter is the subject. We append the Issue (*DataCardValue.Text*)
to it. From there, we define the body of the email. We include the *Issue, Description,
Assigned Technician*, and *Notes*. Since we are sending an HTML email, we use breaks
(*
*) for hard returns and read the *HtmlText* property for the *Description* and *Notes*.
We use the *mailTo:* syntax to allow the user to send a follow-on email and also include a
link to a survey as described in earlier chapters. Here is how the email looks:

To: <User Email>

Subject: Your Ticket Has Been Resolved - <Issue>

Dear <User Display Name>

*We are pleased to inform you that your ticket has been resolved. Here are
the details:*

Issue: <Issue>

Description: <Description>

Assigned Technician: <Technician>

Notes: <Notes>

If you have any questions or would like to address this or another issue,

please call us at <phone number> or email us at <email address>.

Please take our survey (hyperlink)

Thanks,

The Help Desk

Finally, we call the original *Back* method to get to the *Details* or *Browse* screen as appropriate.

My Tickets Application

It didn't take long after releasing this new help ticket solution for users to ask to view their own tickets. We needed to limit it to those users who have an Office 365 account,[8] but it took very little time to edit the application described in this chapter and rename it to *MyHelpTickets*. Figure 9-4 shows the result.

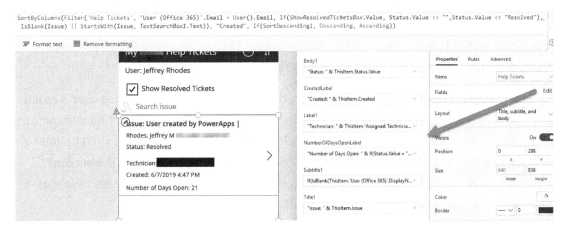

Figure 9-4. *The My Help Tickets application*

The user label has a simple formula for its *Text* property:

---

[8] We will limit to Office 365 users since otherwise we don't have a way to prevent one person from looking up someone else's tickets. Plus, there is no way to launch a Power App application unless you have an Office 365 account/license and the app is shared with you. We got by that with our kiosk application for creating a ticket, but there would be security problems with a kiosk to view tickets. Soon, everyone had accounts anyway.

```
"User: " & User().FullName
```

Rather than a drop-down box showing the different *Status* values, we default to only open tickets but give the option to *Show Resolved Tickets* as well. The *Items* property for the gallery is a bit different than what we saw earlier:

```
SortByColumns(Filter('Help Tickets', 'User (Office 365)'.Email = User().
Email, If(ShowResolvedTicketsBox.Value, Status.Value <> "",Status.Value <>
"Resolved"), IsBlank(Issue) || StartsWith(Issue, TextSearchBox1.Text)),
"Created", If(SortDescending1, Descending, Ascending))
```

We limit our tickets to the current user by making sure the *Email* property of our SharePoint person column matches the email of the current user. If the Show Resolved Tickets box is checked, we take any ticket (make sure the status is not ""). Otherwise, we take all except those with a Resolved status.

As you might have guessed from the warning symbol in Figure 9-4, this initial implementation also suffered from the 500-record limit. Since there were multiple issues here, we fix it a different way. We first set two variables in the *OnStart* event for the application:

```
Set(currentEmail, User().Email); ClearCollect(col, Filter('Help Tickets',
'User (Office 365)'.Email = currentEmail))
```

The first part creates the *currentEmail* variable and sets it to the current user's email. We need this because putting the *User().Email* value into either the *ClearCollect* function or the *Items* property of gallery causes the delegation error and limits us to 500 or 2000 records. The *ClearCollect* function makes a collection variable (*col*) from the second parameter, which is the *Filter* of all help tickets with the user's email address.[9] We can then use *col* in our *Items* property for our gallery control:

```
SortByColumns(Filter(col, If(ShowResolvedTicketsBox.Value, Status.Value
<> "",Status.Value <> "Resolved"), IsBlank(Issue) || StartsWith(Issue,
TextSearchBox1.Text)), "Created", If(SortDescending1, Descending,
Ascending))
```

---

[9] Note that this solution will run into problems if the user ever exceeds 500 or 2000 tickets. But that is much better than a limit of 500 tickets total.

We filter on *col* and don't need to limit to the user's email address since we already took care of that.

For the rest of the application, we delete the *Edit* screen, hide the "edit" and "new" buttons, and fix the errors (e.g., code that references the missing screens).

Summary

In this chapter, we customized the template that Power Apps creates for the SharePoint list to turn it into a Help Desk Technician's application. We added important functionality like displaying the number of days that the ticket is open and notification to the customer when the issue has been resolved. We then saw how just minor edits to this solution could turn it into a "My Tickets" application where users could see the status of their own help tickets.

CHAPTER 10

Using Power BI for the Help Ticketing System

Our help ticketing solution would not be complete without a Power BI solution to monitor our tickets. In this chapter, we connect Power BI to the SharePoint list holding our help ticket data and explore how to best configure it to get the data insights we want such as open tickets and what areas are experiencing the most demand for support.

The Power BI Visualization

Our SharePoint list is an easy-to-use data source. Figure 10-1 shows the results a couple of weeks after going live with this solution.[1]

---

[1] This was in the summer when many of the staff were away. The system still logged about 100 tickets per week.

© Jeffrey M. Rhodes 2022

J. M. Rhodes, *Creating Business Applications with Microsoft 365*,

https://doi.org/10.1007/978-1-4842-8823-8_10

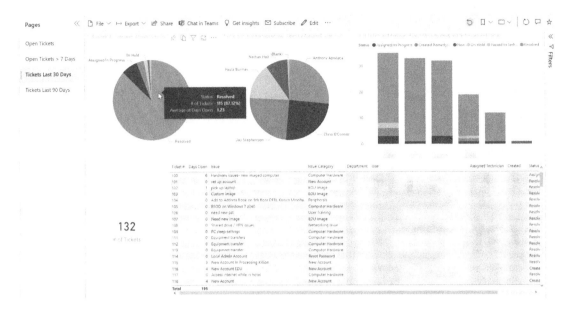

Figure 10-1. *Power BI visualization of tickets within the last 30 days*

Configuring Power BI

As with earlier Power BI solutions, much of the work is in transforming the query. Our first challenge is to get the display name of the *User (Office 365)* People column. As shown in Figure 10-2, we expand the *FieldValuesAsText* and select that column.

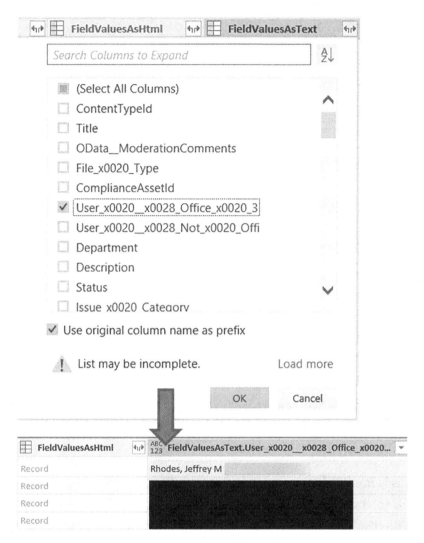

Figure 10-2. *Expanding FieldValuesAsText to get the DisplayName for the User (Office 365) People column*

We rename that column to be *Office 365 User*. We then create a conditional *User* column that will have this *Office 365 User* value if has a value and otherwise contains *User (Not Office 365)*. See Figure 10-3.

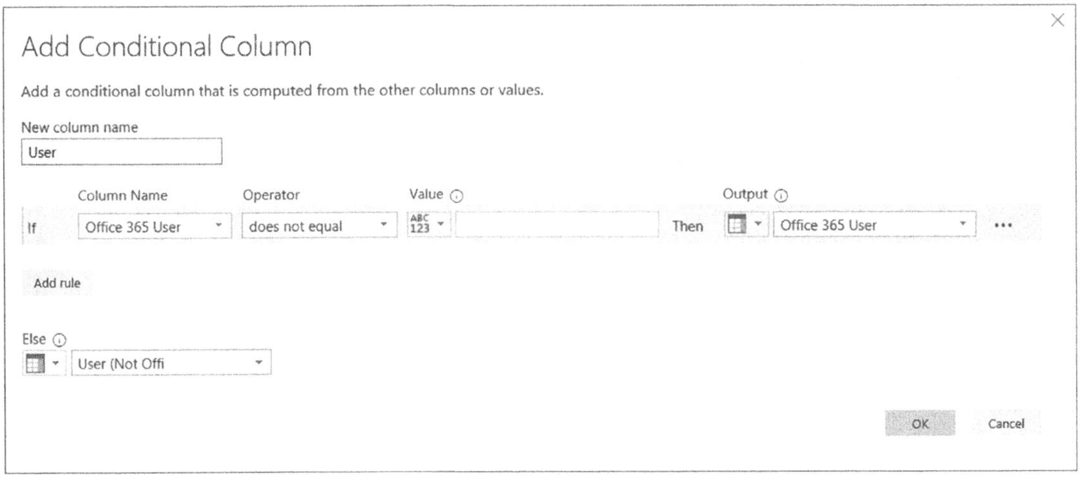

Figure 10-3. *Conditional column that takes the proper value depending on whether the user had an Office 365 account*

As in previous examples, we want a *Days Open* column. But we want to be a bit more sophisticated in that we will stop counting once the ticket is resolved. That gives us this logic:

```
Days Open = if [Status] = "Resolved" then if ([Resolved Date] > [Created])
then [Resolved Date] - [Created] else 0 else DateTime.From(DateTime.
LocalNow()) - [Created]
```

If the status is *Resolved*, then we make sure the *Resolved Date* is greater than the *Created* date. If so, the value is the difference. If not, we give it a value of 0.[2] If the ticket has not yet been resolved, we take the current date and time and subtract *Created* from that. We then change this type to be a whole number. We use this value in the *Open Tickets > 7 Days* page as well as displaying as a Tooltip on all graphs.

In a similar vein, we make a *Days Since Created* column using this logic:

```
DateTime.From(DateTime.LocalNow()) - [Created]
```

---

[2] We need this extra logic because *Resolved Date* is just a date value without a time. This ends up being the same as 00:00 (midnight). So if a ticket is opened and closed the same day, the *Days Open* ends up being negative (since *Created* has both a date and time and is later than midnight). That doesn't make sense, so we use 0 instead.

This allows us to see all tickets created during a time period. As you might guess, this is what we use for the *Tickets Last 30 Days* and *Tickets Last 90 Days* pages back in Figure 10-1.

Our last main change is to rename *Id* to *Ticket #*. This keeps us from having to rename it for each visualization.

Page-Level Filters

Much of the work for the visualization is in the page-level filters. As we see in Figure 10-4, we limit the *Open Tickets* page to tickets where the *Status* is not *Resolved*. Similarly, the *Tickets Last 30 Days* page has a single filter for *Days Since Created <= 30*. We want to include resolved tickets in this case as we want to see the entire workload.

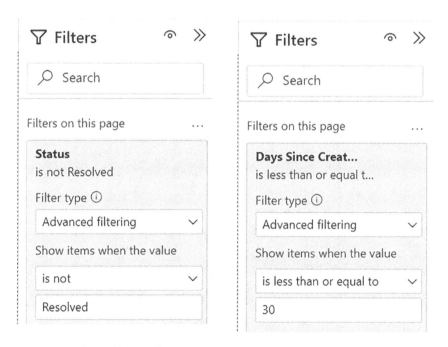

Figure 10-4. *Page-level filters for the Open Tickets and Tickets Last 30 Days pages*

For the *Open Tickets > 7 Days* page, however, we need two filters: *Days Open > 7* and *Status* is not *Resolved*. Power BI used to only allow one page-level filter, but now we can add multiple ones. This is a nice enhancement and avoids us having to add the second one to each visualization on the page. Figure 10-5 shows the two filters.

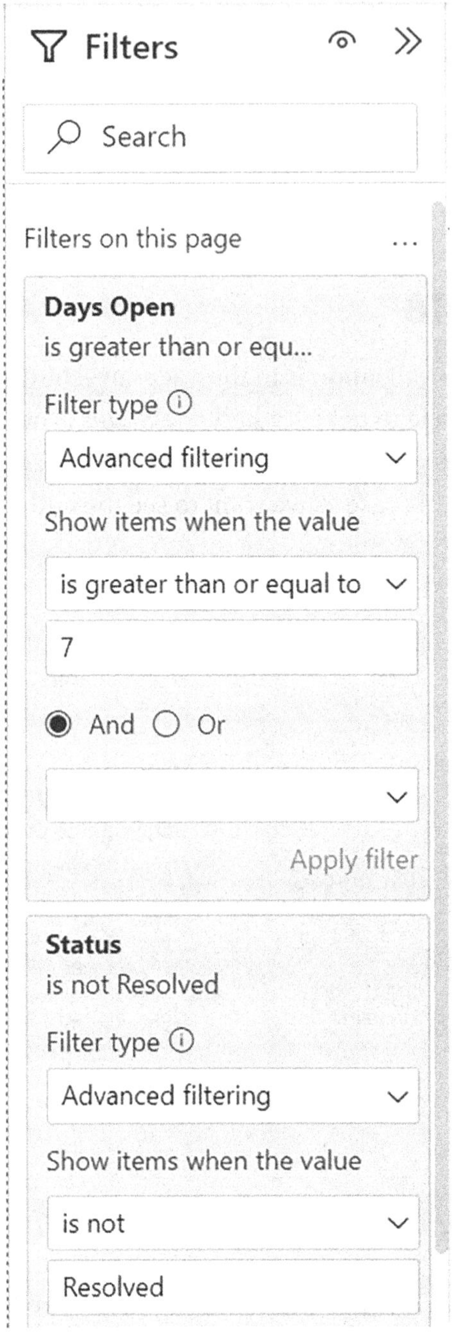

Figure 10-5. *Two page-level filters for the Open Tickets > 7 Days page*

As in past examples, our pie charts have the data we are tracking (*Status* or *Assigned Technician*) as the *Legend*. We then have the *Count of the ID/Ticket #* as the *Values*. We rename this to *# of Tickets* to make the labels more understandable. We show *Average of Days Open* as the *Tooltip*.

The stacked column chart (Figure 10-6) gives us additional information. We show the *Assigned Technician* along the horizontal axis. The Legend is the *Status*. These are each in a different color. The Value is once again the *Count of ID/Ticket #* that we rename to *# of Tickets*. We display *Average of Days Open* as the Tooltip. As you can see in Figure 10-6, all of these values show up as the tooltip when we move our mouse over one of the segments of the bar chart. It also shows the *Table* control showing the detailed information.

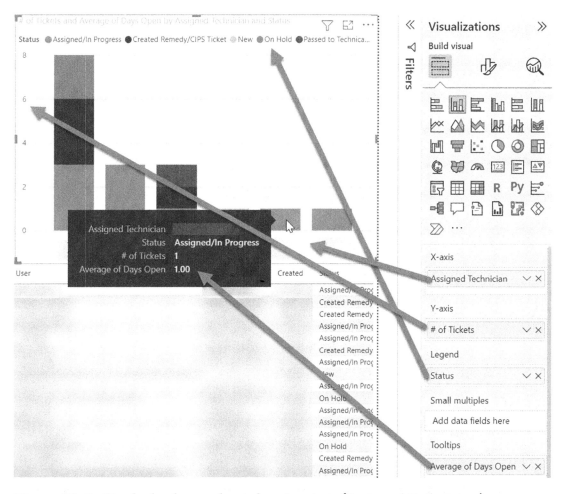

Figure 10-6. *Stacked column chart showing Axis (Assigned Technician), Legend (Status), Value (Count of Ticket #), and Tooltips (Average of Days Open)*

Summary

In this chapter, we learned how to visualize our SharePoint ticket data to get insight into the amount time tickets were open, the ticket mix per technician, the workload, and more. Custom columns like *Days Open* and *Days Since Created* helped us filter the pages to focus on open tickets and workload and show important statistics like the average number of days a ticket was open.

CHAPTER 11

Overcoming Power Apps Delegation Issues with SharePoint and Excel Data Sources

In this chapter, we look at how to address a major issue for Power App developers –
delegation. This is a huge challenge for the most common types of applications we
develop, those with SharePoint data sources. Not being limited to 500 or 2000 records is a
huge improvement for these applications.

For performance reasons, Power Apps will *delegate* processing to its data sources.
Microsoft spells it out this way[1]:

> *Delegation is where the expressiveness of Power Apps formulas meets the
> need to minimize data moving over the network. In short, Power Apps will
> delegate the processing of data to the data source, rather than moving the
> data to the app for processing locally.*

Things get challenging when we want to perform a task like *Filter()* with parameters
that don't support delegation. This chapter will demonstrate this issue and then show
you a nice workaround.

---

[1] See https://docs.microsoft.com/en-us/power-apps/maker/canvas-apps/
delegation-overview

© Jeffrey M. Rhodes 2022
J. M. Rhodes, *Creating Business Applications with Microsoft 365*,
https://doi.org/10.1007/978-1-4842-8823-8_11

Demonstrating Delegation Issues with Excel

Our data source starts as an Excel spreadsheet with links from my Music Genius application for iOS, MacOs, Google Play, and Windows Store.[2] Figure 11-1 shows the first 16 rows of the 3522 in the file.

	A	B	C	D
1	Group	Song	Album	Link
2	10,000 Maniacs	Because the Night		https://itunes.apple.com/us/album/because-the-night-live/id322123519?i=322123715&uo=4&at=11l7qL
3	10cc	I'm Not in Love		https://itunes.apple.com/us/album/im-not-in-love/id383951?i=383943&uo=4&at=11l7qL
4	3 Doors Down	Be Like That		https://itunes.apple.com/us/album/be-like-that/id101627?i=101613&uo=4&at=11l7qL
5	3 Doors Down	Citizen/Soldier		https://itunes.apple.com/us/album/citizen-soldier/id280508706?i=280508708&uo=4&at=11l7qL
6	3 Doors Down	Kryptonite		https://itunes.apple.com/us/album/kryptonite/id101627?i=101602&uo=4&at=11l7qL
7	3 Doors Down	Landing in London		https://itunes.apple.com/us/album/landing-in-london/id422816617?i=42281671&uo=4&at=11l7qL
8	3 Doors Down	Let Me Be Myself		https://itunes.apple.com/us/album/let-me-be-myself/id280508706?i=280508711&uo=4&at=11l7qL
9	3 Doors Down	Let Me Go		https://itunes.apple.com/us/album/let-me-go-rock-version/id422816617?i=42281649&uo=4&at=11l7qL
10	3 Doors Down	Loser		https://itunes.apple.com/us/album/loser/id101627?i=101607&uo=4&at=11l7qL
11	3 Doors Down	That Smell (Live)		https://itunes.apple.com/us/album/that-smell-live/id3502816?i=3502814&uo=4&at=11l7qL
12	3 Doors Down		3 Doors Down	https://itunes.apple.com/us/album/3-doors-down-bonus-track-version/id280508706?uo=4&at=11l7qL
13	3 Doors Down		Away from the Sun	https://itunes.apple.com/us/album/away-from-the-sun/id352412?uo=4&at=11l7qL
14	3 Doors Down		Seventeen Days	https://itunes.apple.com/us/album/seventeen-days-bonus-track/id422816617?uo=4&at=11l7qL
15	3 Doors Down			https://itunes.apple.com/us/artist/3-doors-down/id101604?uo=4&at=11l7qL
16	38 Special	Caught Up in You		https://itunes.apple.com/us/album/caught-up-in-you/id1581039?i=1581002&uo=4&at=11l7qL
17	38 Special	Rockin' into the Night		https://itunes.apple.com/us/album/rockin-into-the-night/id1294596?i=1294592&uo=4&at=11l7qL

Figure 11-1. *Music Genius Excel Data Source*

We ensure our data is an Excel table[3] and then upload this file to a SharePoint document library. We then use the *Excel Online (Business)* data source, as shown in Figure 11-2.

---

[2] See https://apps.apple.com/us/app/music-genius-trivia-on-rock-pop-country-and-more/id930170219 or https://apps.microsoft.com/store/detail/music-genius/9WZDNCRFKO3B.

[3] Unlike linking to an Excel file in Power BI, Power Apps can't read from a worksheet tab. Instead, it needs one or more tables within the Excel file.

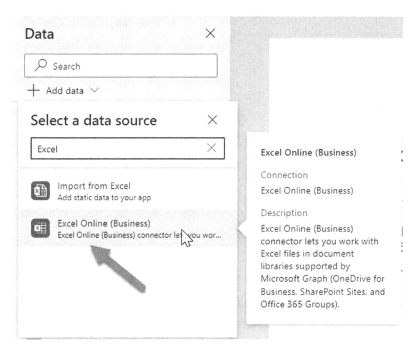

Figure 11-2. *Adding the Excel Online Data Source*

Since there is no index column in the table, the Excel Online connector will create one for us. But we are not able to see it programmatically and thus can't use it for our "getting around delegation" solution. But we could have added one and used the same solution as we will show later for SharePoint.

Figure 11-3 shows when there are no delegation issues.

Figure 11-3. *Excel Example with No Delegation Issues*

It might look like we have issues, since the number of items shows only 100. Here is the *Text* of that label:

```
"Number of Items: " & CountRows(MusicGallery.AllItems)
```

But Power Apps is just loading the number of rows needed by the gallery. If we scroll down, the number jumps to 200, 300, etc. That is because the Filter argument (*StartsWith()*) for the gallery's *Items* property can be fully delegated to Excel:

```
Filter(Table1, StartsWith(Song, SearchBox.Text))
```

Similarly, I could have used the *in* operator and still been delegable:

```
Filter(Table1, SearchBox_1.Text in Song)
```

But when I add an *Or* to our filter, so that we can look for either the song or the group, we run into delegation issues:

```
Filter(Table1, SearchBox_1.Text in Song || SearchBox_1.Text in Group)
```

Figure 11-4 shows the delegation warning.

Figure 11-4. *Delegation Warning with the Or Operator*

Note that the *Number of items* changes to 500, which is the default *Data row limit,* as shown in Figure 11-5.

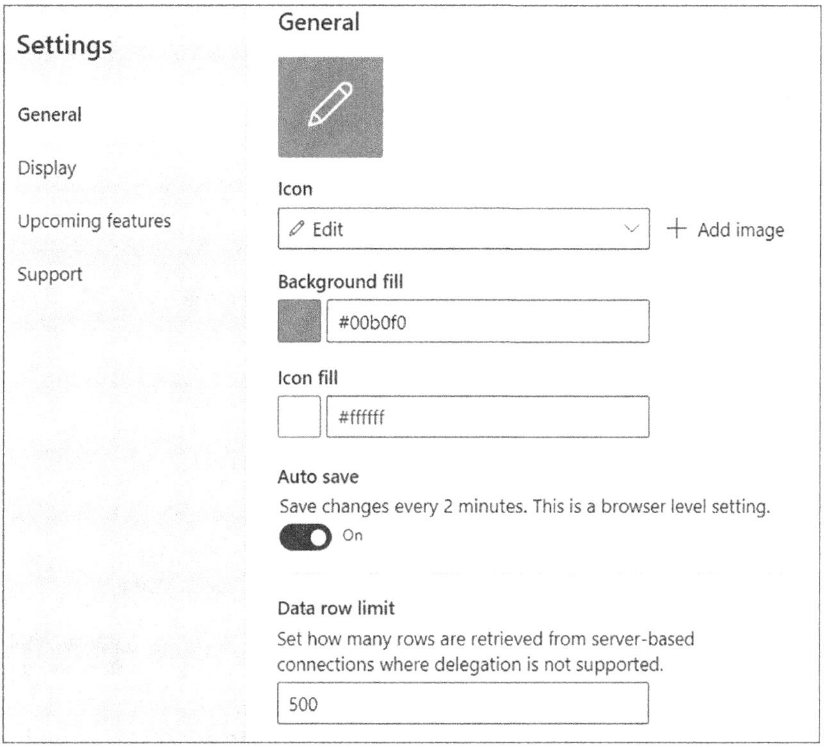

Figure 11-5. *Data Row Limit Setting in Power Apps*

We can increase this value to 2000, but we are stuck beyond that. Power Apps goes ahead and grabs that number of records, but all filtering occurs with just those 500 or 2000 records.

Demonstrating Delegation Issues with SharePoint

Before we copy our spreadsheet into a SharePoint list and demonstrate the delegation issue, we skip forward toward our solution[4] by noting that we need a numeric column other than the SharePoint list's *Id* column in order to read our data source and load it into a collection. For that, we will need a Power Automate flow to run each time we create a SharePoint list item. We might as well create that first so we get this *ID_Numeric* column to load for each row we paste in.

We create the *MusicGeniusLinks* list with the columns to match the Excel spreadsheet (*Group, Song, Album, Link*) as well as the new ID_Numeric column. As shown in Figure 11-6, we create an *automated cloud flow* with the trigger of *when an item is created*.

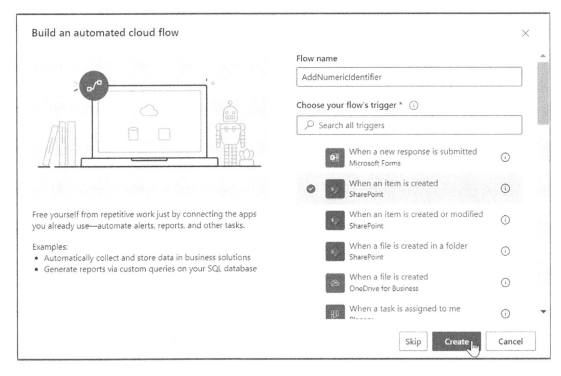

Figure 11-6. *Creating the Power Automate Flow to Update ID_Numeric*

---

[4] See https://tinyurl.com/twzvbgl for the original concept. My former colleague, Anthony Apodaca, found the solution and created the initial implementation.

We choose the site address and the name of our list, add a step, and then search for SharePoint actions (Figure 11-7).

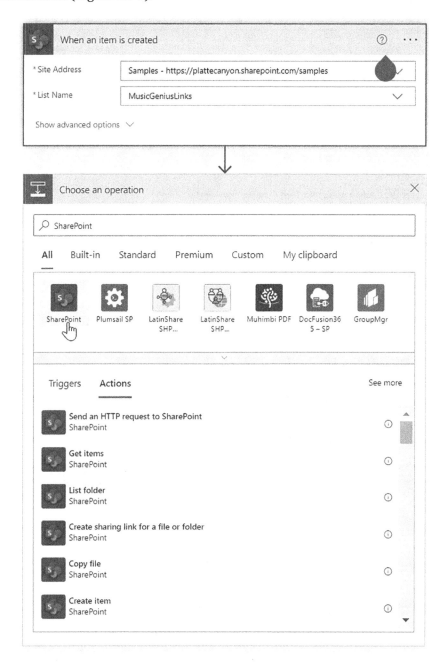

Figure 11-7. *Selecting SharePoint Actions*

We search for *Update* so we can find the *Update item* action (Figure 11-8).

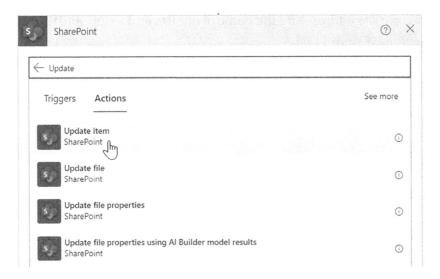

Figure 11-8. *Updating the SharePoint Item*

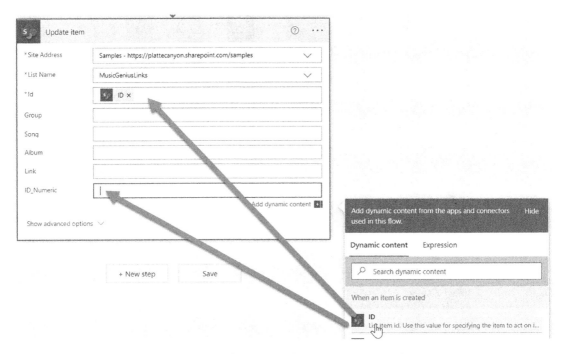

Figure 11-9. *Adding ID to both the ID and ID_Numeric columns*

We need to give values for each required column (shown by the * to the left of the column name). We choose *ID* for both the Id column[5] AND the new *ID_Numeric* column.

Now that we have our flow set up, it is time to import our data. As shown in Figure 11-10, I like to copy the Excel rows and then go to grid view in SharePoint and then select the columns I want to paste.[6]

Figure 11-10. *Pasting Excel Data into the SharePoint List*

We then paste via Ctrl + V. This ends up taking quite a bit of time as our flow has to run for each of our 3522 rows. We can go back to Power Automate and check our run history to make sure all is working correctly (Figure 11-11).

28-day run history ⓘ		All runs
Start	Duration	Status
May 31, 04:00 PM (1 sec ago)	52 ms	Succeeded
May 31, 04:00 PM (1 sec ago)	08 ms	Succeeded
May 31, 04:00 PM (1 sec ago)	24 ms	Succeeded
May 31, 04:00 PM (1 sec ago)	54 ms	Succeeded
May 31, 04:00 PM (1 sec ago)	26 ms	Succeeded
May 31, 04:00 PM (1 sec ago)	25 ms	Succeeded
May 31, 04:00 PM (1 sec ago)	27 ms	Succeeded

Figure 11-11. *Power Automate Flow Run History*

---

[5] Notice that this is how Power Automate figures out which column to update. This is similar to a SQL update query: *Update MusicGeniusLinks Set ID_Numeric = ID where Id = ID.*

[6] Selecting the first one and then using Shift - Right Arrow to select each cell is a useful technique. Be sure the columns you are pasting are contiguous. Note how I did NOT include the automatically generated *ID* column nor the *ID_Numeric* that will be set by the Power Automate flow.

Once the list is fully populated, we connect it as a data source in Power Apps. We get the same delegation success/failures based on how we *Filter()* as we had with Excel (Figures 11-3 and 11-4). But now we have another workaround. As we see in Figure 11-12, we have a *LoadCollectionButton* that contains all our code. We programmatically execute this code in response to the *OnVisible* event for our screen using this syntax:

```
Select(LoadCollectionButton)
```

We use the button because there are other times[7] where we also want to reload the collection, such as when we click on a "Refresh" button and after we add, edit, or delete records from our data source.

Figure 11-12. *Selecting the LoadCollectionButton in the OnVisible Event*

Let's look at each section of our *OnSelect* code, starting with the *Reset* functionality in Listing 11-1.

Listing 11-1. Load Collection Code: Reset

```
// Thanks to Microsoft for this post and to Anthony Apodaca for finding/
implementing it:
// https://powerusers.microsoft.com/t5/Building-Power-Apps/500-item-limit-
in-CDM-entity-search-filter-need-to-switch-to-asp/m-p/22980#M9872

// Start Process
Refresh(MusicGeniusLinks);
// in case just added an item
```

---

[7] Putting the code in a button takes the place of a module or class library in other environments, where we could call code that needs to execute in from different areas of the application.

```
// unload staging collections
Clear(colNumTemp);
Clear(colDummy);
Clear(colNumbersTable);
Clear(varCounter);
Clear(colIterations);
Clear(linksCollection);
```

We start with some comments and then *Refresh* our data source. This is needed in case we or another user recently added, edited, or deleted a record. We then clear all the variables/collections that we use in the code to come. *linksCollection* is our final output and what we will use in our filter. Since it is a collection internal to Power Apps, it does not have the same delegation restrictions as our Excel or SharePoint data sources.[8]

Next, we create our *colNumTemp* collection (Listing 11-2).

Listing 11-2. Load Collection Code: Generate colNumTemp

```
// Generate series. This can retrieve ~ 500,000 to 2 million records
Collect(
    colNumTemp,
    [
        1,
        2,
        3,
        4,
        5,
        6,
        7,
        8,
        9,
        10
    ]
);
```

---

[8] The corollary is that all of our data is stored in memory in Power Apps. So be careful not to store so many records that you overwhelm your devices, particularly if you are planning to have your application available on smaller mobile devices.

This is basically an array of ten cells that will hold sets of records. We can go to File ➤ Collections in Power Apps to see a preview of how it looks (Figure 11-13).

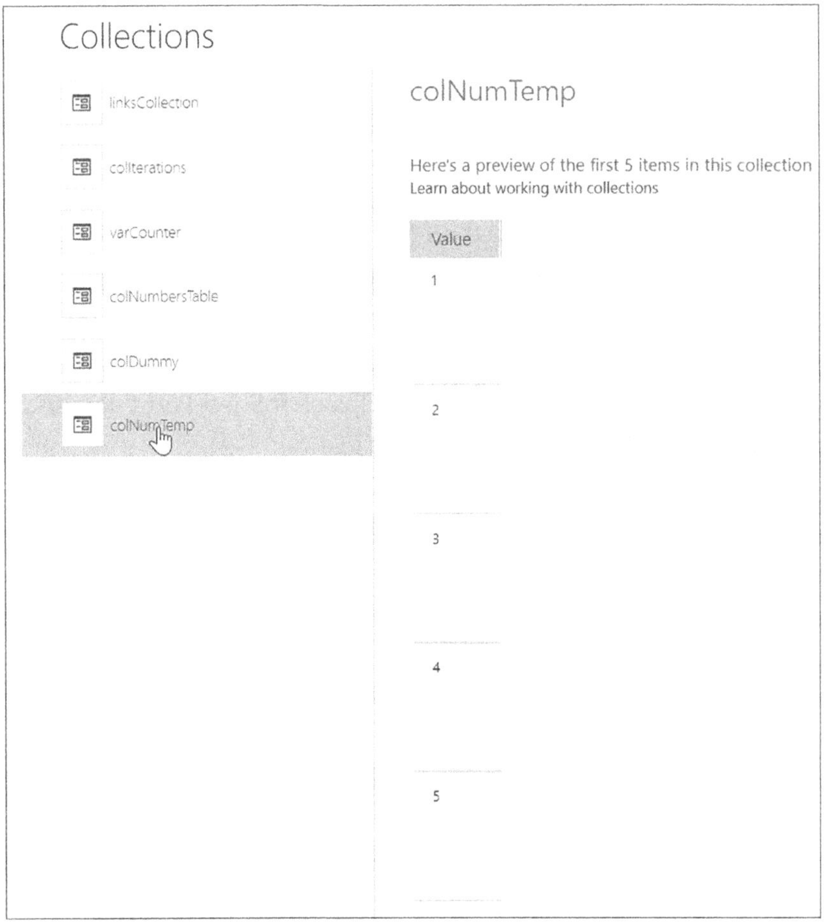

Figure 11-13. *The first five items in the colNumTemp collection*

Our next task is to generate another collection, colNumbersTable (Listing 11-3).

Listing 11-3. Load Collection Code: Generate colNumbersTable

```
ForAll(
    colNumTemp,
    ForAll(
        colNumTemp,
        ForAll(
```

```
        colNumTemp,
        Collect(
            colDummy,
            {dummy: 1}
        );
        Collect(
            colNumbersTable,
            {Number: CountRows(colDummy)}
        )
    )
)
);
// End Generate Series
```

This is our first introduction to the *ForAll()* function.[9] It has two parameters, the *Table* to be operated on and the *Formula* to use. Let's start with the inside set of code:

```
    ForAll(
        colNumTemp,
        Collect(
            colDummy,
            {dummy: 1}
        );
```

This operates on the *colNumTemp* collection that we created earlier. For each value (1, 2, 3, etc.), it creates a *colDummy* collection, with a single item named *dummy* and a value of *1*. Figure 11-14 shows how this looks in the preview mode.

---

[9] See https://docs.microsoft.com/en-us/power-apps/maker/canvas-apps/functions/function-forall.

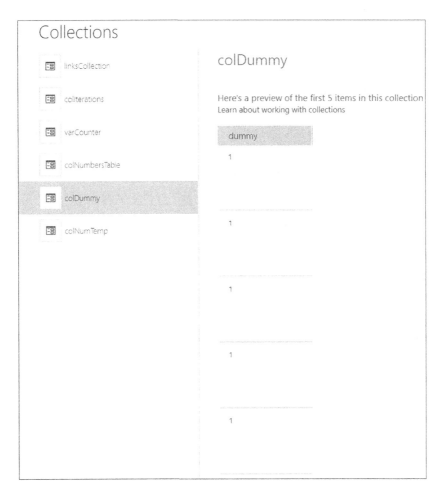

Figure 11-14. *The colDummy collection*

The effect of naming the item changes the heading from *Value* (Figure 11-13) to *dummy*. Since we are using *Collect* rather than *ClearCollect*, each time that *ForAll()* loops, it will add records to the collection. Similarly, this code runs next:

```
Collect(
    colNumbersTable,
    {Number: CountRows(colDummy)}
)
```

This adds items to the *colNumbersTable* collection and creates a *Number* with a value of the number of rows in the *colDummy* collection (1 then 2 then 3, etc.). Figure 11-15 shows the result.

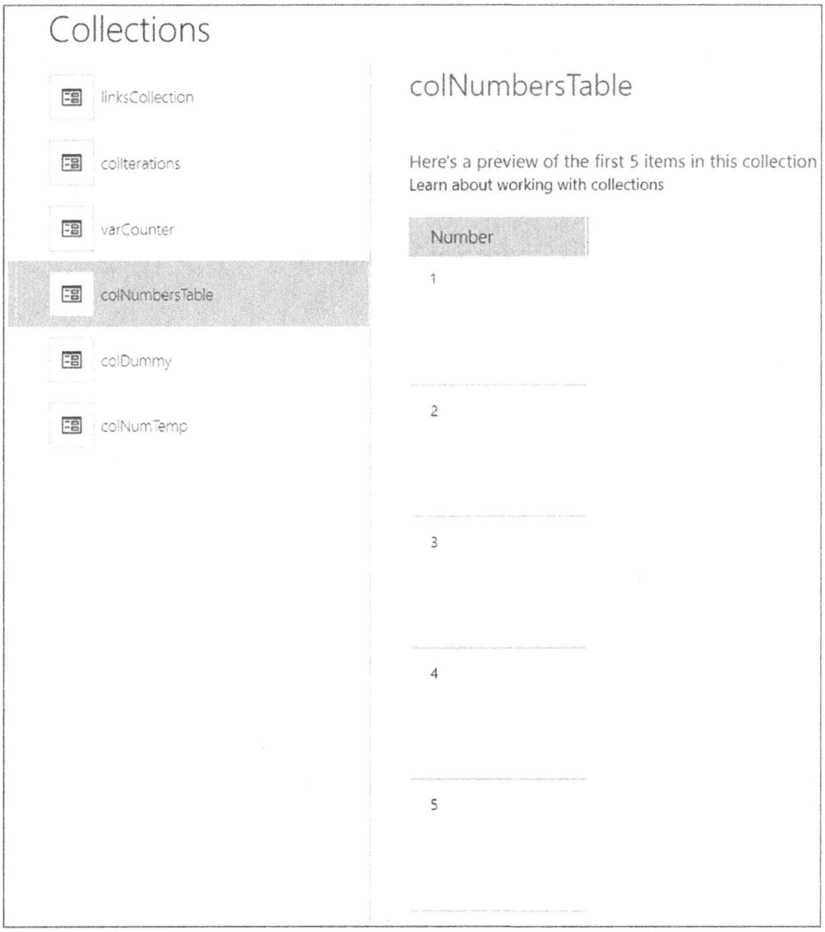

Figure 11-15. *The colNumbersTable collection*

The result so far is that both *colDummy* and *colNumbersTable* have 10 rows. *colDummy* has a 1 in each item while *colNumbersTable* has 1, 2, 3, etc. But this was all inside two more *ForAll()* loops, as we see in the following.

```
ForAll(
    colNumTemp,
    ForAll(
        colNumTemp,
        <run code above>
    )
);
```

The inside loop runs ten more times, giving us 100 items in both *colDummy* and *colNumbers*. The outside loop runs ten times as well, leading to 1000 items in both collections.

Next up are some variables to keep us organized. Since they only need to live on the current screen, we use context variables, as shown in Listing 11-4.

Listing 11-4. Load Collection Code: Set Variables

```
// Obtain first and last record
UpdateContext(
    {
        FirstRecord: First(
            Sort(
                MusicGeniusLinks,
                ID,
                Ascending
            )
        )
    }
);
UpdateContext(
    {
        LastRecord: First(
            Sort(
                MusicGeniusLinks,
                ID,
                Descending
            )
        )
    }
);
// Begin iteration
UpdateContext(
    {
        Iterations: RoundUp(
            (LastRecord.ID - FirstRecord.ID) / 500,
```

```
            0
        )
    }
);
//Create new collection to temporarily store our first ID to capture
ClearCollect(
    varCounter,
    {min_Num: FirstRecord.ID}
);
```

Looking first at the *FirstRecord* variable, the *Sort()* function takes three parameters: the table, the formula, and an optional sort order (*Ascending* or *Descending*). Power Apps again delegates this operation to the data source (SharePoint in this case), but luckily SharePoint doesn't impose the 500- or 2000-item cap in this case. Since we want the first record, we sort *Ascending*. Our formula is to do our sorting by the *ID* column. We then use the *First()* function to grab the first item. For *LastRecord*, we just change the sort to *Descending*, which puts the highest *ID* first.[10]

Our next challenge is to figure out how many *Iterations* we are going to need to read all our records. We use this formula:

```
RoundUp((LastRecord.ID - FirstRecord.ID) / 500, 0)
```

In our case, *LastRecord.ID* = 3522 and *FirstRecord.ID* = 1. This gives us 7.04 but we round up to 8 (with no decimal places).[11] It is important that the divisor (500 here) either match or is smaller than the *Data row limit* (see Figure 11-5). Otherwise, delegation limits will kick in again.[12] Figure 11-16 shows how we can see these variable values within the Power Apps environment.

---

[10] We could have kept an *Ascending* sort and switched to the *Last()* function instead.

[11] Note that this gives us the maximum number of records per iteration. In a list that can have deletions, there will be some missing IDs. In other words, IDs 7, 12, 19, etc. might have been deleted.

[12] I had this problem when creating this demo as my saved code had 2000 instead of 500, but I had forgotten that I had changed the original application to have a *Data row limit* of 2000. This changed Iterations to 2 and left me with only 1000 records (1 - 501 and then 1001 - 1501). It took me some time to figure out what was wrong.

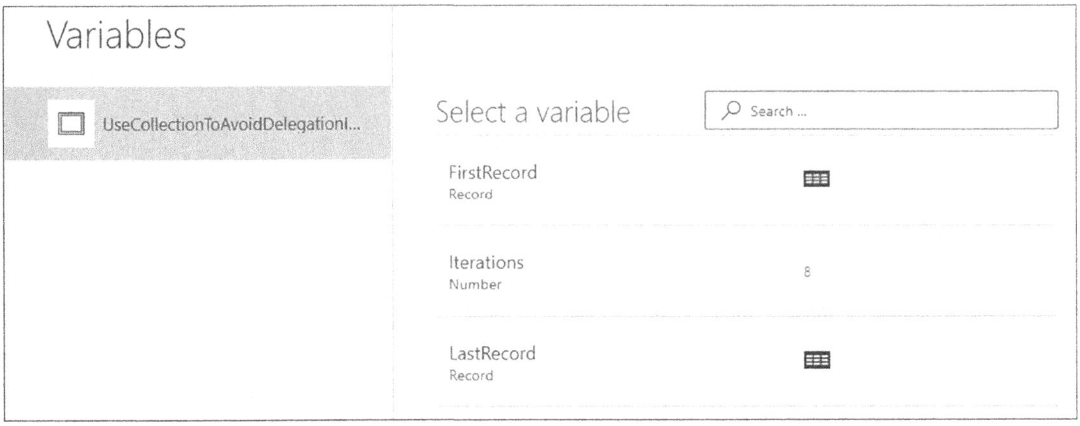

Figure 11-16. *FirstRecord, LastRecord, and Iterations Variables*

Our last variable, *varCounter,* stores which ID we are on. We name its value *min_Num* and set it to *FirstRecord.ID*. We can already guess that we will loop through sets of records and update this variable to keep track of where we are.

We are now ready to finally start reading all our data. Listing 11-5 shows our code.

Listing 11-5. Load Collection Code: Loop to Read Records

```
/* Using a ForAll loop where column number is less than or equal to the
number of iterations
Update iteration collection with current iteration number, min, and
max numbers
Update counter collection */
ForAll(
    Filter(
        colNumbersTable,
        Number <= Iterations
    ),
    Collect(
        colIterations,
        {
            Number: Last(
                FirstN(
                    colNumbersTable,
                    CountRows(colIterations) + 1
```

```
                )
            ).Number,
            min_Num: First(varCounter).min_Num,
            max_Num: First(varCounter).min_Num + 499
        }
    );
    Patch(
        varCounter,
        First(varCounter),
        {
            min_Num: Last(
                FirstN(
                    colIterations,
                    CountRows(colIterations) + 1
                )
            ).max_Num + 1
        }
    )
);
// End iteration capture
```

Recall that the *ForAll()* function requires a *Table* and a *Formula*. Our table is the result of this line:

```
Filter(colNumbersTable, Number <= Iterations)
```

Since *Iterations* is 8 in our case, this gives a table with 1 in the first item, 2 in the second, and on up to 8 in the eighth item. See Figure 11-15. For each value (1–8), we run this code:

```
Collect(
        colIterations,
        {
            Number: Last(
                FirstN(
                    colNumbersTable,
                    CountRows(colIterations) + 1
```

```
            )
        ).Number,
        min_Num: First(varCounter).min_Num,
        max_Num: First(varCounter).min_Num + 499
    }
)
```

We build a new collection, *colIterations*, item by item. It has three columns: *Number*, *min_Num*, and *max_Num*. Let's look at *Number* first:

```
Number: Last(FirstN(colNumbersTable, CountRows(colIterations) + 1)).Number
```

Working from the inside, the *FirstN()* function takes a table as the first parameter and the number of records to return as the second parameter. As we saw earlier, *colNumbersTable* has eight items in our case. colIterations starts with 0 rows and adds a row each time. So we read one record the first time, two the second time, and so forth. Since we get the *Last()* record and then grab its *Number* value, this will be 1, 2, 3, etc.

For *min_Num*, we refer back to Listing 11-4 to note that *varCounter.min_Num* means the *ID* of our *FirstRecord* variable. So this will be 1 the first time around. To get *max_Num*, we add 499 to it. It is important that this is one less than the value we used in defining our Iterations variable in Listing 11-4. That was 500 in our case.

All that is left is for us to update our varCounter collection variable so we can store the beginning and ending IDs for each set of records:

```
Patch(varCounter, First(varCounter),
    {
        min_Num: Last(
            FirstN(
                colIterations,
                CountRows(colIterations) + 1
            )
        ).max_Num + 1
    }
)
```

The *Patch()* function is used to update data sources, but that can be a collection as well. It has three parameters: the data source, which record to update, and the value(s) to be changed. *varCounter* is the data source and its first record is what to update. Since our formula for *min_Num* parallels that for the *colIterations* collection, we can refer to Figure 11-17 for insight into the values.

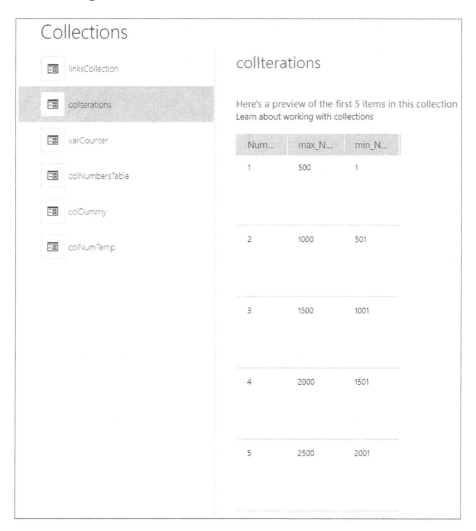

Figure 11-17. *The colIterations collection*

The first time around, we are in the first row and *max_Num* will be 500. *varCounter. min_Num* will equal that value + 1 (e.g., 501).

The *ForAll()* loop will start again and jump to populate the next row of *colIterations* with the first five items showing in Figure 11-17.

With all this legwork out of the way, we can now load our linksCollection with the code in Listing 11-6.

Listing 11-6. Load Collection Code: Creating linksCollection

```
/* Finally, with a ForAll loop we collect all our items
** Cannot use ID column to do delegations! **
We use ID_Numeric instead */
ForAll(
    colIterations,
    Collect(
        linksCollection,
        Filter(
            MusicGeniusLinks,
            ID_Numeric >= min_Num && ID_Numeric <= max_Num
        )
    )
);
```

We start with some comments and then use our old standby, *ForAll()*. We loop through each record of colIterations (Figure 11-17) and use the *Collect()* to build our *linksCollection* in sets of 500 records. We see now why we created our Power Automate flow to populate the *ID_Numeric* column of SharePoint list. We use it to *Filter()* our list and get the records we want. Note that this filter is subject to delegation limits and thus our *min_Num* and *max_Num* values need match our *Data row limit* as discussed in Footnote 12. Here is how our filter line looks for the first two iterations of our *ForAll()* loop:

```
Filter(MusicGeniusLinks, ID_Numeric >= 1 && ID_Numeric <= 500)

Filter(MusicGeniusLinks, ID_Numeric >= 501 && ID_Numeric <= 1000)
```

The Final Result

Now that we have a *linksCollection* that contains all our data locally, we just need to change the Items property of our gallery to use that collection instead of our Excel or SharePoint data source:

```
Filter(linksCollection, SearchBox_2.Text in Song || SearchBox_2.Text
in Group)
```

Figure 11-18 shows our completed app. Since our Excel file was sorted by *Group*, we test by searching for ZZ Top and notice that we are retrieving items 3478 and 3479, way above even the maximum 2000 record limit if we were querying SharePoint directly. Whew!

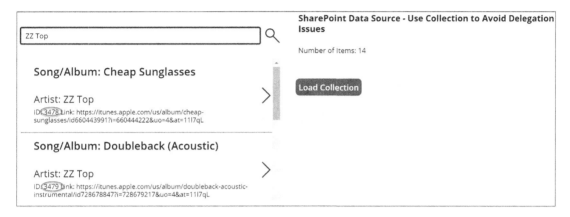

Figure 11-18.   *Power App showing records above the delegation limit*

Summary

In this chapter, we learned how to use Power App collections and methods like *Collect()*, *ClearCollect()*, *ForAll()*, and *Patch()* to avoid the dreaded delegation issues with SharePoint or Excel data sources. While there is a bit of code, you will be able to breathe a sigh of relief once you have this nailed down. Otherwise, what looked to be the perfect solution to a key business problem instead could fail once you exceeded 2000 records. Once you have this technique at your disposal, you can then look closely at your data to decide when it makes sense to add this extra step to your applications.

CHAPTER 12

Creating a Class Sign-Up Solution in SharePoint and Power Apps

This chapter demonstrates how to use SharePoint and Power Apps together to schedule appointments when there is a fixed capacity. I originally created this solution in InfoPath for handling classroom-based training events with only a specific number of seats in a classroom or auditorium. Once Power Apps came out, I switched to it instead. The gist of the approach is one SharePoint list that holds the classes or other training events (including the capacity of the event) and another list that contains the attendees as well as what event(s) they are signed up for. Views on the list (or Power BI) provide a training roster. A user or an owner deleting a registration frees up a spot for someone else. This could apply to human resources briefings, imaging appointments for updating computers, vaccinations, tax return appointments, and much more.

The SharePoint Lists

Our first step is to create a custom list that I will name *Classes*. In addition to the default *Title* column, we add *Class Date*, *Location*, and *Capacity* columns. As shown in Figure 12-1, we set the format to *Date & Time* and the display to *Standard*.[1]

---

[1] We need the time so that the user knows what time the class starts. The standard format avoids terms like *tomorrow*, *2 hours*, etc.

© Jeffrey M. Rhodes 2022
J. M. Rhodes, *Creating Business Applications with Microsoft 365*,
https://doi.org/10.1007/978-1-4842-8823-8_12

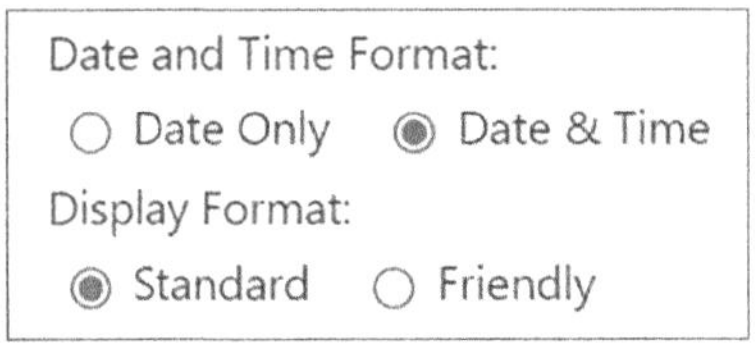

Figure 12-1. *Setting the date format to Date & Time and Standard*

Looking ahead to when we display a list of available classes, we need a column that will show both the title and the date/time.[2] So we add a *Calculated* column we will call *Expanded Title*. One challenge is that our drop-down list in Power Apps will have a default value. To avoid users being defaulted to the wrong class (and instead force them to make a selection), we create a class with a dash as the *Title*.[3] Our formula[4] is

```
=IF(Title="-",Title,Title&" ("&TEXT([Class Date],"MMM DD yyyy, h:mm AM/
PM")&")")
```

This formula takes the title of the class, add a left parenthesis, formats the *Class Date* with a three-letter month, two-digit day, four-digit year, and then the hours and minutes with AM or PM.

Figure 12-2 shows the resulting list with some test data, including the bottom class that is in the past as of the time of this writing.

---

[2] We could put the date and time into the title, but that is messy and subject to error. Plus, we will do logic later to only show classes that are in the future. Trying to get that information out of the title is problematic, but easy when we use our *Class Date* column.

[3] Shane Young demonstrates this technique at `www.youtube.com/watch?v=43ekj5MlNJU`. He makes a good point that using a dash is easier for debugging than using a space.

[4] On more complicated formulas like this, I recommended copying the formula to the clipboard before clicking the *OK* button. That way, you can paste it back in and correct if you get a syntax error and have to start over.

Classes ☆

ID ∨	Title ∨	Class Date ∨	Location ∨	Capacity ∨	Expanded Title ∨
4	-	12/31/2099 12:00 AM			-
2	Microsoft 365 Training	8/14/2022 2:00 PM	Room 6J23	10	Microsoft 365 Training (Aug 14 2022, 2:00 PM)
1	Microsoft 365 Training	8/6/2022 9:00 AM	Room 6J23	5	Microsoft 365 Training (Aug 06 2022, 9:00 AM)
3	Microsoft 365 Training	6/4/2022 10:00 AM	Room 6J23	5	Microsoft 365 Training (Jun 04 2022, 10:00 AM)

Figure 12-2. *The Classes list with some default data, a default value, and an event in the past for testing*

This past event should NOT show up as available in our sign-up form. It will be helpful for making the class roster views to have the ID of the class, which is why we added that column to the default view. We also sort by *Class Date* in descending order so the oldest classes are at the bottom.

Next, we add an *Attendees* custom list. We don't need the default *Title* column, so we will rename it to *Phone* and make it optional. If all our attendees have Microsoft 365 accounts, we can make an *Attendee* column of type *Person.*[5] Otherwise, we can add individual columns for Name and Organization. Most importantly, we link to the *Classes* list by creating a Lookup column, as shown in Figure 12-3. Power Apps struggles a bit with Lookup columns, so we grab all the columns that we need up front. It also turns out that working with any column other than the primary lookup column (*Expanded Title* in this case), causes delegation issues. So choose carefully and be ready to rework if you run into any issues.

---

[5] This avoids the need to ask for email address or other information contained in the user's account. It also avoids issues with the same or similar name (and figuring out who really signed up).

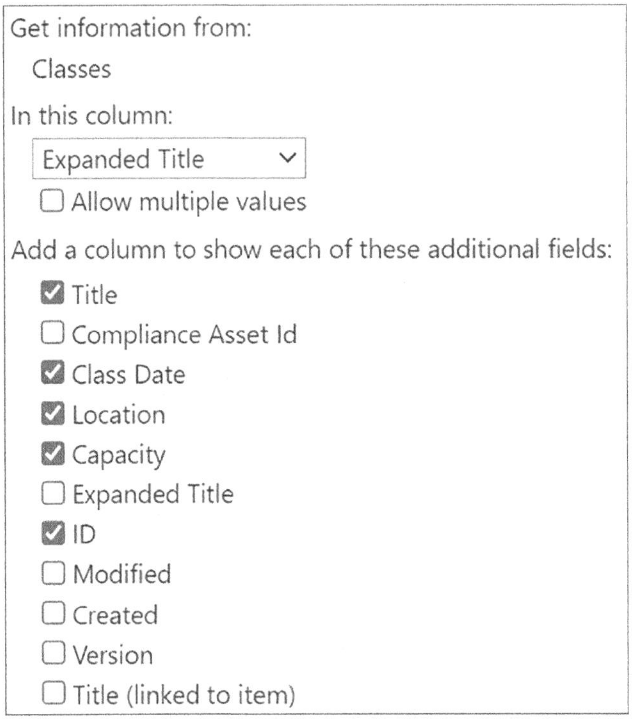

Get information from:

Classes

In this column:

Expanded Title   ∨

☐ Allow multiple values

Add a column to show each of these additional fields:

☑ Title
☐ Compliance Asset Id
☑ Class Date
☑ Location
☑ Capacity
☐ Expanded Title
☑ ID
☐ Modified
☐ Created
☐ Version
☐ Title (linked to item)

Figure 12-3. *Lookup column linking to the Expanded Title and other columns of the Classes list*

Our next step is to go to the *Advanced Settings* for the list (Figure 12-4) and choose *Read all items* and *Create items and edit items that were created by the user*.

Item-level Permissions

Specify which items users can read and edit.

Note: Users with the Cancel Checkout permission can read and edit all items. Learn about managing permission settings.

Read access: Specify which items users are allowed to read

◉ Read all items
○ Read items that were created by the user

Create and Edit access: Specify which items users are allowed to create and edit

○ Create and edit all items
◉ Create items and edit items that were created by the user
○ None

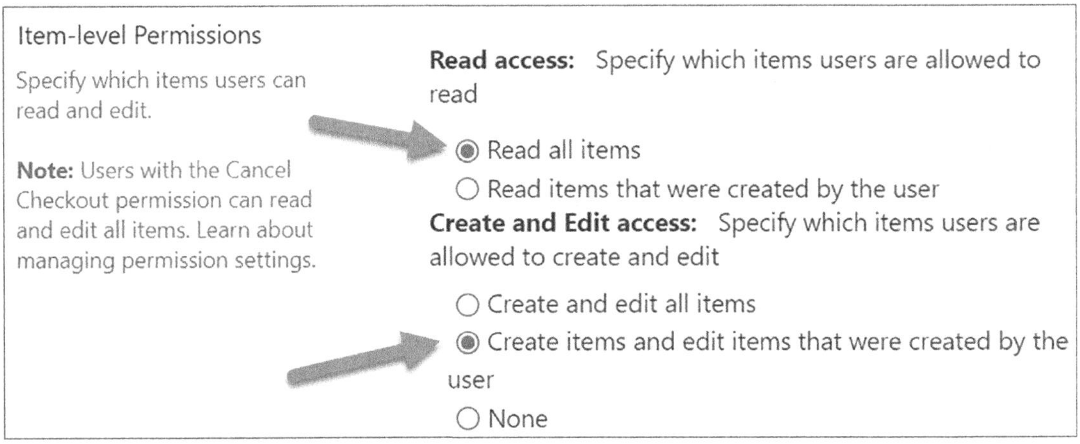

Figure 12-4. *Setting proper Read and Edit SharePoint List Permissions*

The first is needed so we can figure out the capacity from Power Apps. The second prevents issues just in case users found the SharePoint list directly and tried to edit someone else's registration.

Figure 12-5 shows the default *New item* SharePoint form. It is inadequate as it shows the past classes and does not have any logic to check the capacity of the class.

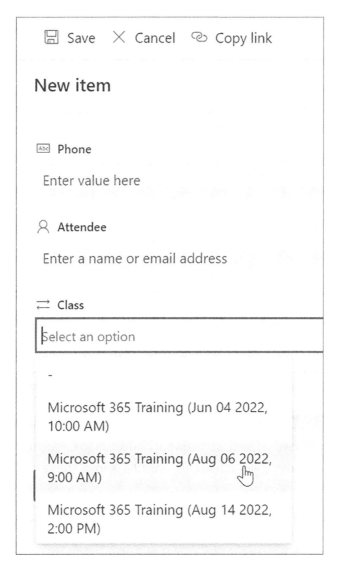

Figure 12-5. *Default SharePoint New item form*

While we could customize this form with Power Apps, that would require us to send users to the SharePoint list URL directly. I prefer to use SharePoint as a backup data source and send the user to either the Power Apps URL or, better, embed the form as a tab in the appropriate team.

Creating the Power Apps Form

As we have seen in past examples, we create a new Canvas application in Power Apps with the *Tablet* format (though *Phone* would work too here as we don't need much screen real estate). We connect *both* our SharePoint lists as data sources, as shown in Figure 12-6.

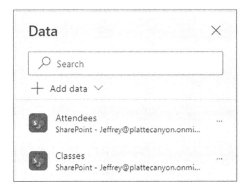

Figure 12-6. *Connecting to both the Classes and Attendees data sources*

The Home Screen

For our design, we will have a *Home* screen that allows us to create a registration and, if existing registrations exist, delete them. Figure 12-7 shows the result with existing registrations.

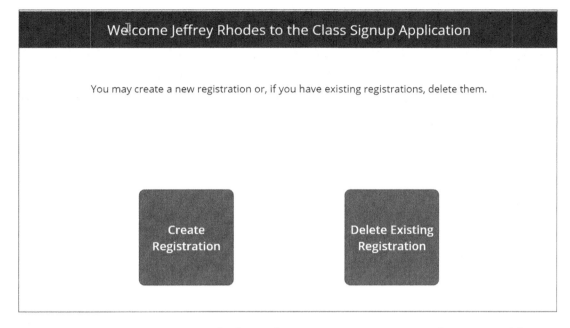

Figure 12-7. *Home Screen with the Delete Existing Registration button visible*

Notice how we customize the top label by including the user's name in its *Text* property:

```
"Welcome " & User().FullName & " to the Class Signup Application"
```

Deciding whether to show the *Delete Existing Registration* button is not trivial, largely due to delegation constraints. We handle the screen's *OnVisible* event so that our code runs each time the user returns to this screen. Our first attempt is shown in Listing 12-1.

Listing 12-1. Building a collection to determine if there are future registrations for the current user

```
ClearCollect(
    colUserTraining,
    Filter(
        Attendees,
        Attendee.Email = User().Email,
        DateTimeValue('Class:Class Date'.Value) >= Now()
    )
)
```

Starting in the middle, we *Filter()* the *Attendees* list to see if the current user has any registrations. That part is fine, but it is the next filter (*DateTimeValue('Class:Class Date'.Value) >= Now()*) that gives us delegation warnings. This comes from the fact that 'Class:Class Date' comes from the lookup column. Since it is entirely likely that there will be more than 500 or 2000 registrations, we need to find another solution. This involves splitting the logic, as shown in Listing 12-2.

Listing 12-2. Splitting our logic to avoid delegation warnings

```
ClearCollect(
    colUserTraining,
    Filter(
        Attendees,
        Attendee.Email = User().Email
    )
);
// This has every user training but some of those can be in the past. Need
to create new collection with just future registrations
ClearCollect(
    colUserFutureTraining,
    Blank()
);
If(
    Count(colUserTraining.ID) > 0,
    ClearCollect(
        colUserFutureTraining,
        ForAll(
            colUserTraining,
            If(
                DateTimeValue('Class:Class Date'.Value) >= Now(),
                {
                    ID: ID,
                    Phone: Phone,
                    Attendee: Attendee,
                    Class: Class,
                    'Class:Title': 'Class:Title',
```

```
          'Class:Location': 'Class:Location'
        }
      )
    )
  )
)
```

We return to just the initial logic so that *colUserTraining* contains all registrations (past and future) for the current user. We then create *colUserFutureTraining* to be *Blank()*. We check the count of *colUserTraining* as there is no point proceeding if there are no registrations for the user. If there are registrations, we use the *ForAll()* loop once again to operation on *colUserTraining*. Recall that the return value of *ForAll()* is a table defined by the second parameter, the formula. We check to see if the *Class Date* is in the future (>= *Now()*). If so, we create a new record in *colUserFutureTraining* with the columns we want: *ID*, *Phone*, *Attendee*, *Class*, *Class:Title*, and *Class:Location*. We will use the *colUserFutureTraining* collection when we get to the *Delete Registration* screen later in the chapter, but for now note how it controls the *Delete Existing Registration* button's *Visible* property:

```
Count(colUserFutureTraining.ID) > 0
```

Our only other logic is navigating to the corresponding screens in response to the *OnSelect* event for our *Create* button:

```
Navigate(NewScreen)
```

as well as our *Delete* button:

```
Navigate(DeleteScreen)
```

The New Screen

We jump to this screen to create a registration. The *Class* defaults to – so the user has to make a selection as discussed earlier in the chapter. The key functionality is then to read the *Attendees* list and determine 1) if any slots are available and 2) if the user has already registered? If neither of these, then we show the *Save* button and allow the user to register. This is shown in Figure 12-8.

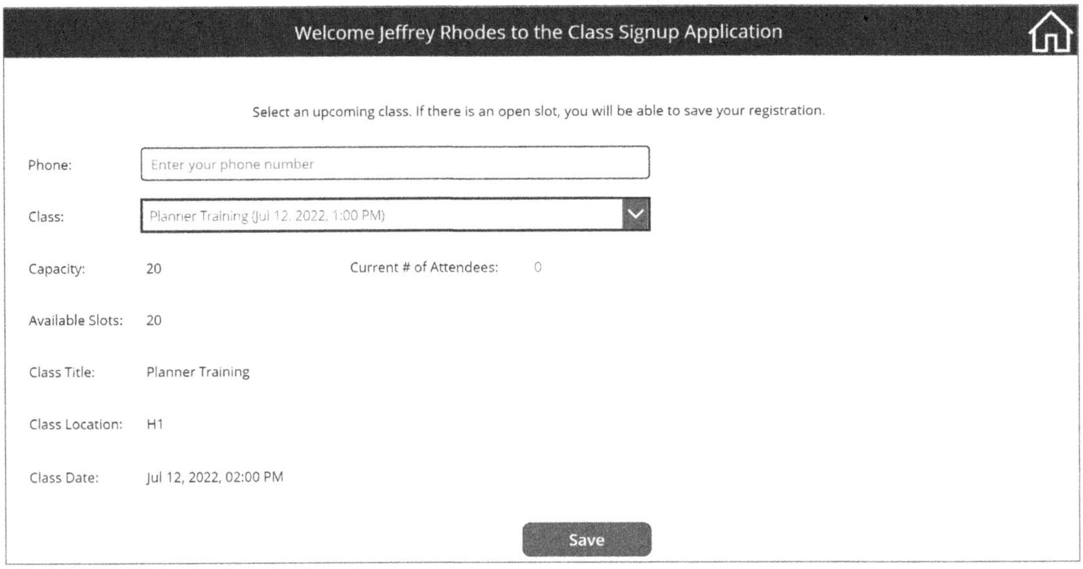

Figure 12-8. *Selecting a class with available slots*

If there are no more slots or the user is already registered, we show the appropriate message and leave the *Save* button hidden. These are shown in Figure 12-9 and Figure 12-10, respectively.

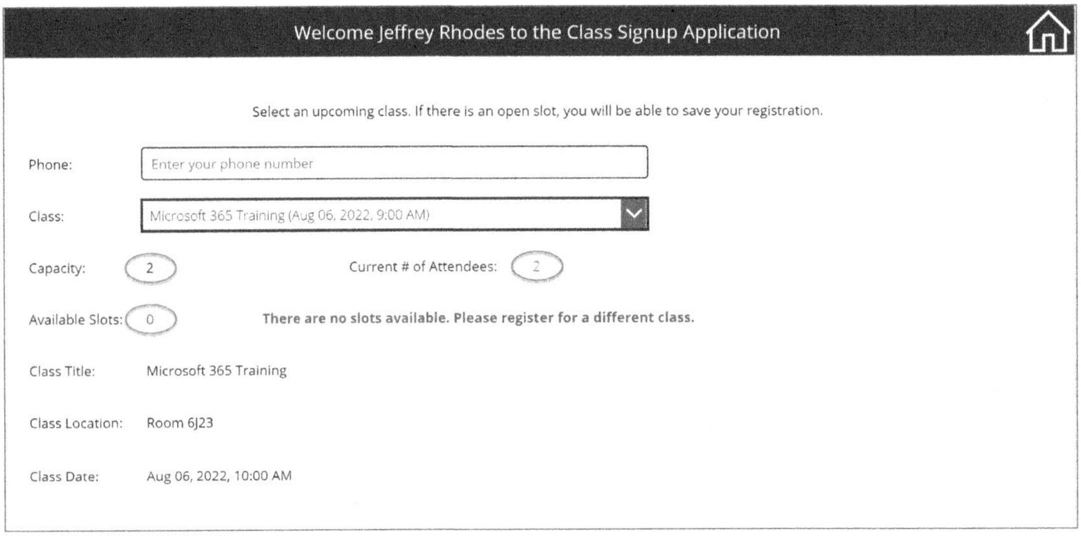

Figure 12-9. *No Slots Available and Unable to Save*

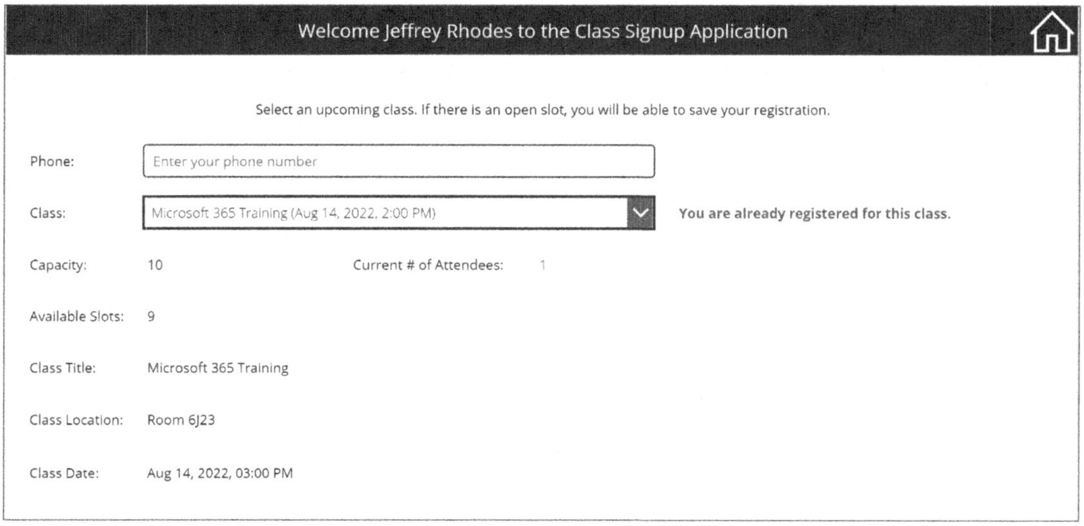

Figure 12-10. *Already Registered and Unable to Save*

Let's look at each of the key controls in turn. For the *Class* drop-down, the key setting is for the *Items* property:

```
Sort(
    Filter(
        Classes,
        'Class Date' > Now()
    ),
    Title,
    Ascending
)
```

We filter out past classes and then sort by the *Title*.[6] We choose *Ascending* so our – is the first item, since *Default* = "1". It will be helpful to store our selected class as a variable and thus handle the *OnChange* event:

```
Set(varSelectedClass, ClassesBox.Selected)
```

While there are other properties of the drop-down list like *SelectedText*, we want *Selected* in this case as we want our entire record. We will use this extensively in the following text.

---

[6] You might think we would sort by the *Expanded Title* since it shows the date and time too. However, that gives us another delegation warning, presumably since it is a calculated column.

Next is our *Already Registered* label. Its Visible property is

```
!IsBlank(varSelectedClass) && Count(
    Filter(
        Attendees,
        Class.Value = varSelectedClass.'Expanded Title',
        Attendee.Email = User().Email
    ).ID
) > 0
```

Since we don't want to show this label if there is no selection yet, we check if *varSelectedClass* is blank. We then *Filter()* our Attendees list looking for both the selected class AND our current user.[7] Note how we compare Attendee/User Email properties as that is simpler than other options.

For *Capacity*, we set the *Text* to be "" if we haven't yet selected a class and otherwise read the *Capacity* value from our SharePoint list.

```
If(varSelectedClass.Title = "-" || IsBlank(varSelectedClass), "",
varSelectedClass.Capacity)
```

We use this same format for *Class Title* and *Class Location*.

The *Current # of Attendees* is a little more involved. Here is its Text property:

```
If(
    varSelectedClass.Title = "-" || IsBlank(varSelectedClass),
    "",
    Count(
        Filter(
            Attendees,
            Class.Value = varSelectedClass.'Expanded Title'
        ).ID
    )
)
```

---

[7] You might think we would compare *ID* properties rather than the *Class.Value* and *'Expanded Title.'* But that again causes delegation issues. That's one reason we chose to link to *Expanded Title* back in Figure 12-3.

Again, we check to see if we have selected a class. If so, we *Filter()* the *Attendees* list for the currently selected class. The *Count* of this filtered list is our number of attendees.

We are now ready to do a little math to get to our *Available Slots*. Here is its *Text* property:

```
If(
    varSelectedClass.Title = "-" || IsBlank(varSelectedClass),
    "",
    Value(ClassCapacityLabel.Text) - Value(NumberOfAttendees.Text)
)
```

We again check to make sure we have selected a class. If so, we convert our text to a number with the *Value()* function and subtract the number of attendees from the capacity.

We use our calculation to determine whether to show the "No Slots Available" message. Here is its *Visible* property:

```
If(
    IsBlank(AvailableSlotsLabel.Text),
    false,
    Value(AvailableSlotsLabel.Text) <= 0
)
```

The value should never be less than zero, but just to be on the safe side, we show the label if the available slots is less than or equal to zero.

While the *Class Title* and *Class Location* labels are similar as we mentioned previously, the *Class Date* has some interesting *Text* to format the value correctly:

```
If(
    varSelectedClass.Title = "-",
    "",
    Text(
        varSelectedClass.'Class Date',
        "mmm dd, yyyy, hh:mm AM/PM"
    )
)
```

We use the *Text()* method and then pass a similar syntax to what we used for the SharePoint calculated column earlier in the chapter.

Last but not least is our *Save* button. Rather than repeat all the previous logic related to whether there are slots available or the attendee is already registered, we link its *Visible* property to whether those labels themselves are showing (as well as checking for whether the title is -):

```
!NoAvailableSlotsLabel.Visible && !AlreadyRegisteredLabel.Visible &&
varSelectedClass.Title <> "-"
```

We are now ready to save our registration back to SharePoint, as shown in Listing 12-3.

Listing 12-3. OnSelect code for saving a class registration

```
Patch(
    Attendees,
    Defaults(Attendees),
    {
        Attendee: {
            '@odata.type': "#Microsoft.Azure.Connectors.SharePoint.
SPListExpandedUser",
            ODataType: Blank(),
            Claims: Concatenate(
                "i:0#.f|membership|",
                User().Email
            ),
            DisplayName: User().FullName,
            Email: User().Email,
            Department: "",
            JobTitle: "",
            Picture: ""
        },
        Class: {
            '@odata.type': "#Microsoft.Azure.Connectors.SharePoint.
SPListExpandedReference",
            Id: varSelectedClass.ID,
```

```
            Value: varSelectedClass.'Expanded Title'
        },
        Title: PhoneBox.Text
    }
);
Reset(PhoneBox);
Set(
    varSelectedClass,
    Blank()
);
Navigate(HomeScreen)
```

As we have seen previously, we use the *Patch()* method with the first parameter being the data source (*Attendees* list) and the second being the record. For a new record, we use the *Default(Attendees)* syntax to write the default values of any columns we do not specify in the third parameter. We have previously seen how to write a SharePoint *Person* column, which is what we do for *Attendee*. What we haven't seen yet is how to write a Lookup column. Here is that part again:

```
Class: {
            '@odata.type': "#Microsoft.Azure.Connectors.SharePoint.
SPListExpandedReference",
            Id: varSelectedClass.ID,
            Value: varSelectedClass.'Expanded Title'
        }
```

This is similar to the *Person* column except that we need to pass the *Id* and *Value*. The *Value* needs to be the column we selected in Figure 12-3, which was *Expanded Title*. We then write the *Phone* value. So that we are ready to select another class, we *Reset()* the *PhoneBox* control, set the *varSelectedClass* variable back to *Blank()*, and then return to the *Home* screen.

Finally, we look at the OnSelect code for the *Home* button at the upper right:

```
Set(
    varSelectedClass,
    Blank()
);
Navigate(HomeScreen)
```

We again clear the *varSelectedClass* variable and then return to the *Home* screen.

The Delete Screen

As we saw earlier, we can only get to this screen if the user has at least one future class registration. Figure 12-11 shows how it looks with two registrations.

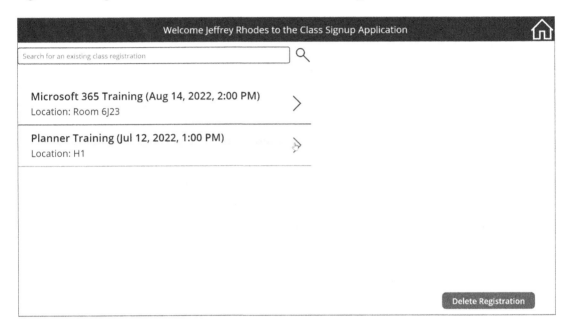

Figure 12-11. *Delete Registration Screen*

For our gallery, we take advantage of the *colUserFutureTraining* variable we configured in the *OnVisible* event for the Home screen (see Listing 12-2). Here is the gallery's Items property:

```
Filter(
    colUserFutureTraining,
    SearchClassesBox.Text in Class.Value
)
```

We *Filter()* the collection by whatever we type into the *SearchClassesBox* input control. We don't have to worry about delegation warnings since we are filtering a collection and not a data source. We also handle the *OnSelect* event and set a new *varSelectedItemToDelete* variable:

```
UpdateContext({varSelectedItemToDelete: ClassesGallery.Selected})
```

Rather than our normal global variable, I used a context variable to try to ensure that it would not survive once I return to the *Home* screen. This is to avoid the possible situation where the user leaves the screen, comes back, and then clicks the *Delete* button without making a new selection. To be on the safe side, I clear the variable when leaving the screen as well.

To give a visual indication of which item is selected, we set the Fill property of our Title to be:

```
If(ThisItem.IsSelected && !IsBlank(varSelectedItemToDelete), Color.Yellow,
RGBA(0, 0, 0, 0))
```

We check the *IsSelected* property (which is true immediately for the first item in the gallery) AND the *varSelectedItemToDelete* variable (which is not set until the user clicks on the > in the gallery) and then set the color to yellow when both are true. This reminds the user to actually select the class registration they want.

We reuse this same variable to control the *Visible* property of our *Delete* button:

```
!IsBlank(varSelectedItemToDelete)
```

So that button won't show up until the user selects a class registration. Listing 12-4 shows the *OnSelect* code for the button.

Listing 12-4. Delete button OnSelect code

```
Remove(
    Attendees,
    LookUp(
        Attendees,
        ID = varSelectedItemToDelete.ID
    )
);
UpdateContext({varSelectedItemToDelete: Blank()});
Navigate(HomeScreen)
```

We use the helpful *Remove()* method. Its first parameter is the data source (our *Attendees* list) and its second parameter is the record to remove. For that, we use the *LookUp()* method and find the record with the *ID* that matches up to what we selected in the gallery. We then clear our *varSelectedItemToDelete* context variable, just to be safe. From there we navigate back to our *Home* screen. Note that it will free up capacity for other students.

The *OnSelect* code for our *Home* button is identical to the end part of the preceding script, obviously not deleting the record first:

```
UpdateContext({varSelectedItemToDelete: Blank()});
Navigate(HomeScreen)
```

That does it.

Summary

In this chapter, we learned how to use two SharePoint lists and Power Apps to create a solution for only allowing users to sign up for a class or other type of event/appointment with available slots. When the user or an owner deletes a registration, that frees up a slot for someone else. Logic within Power Apps allows us to calculate availability, display a message when there are no slots, and more. Views in SharePoint or, even better, Power BI reports, allow us to easily generate a roster of registered attendees per event. We will explore that in the next chapter.

CHAPTER 13

Working with SharePoint Lookup Columns in Power BI

Let's continue our example from the last chapter by visualizing our data. It gives us a good opportunity to explore how we work with lookup columns, such as the *Class* lookup column in the *Attendee* list. In this chapter, we will connect to our two lists, transform our data, and then create rosters and other visualizations of our data. After selecting a desired event, users can then export an attendee list, if desired.

Connecting to Our Data Sources

As with past examples, we choose *SharePoint Online List* as our data source via the *Get data* button in Power BI Desktop and then the *2.0* Implementation. Even though we could work entirely with the *Attendees* list since we included additional columns like *Location* and *Capacity*, I prefer to bring both lists in as sources,[1] as shown in Figure 13-1.

---

[1] This avoids having to rename columns and also allows us to do visualizations on both lists independently, if desired. If you must work with older SharePoint versions and thus need to use the *1.0* implementation, joining the two lists avoids errors and has even more advantages.

© Jeffrey M. Rhodes 2022
J. M. Rhodes, *Creating Business Applications with Microsoft 365*,
https://doi.org/10.1007/978-1-4842-8823-8_13

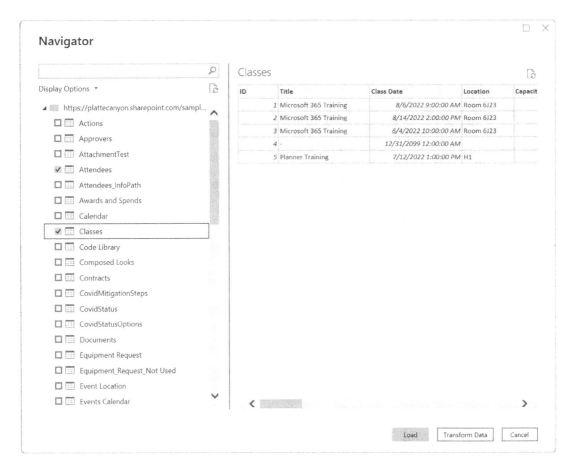

Figure 13-1. *Connecting to the two related SharePoint Lists*

We Load the data and then go to the Model ⊞ view on the left side of Power BI Desktop. As shown in Figure 13-2 we drag between *ID* in the *Attendees* list and *Class:ID* in the *Classes* list.

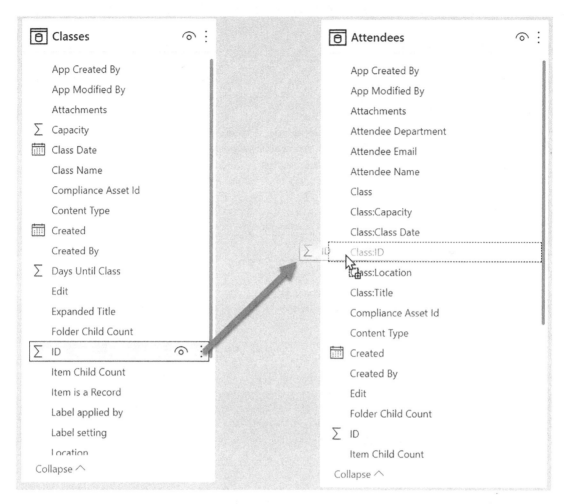

Figure 13-2. *Creating the join link between ID and Class:ID*

We can review the properties of the link, as shown in Figure 13-3, to make sure that all is how we want it.

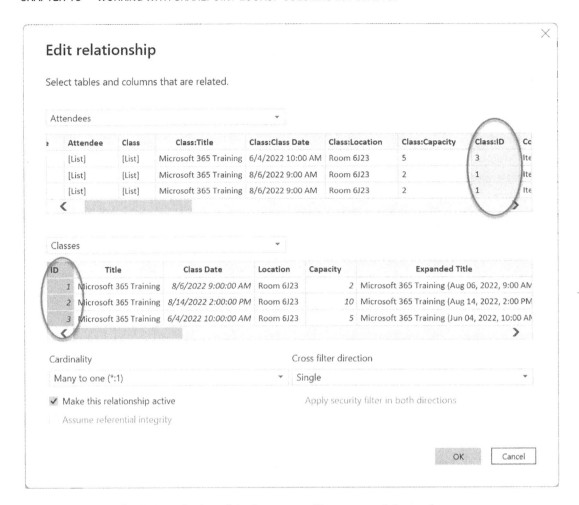

Figure 13-3. *The join relationship between Classes and Attendees*

Power BI will tell us if there is an issue with the data that prevents creating the relationship. We will then be able to use fields from both lists in our visualizations.

We then go to *Transform data*. As we see in Figure 13-4, we can ignore or even hide the various *Class* columns. But we do need to expand the list shown in the *Attendee* column.

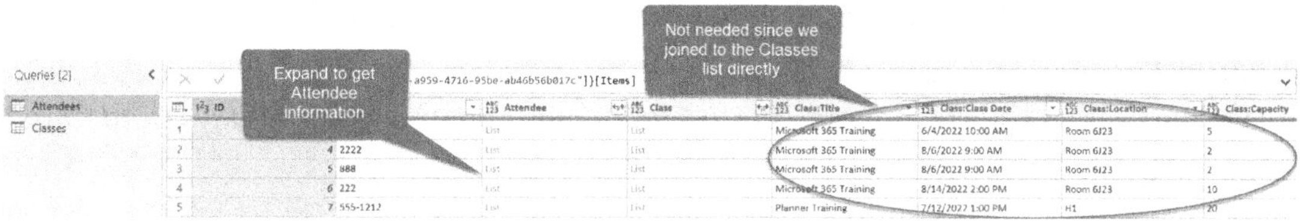

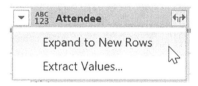

Figure 13-4. *Class information not needed but will expand Attendee List*

We click the *Expand* button 🔛 next to the *Attendee* column and *Expand to New Rows,* as shown in Figure 13-5.

Figure 13-5. *Expand Attendee to new rows*

That changes the contents from a *List* to a *Record*. We click it again, as shown in Figure 13-6 to get the information we want: *title, email,* and *department.*

Figure 13-6. *Choose Attendee record items to make into new columns*

We then rename the columns to be *Attendee Name, Attendee Email,* and *Attendee Department.*

On the Classes list, we rename *Title* to *Class Name* and then add the *Days Until Class* custom column (Figure 13-7).

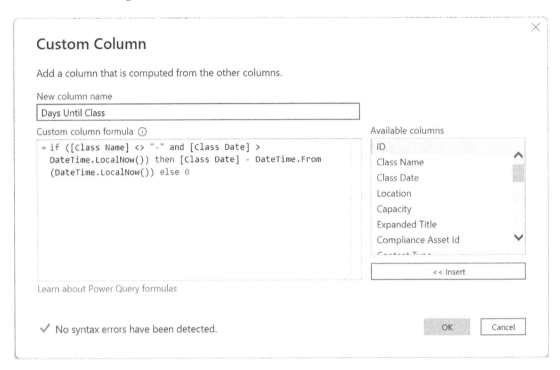

***Figure 13-7.** Days Until Class custom column*

As Listing 13-1 shows, the syntax has a few more permutations than normal.

Listing 13-1. Days Until Class syntax

```
if ([Class Name] <> "-" and [Class Date] > DateTime.LocalNow()) then [Class
Date] - DateTime.From(DateTime.LocalNow()) else 0
```

Since we have one record ("-") that we want to ignore,[2] we only want to do our logic of the *Class Name* is not "-". We also don't want to deal with any classes that have already taken place. So we make sure the *Class Date* is later than the current date and time. If both of these are true, we subtract the current date/time from the *Class Date.*

---

[2] You might recall that this is due to Power Apps defaulting to one of our list items and we didn't want the default to be a real class.

Otherwise, we just put 0 in the column. We then change the type of the column to *Whole Number* for ease of display. That completes our data transformations. We click *Close & Apply* to return to the main Power BI window.

Visualizing Our Data

We'd like to create *Upcoming Classes* and *Past Classes* visualizations. Figure 13-8 shows the filters that will apply to all pages as well as just the *Upcoming Classes* page.

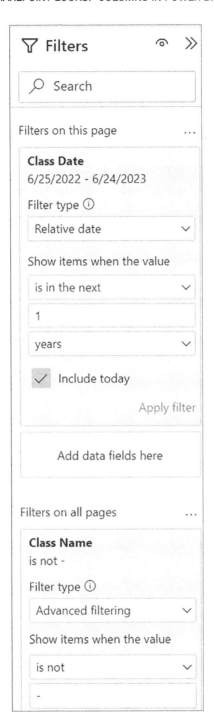

Figure 13-8. *Current page and all page filters*

So that we can exclude past classes, we choose a *Relative date* filter type and show items where the *Class Date is in the next 1 year*. Since we never want to show the default "-" Class, we only include items where *Class Name is not* – on all pages.

Now we see the benefits of joining our two lists. As shown in Figure 13-9, we show the number of attendees per class meeting by using *Expanded Title*[3] from *Classes* and *ID* from *Attendees*.

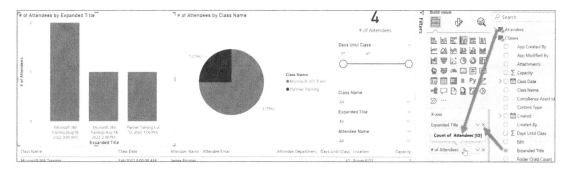

Figure 13-9. *Visualization using columns from both the Attendees and Classes lists*

Similarly, we have slicers and table visualizations that take from one or both of these lists. Figure 13-10 shows how the Upcoming Classes visualization looks after we publish to the Power BI service.

---

[3] We want *Expanded Title* rather than *Class Name* because the former has the date and time in it so each meeting shows up separately. You can see that with the two *Microsoft 365 Training* events in Figure 13-9.

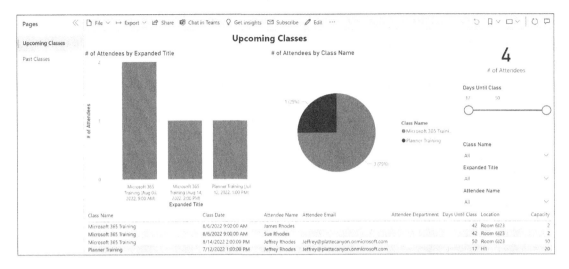

Figure 13-10. *Upcoming Classes visualization*

Notice how we could use our *Days Until Class* information to do special pages with "Classes Next Week" or "Classes Next Month."

One common use of a visualization like this is to create a class roster. Figure 13-11 shows how we can select a particular class date (*Expanded Title*) and then export the table as a roster.

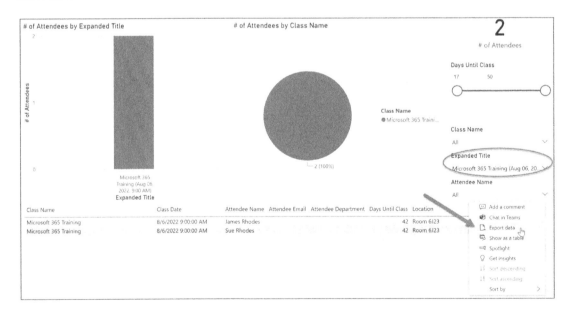

Figure 13-11. *Exporting a Class Date Roster*

For the *Past Classes* page, we duplicate the current page and change the filter to be *Class Date is in the* **last** *1 year*. We then delete the *Days Until Class* slicer and column since that value is always 0 (see Listing 13-1). Figure 13-12 shows the visualization after publishing to the Power BI service.

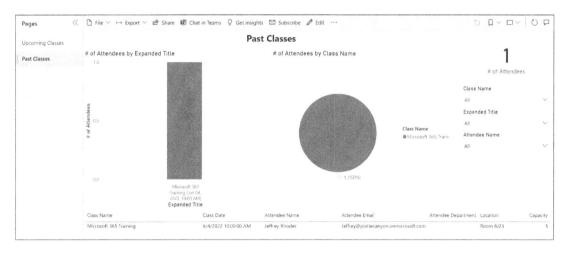

Figure 13-12. *Past Classes visualization*

Summary

In this chapter, we learned how to connect to our two SharePoint lists, join them in our model in order to grab data from both lists in the same visualizations, transform the data with customer columns such as *Days Until Class*, and then add slicers and a data card for an effective display. This is particularly useful for generating rosters of those who signed up for particular events.

CHAPTER 14

Visualizing Learning Management Data from SQL Server Using Power BI

I have done quite a bit of reporting over the years, from text-based reports with ToolBook applications, Crystal Reports from within VB 6 applications, SQL Server Reporting Services, and, one of my favorites prior to Power BI, Microsoft Report Viewer. In this chapter, I wanted to explore how a Report Viewer implementation might be adapted for Power BI. So I chose one of our own products, our Tracker.Net Learning Management System (LMS).[1] It expands on our previous "direct to SQL Server" example. We have a simpler database structure and show how we can test our query in SQL Server Management Studio and then implement it directly within Power BI. We also look at the important topic of how to edit your drill-down interactions so they filter the other visuals rather than highlight their matching values.

---

[1] See http://trackernet.net for more information.

© Jeffrey M. Rhodes 2022
J. M. Rhodes, *Creating Business Applications with Microsoft 365*,
https://doi.org/10.1007/978-1-4842-8823-8_14

Report in Tracker.Net

Let's first take a quick look at the original interface. As shown in Figure 14-1, Tracker.Net allows a user with "Reporter" access to select between Student, Lesson, Course, Class, Organization, and Division reports. Here we select all the lessons and then choose the *Student Information* * report.[2]

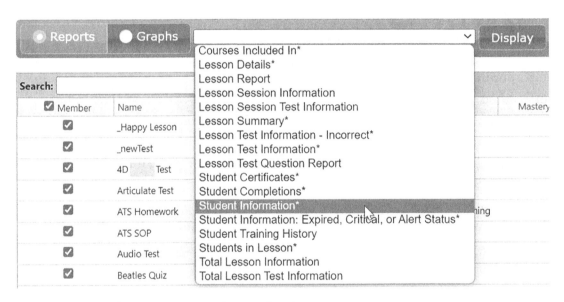

Figure 14-1.   Selecting a Report in Tracker.Net

The user then selects the *Display* button to see the result in Figure 14-2. Microsoft's Report Viewer control gives the interface with the layout controlled by its *.rdlc file.[3]

---

[2] The * indicates that the report is independent of the selected date range.

[3] This is an XML file edited by Visual Studio with optional Visual Basic code embedded within <Code> tags.

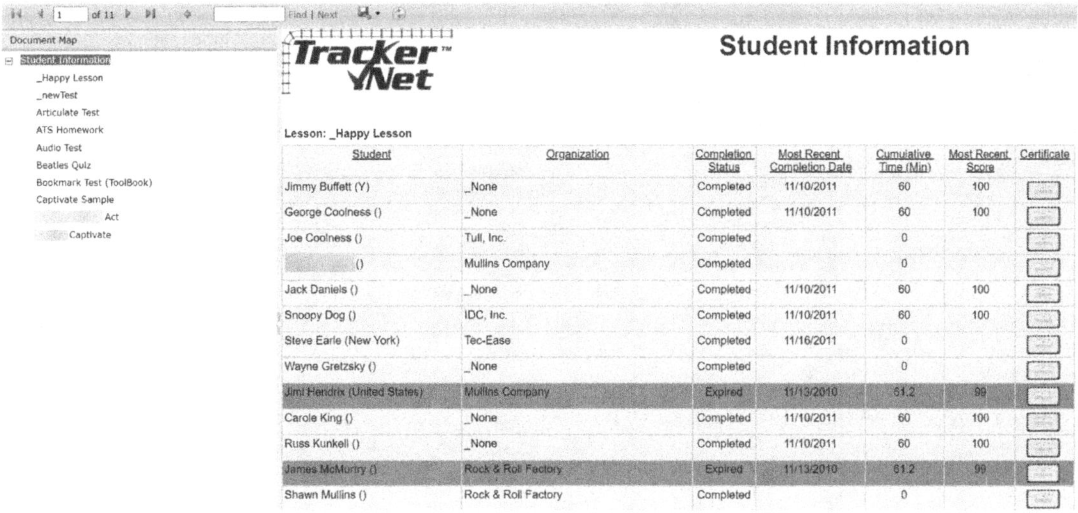

Figure 14-2. *Microsoft Report Viewer Display in Tracker.Net*

Since I am using what Report Viewer calls *ProcessingMode.Local*, our .NET code connects to the database directly, runs our query (taking account of the selected lesson(s) and the report requested),[4] and then sets the report's *DataSource* property. Figure 14-3 shows how this looks in SQL Server Management Studio when grabbing all lesson data.

---

[4] For extensibility reasons, Tracker.Net stores the query files separately as text files and reads them into memory once used. End users can then customize both the .rdlc and query files if needed. There are unique rdlc files for each of the four supported languages and they can be further localized as needed.

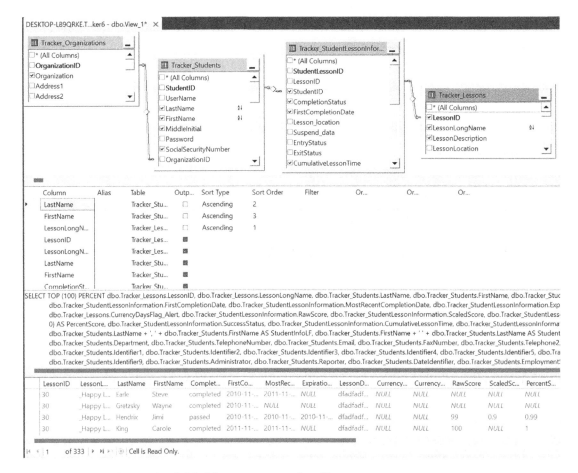

Figure 14-3. *Query in SQL Management Studio*

Notice how the query joins the *Organizations, Students, StudentLessonInformation,* and *Lessons* tables. Notice also how there are 333 total records. We will check this when we get to Power BI. Listing 14-1 shows the Standard Query Language (SQL) query:

Listing 14-1. SQL Query joining the Organizations, Students, StudentLessonInformation, and Lessons tables

```
SELECT TOP (100) PERCENT Tracker_Lessons.LessonID, Tracker_Lessons.
LessonLongName, Tracker_Students.LastName, Tracker_Students.
FirstName, Tracker_StudentLessonInformation.CompletionStatus,
Tracker_StudentLessonInformation.FirstCompletionDate, Tracker_
StudentLessonInformation.MostRecentCompletionDate, Tracker_
StudentLessonInformation.ExpirationDate, Tracker_Lessons.LessonDescription,
```

186

Tracker_Lessons.CurrencyDaysFlag_Critical, Tracker_Lessons.
CurrencyDaysFlag_Alert, Tracker_StudentLessonInformation.RawScore, Tracker_
StudentLessonInformation.ScaledScore, Tracker_StudentLessonInformation.
RawScore / NULLIF (ISNULL(Tracker_StudentLessonInformation.MaxScore,
100), 0) AS PercentScore, Tracker_StudentLessonInformation.SuccessStatus,
Tracker_StudentLessonInformation.CumulativeLessonTime, Tracker_
StudentLessonInformation.StudentID, Tracker_Organizations.Organization,
Tracker_Students.LastName + ', ' + Tracker_Students.FirstName AS
StudentInfoLF, Tracker_Students.FirstName + ' ' + Tracker_Students.LastName
AS StudentInfoFL, Tracker_Students.MiddleInitial, Tracker_Students.
SocialSecurityNumber, Tracker_Students.Department, Tracker_Students.
TelephoneNumber, Tracker_Students.Email, Tracker_Students.FaxNumber,
Tracker_Students.Telephone2, Tracker_Students.CellPhone, Tracker_Students.
Pager, Tracker_Students.Identifier0, Tracker_Students.Identifier1,
Tracker_Students.Identifier2, Tracker_Students.Identifier3, Tracker_
Students.Identifier4, Tracker_Students.Identifier5, Tracker_Students.
Identifier6, Tracker_Students.Identifier7, Tracker_Students.Identifier8,
Tracker_Students.Identifier9, Tracker_Students.Administrator, Tracker_
Students.Reporter, Tracker_Students.DateIdentifier, Tracker_Students.
EmploymentStatus, Tracker_Lessons.UseCEUCertificate, Tracker_Lessons.
CreditValue, Tracker_Lessons.CreditType, Tracker_Lessons.AccreditationInfo

FROM   Tracker_Lessons INNER JOIN Tracker_Students INNER JOIN Tracker_
StudentLessonInformation ON Tracker_Students.StudentID = Tracker_
StudentLessonInformation.StudentID INNER JOIN Tracker_Organizations ON
Tracker_Students.OrganizationID = Tracker_Organizations.OrganizationID ON
Tracker_Lessons.LessonID = Tracker_StudentLessonInformation.LessonID

WHERE (Tracker_Lessons.Inactive IS NULL OR Tracker_Lessons.Inactive =
0) AND (Tracker_Students.EmploymentStatus IS NULL OR Tracker_Students.
EmploymentStatus = 0)

ORDER BY Tracker_Lessons.LessonLongName, Tracker_Students.LastName,
Tracker_Students.FirstName

We join the four tables, do some logic so that we don't divide by zero when calculating the percentage test score, concatenate names in both *Last Name, First Name* and *First Name Last Name* format, and then exclude inactive students and lessons in our WHERE clause.

Connecting to and Transforming the Data

We are now ready to move to Power BI. We create a new report in Power BI Desktop and choose to get data from SQL Server, as shown in Figure 14-4.

Figure 14-4. *Get Data from SQL Server*

Figure 14-5 shows resulting dialog.

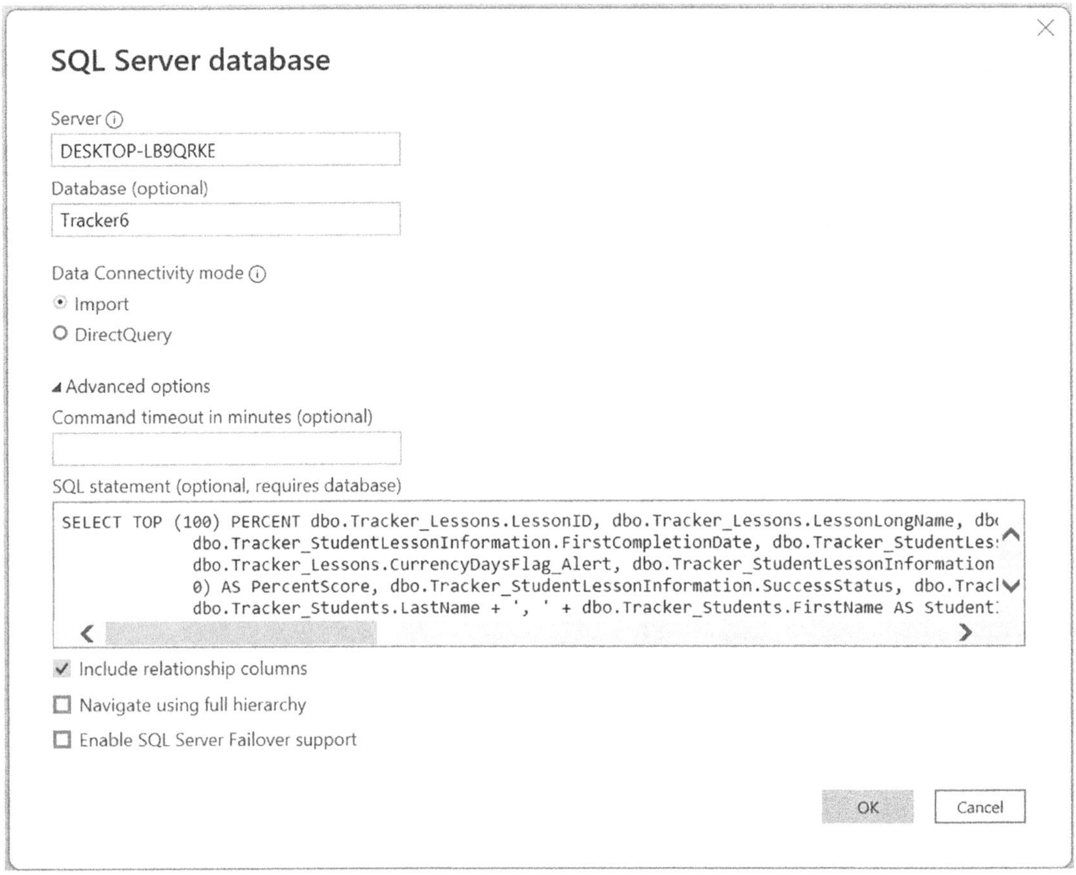

Figure 14-5. *SQL Server Query Inside Power BI*

We enter the Server,[5] Database, .and the *Data Connectivity mode.* Since this is a small data set, importing the entire query will work fine. For larger data sets, we could use *DirectQuery,* which does not load any data during development, but instead just loads the tables and columns. It then queries the data when used. We open the *Advanced options* and then paste in the query from Management Studio (shown back in Listing 14-1).

As is our standard practice, we *Transform data* and proceed to rename columns. Since we are only interested in the date and not the time, we change the type to Date, as shown in Figure 14-6.

---

[5] We use a name here, but this can be a complete URL such as *tcp:*sql123.someurl.com if that has been configured in SQL Server Management Studio. The huge advantage of a URL is that we could configure our Power BI report to have scheduled refreshes.

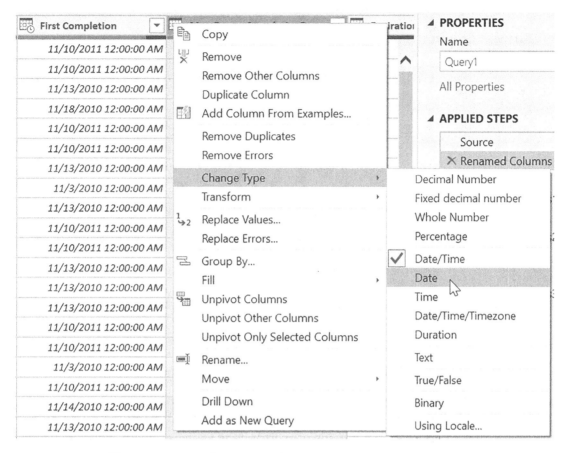

Figure 14-6. *Changing Type from Date/Time to Date*

We add an index column for use in our visualization. Back in the Report Viewer example, we could use the .rdlc file to format the score as shown here:

```
<Value>=IIF(isNumeric(Fields!RawScore.Value),
Round(100*(Fields!PercentScore.Value), 1), "")</Value>
```

This checks if the *RawScore* is numeric and, if so, multiples our *PercentScore* by 100 and rounds it to one decimal place. If not, it makes the value blank. In Power BI, it is easier to implement this as a custom Score column, as shown in Figure 14-7.

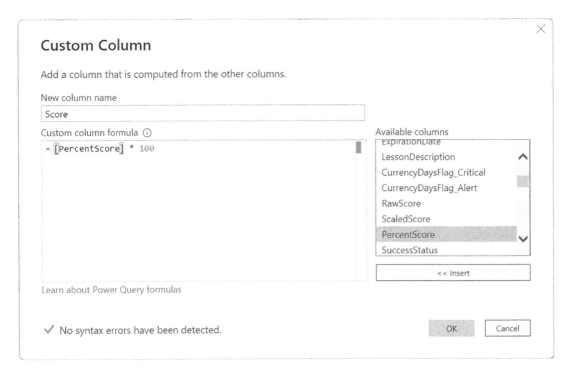

Figure 14-7. Custom Score column

This takes the *PercentScore* column (which has a value like 0.86) and multiplies it by 100. Power BI is smart enough not to have an error if the value is *null*. In that case *Score* will be *null* as well.

Our last data task is to go to the Data screen and change the Date format of our date columns to *Short Date,* as shown in Figure 14-8.

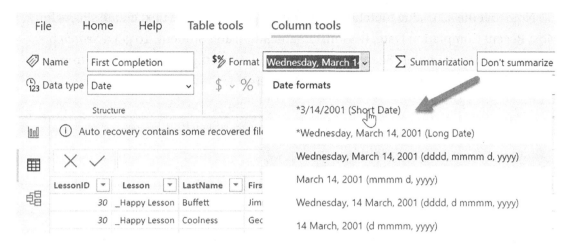

Figure 14-8. *Changing the Date Format to Short Date*

Visualizing the Data

We are now ready to start creating our visualizations. Figure 14-9 shows both the final result and the selected card that shows the count of our *Index* column (renamed to say *# of Students*).

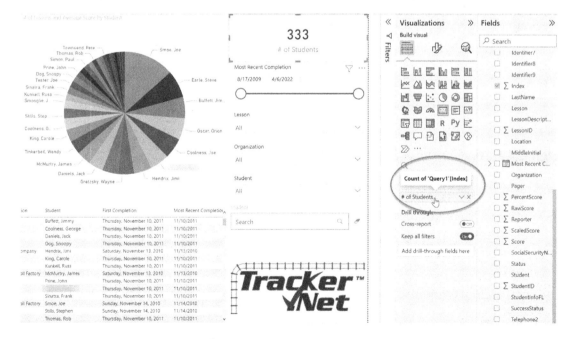

Figure 14-9. *Power BI Visualization*

Note that the 333 value matches our query (Figure 14-3). We next create slicers for Most Recent Completion Date, Lesson, Organization, and Student. To get a *Search* box, we *Get more visuals*, enter "Search" in the box, and select the *Text Filter* visual from Microsoft. These are shown in Figures 14-10 and 14-11.

Figure 14-10. *Getting Additional Power BI Visuals*

Figure 14-11. *Adding a Search Visual*

This allows you to search for a particular student.[6] Figure 14-12 shows the result of searching for "Jim."

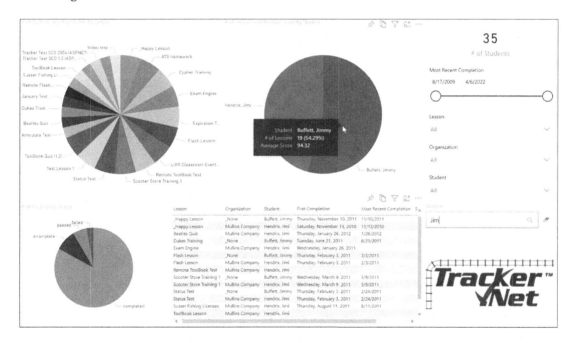

Figure 14-12. *Search Showing Tooltip of Lesson Info*

---

[6]We could have additional Search boxes for lessons, organizations, etc., if desired.

Notice how the tooltip of the # *of Lessons* and *Average Score* shows up when we hover over a user, in this case Jimmy Buffett.[7] Notice how the other visuals are updated as well with only the lessons, statuses, and detailed information associated with Jimi Hendrix and Jimmy Buffett.

Updating the Drill-Down Interactions

Our last task is to adjust what happens when we drill down on particular lessons, students, or statuses. Figure 14-13 shows the default experience of "highlighting" the related visuals.

Figure 14-13. *Default Highlight Drill Down Interaction*

---

[7] You might have noticed that I like to use some of my favorite music artists as test users. With such a high set of test scores, I think Jimmy has earned both a margarita and a cheeseburger ☺.

We have clicked on _Happy Lesson. The *Student* and *Status* visual are grayed out with the matching areas highlighted. This is sub-optimal to me at least. Instead, we'd like to see what students took that lesson and what statuses are associated with that lesson. To get that behavior, we select the lessons visual, go to the *Format* tab, and click *Edit interactions*. We than click on the popup Filter button on each of the other visuals.[8] This is shown in Figure 14-14. Note that the Table only has the filter option, so we don't need to edit anything there.

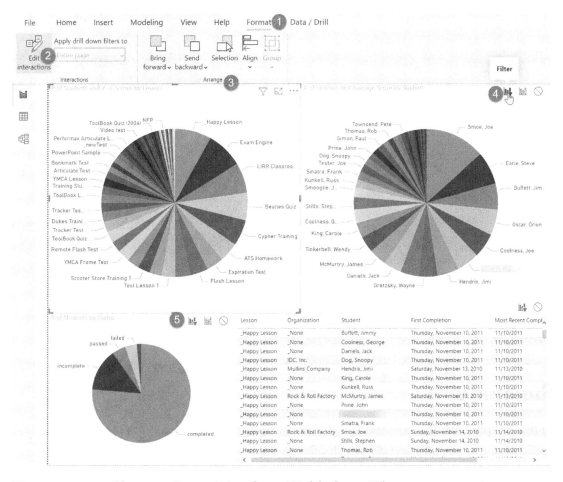

Figure 14-14. *Changng Interaction from Highlight to Filter*

---

[8] This can be a bit temperamental if the visuals are bumping up against each other. If you have trouble, try making the visuals you are trying to switch from *Highlight* to *Filter* smaller.

Figure 14-15 shows the result. Notice how this is a much cleaner interface and only shows the data associated with the _Happy Lesson_ we selected.

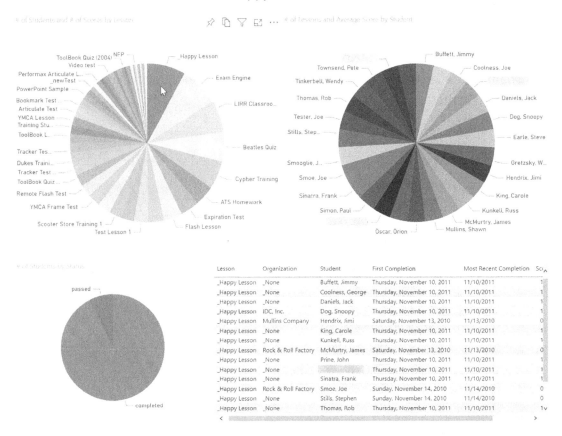

Figure 14-15. *Filter Drill Down Interaction*

Summary

In this chapter, we transformed an older reporting approach into Power BI. We connected to a real-life SQL Server database, transformed our data with a custom column, updated data types, an index column, and by renaming our columns for clarity. We customized our data display format and then visualized our data with the normal mix of cards, slicers, charts, and tables. We added a Search control to allow the user to search for key data like the student and lesson names. We then saw how to change our drill-down interaction from highlight to filter, which I find preferable in most cases.

CHAPTER 15

Dynamic Information in Power Apps and Sending an Adaptive Card to Teams Using Power Automate

This chapter illustrates how to use Power Apps, Power Automate, SharePoint, and Teams together to solve real-world requirements. It is based on an actual COVID-19 notification application. The gist of the design is that the decision-maker goes into a particular SharePoint list and selects the current level (1–4) and adds any additional instructions. The level has a set of associated steps on restrictions such as whether personnel are on-site or remote. Whenever the status changed, there is automated post to Teams via Power Automate with the summary and a link to a Power App that displays the color-coded status and all the restrictions and instructions. We deployed the solution quickly with no licensing costs[1] to rave reviews.

---

[1] All users needed a Microsoft 365 license but not a Power Apps per user or Dynamics license that might come into play if we were using model-driven apps or Dataverse as a data source.

© Jeffrey M. Rhodes 2022
J. M. Rhodes, *Creating Business Applications with Microsoft 365*,
https://doi.org/10.1007/978-1-4842-8823-8_15

Configuration in SharePoint

Let's start with the configuration of our data sources in SharePoint. Figure 15-1 shows *CovidStatusOptions* list.

CovidStatusOptions ☆			
Title ∨	Color ∨	TextColor ∨	StatusNumber ∨
Level 1	Green	White	1
Level 2	Yellow	Black	2
Level 3	Red	White	3
Level 4	Black	White	4

Figure 15-1. *CovidStatusOptions SharePoint List*

We give each status a *Title* (Level 1–4) and then a *Color* and *TextColor* (to be used later in Power Apps). To avoid a "brittle" application that breaks if we rename our statuses, we make a numeric *StatusNumber* column as well.

Our next step is to use this as a lookup column for our *CovidStatus* list. As shown in Figure 15-2, we want to have access to the TextColor and Color columns as well as ID. So we include them as well.

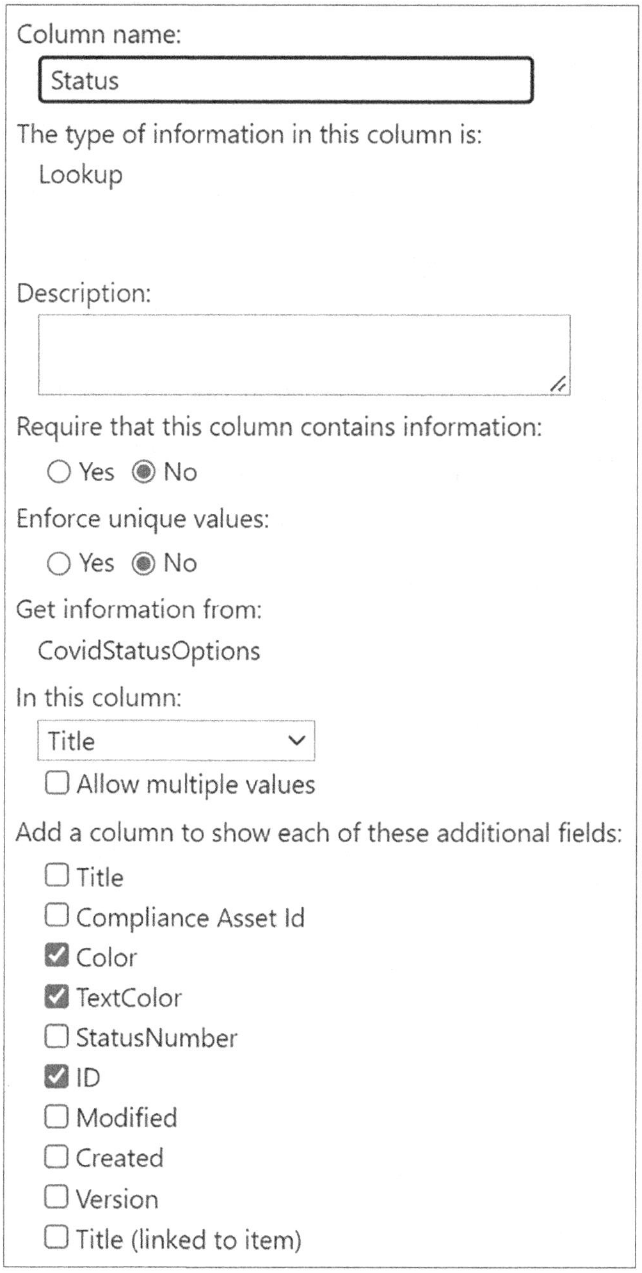

Column name:

Status

The type of information in this column is:

Lookup

Description:

Require that this column contains information:

○ Yes ◉ No

Enforce unique values:

○ Yes ◉ No

Get information from:

CovidStatusOptions

In this column:

Title ⌄

☐ Allow multiple values

Add a column to show each of these additional fields:

☐ Title
☐ Compliance Asset Id
☑ Color
☑ TextColor
☐ StatusNumber
☑ ID
☐ Modified
☐ Created
☐ Version
☐ Title (linked to item)

Figure 15-2. *Status Lookup Column*

Figure 15-3 shows the resulting list. It only has a single record with a title of *Current Status.*

CovidStatus ☆					
○ Title ∨	Status ∨	AdditionalGuid... ∨	Status:Color ∨	Status:TextColor ∨	Status:ID ∨
Current Status	Level 2	Additional Information: 1. Wash hands 2. 6-fit social	Yellow	Black	2

Figure 15-3. *CovidStatus SharePoint List*

In addition to the lookup Status column and its associated information, we have
an *AdditionalGuidance* column where the senior leader updating the status can give
specific information about current restrictions not generally associated with the Covid
level. We make this column *Enhanced rich text* so that we can add formatting, graphics,
etc., if needed. Figure 15-4 shows how the leader would edit the status and the additional
guidance.

Figure 15-4. *Editing the Current Covid Status*

Our last SharePoint list is *CovidMitigationSteps,* as shown in Figure 15-5.

CovidMitigationSteps ☆				
Status ∨	Title ∨		Description ∨	Status:ID ∨
Level 1	Dining Out		In person and take out	1
Level 1	Remote Teaching		Up to 50%	1
Level 2	Dining Out		Take out only	2
Level 2	Remote Teaching		Can shift to remote and go over 50%	2

Figure 15-5. *CovidMitigationSteps SharePoint List*

This has the same *Status* lookup column, but we only bring along the *ID* column this time. We then list as many common steps (*Dining Out* and *Remote Teaching* in this example) as needed for each level. These and the *Additional Guidance* from Figure 15-3 will show up in the Power App that we will cover next.

Creating the Status Application in Power Apps

We again create a *Blank app* ➤ *Blank canvas app* ➤ *Tablet* format in Power Apps. Our next step is to connect to the *CovidMitigationSteps* and *CovidStatus* lists, as shown in Figure 15-6. We don't need to connect to *CovidStatusOptions* since we brought its info over to *CovidStatus* via our lookup column.

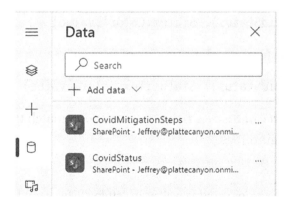

Figure 15-6. *Connecting to CovidMitigationSteps and CovidStatus from Power Apps*

Our next step is to display the current status in a label (Figure 15-7).

Figure 15-7. *Setting the Text Based on our Current Status*

We use the fact that the *CovidStatus* list only has one record and use the *First()* method to grab the first item. We then read the *Status* column and its *Value*. Notice how Power Apps shows us that this *Value* is text and is "Level 2." More challenging is getting the Fill property, as shown in Figure 15-8. The tricky part here is getting from the text value of "Yellow" to the actual color of *Yellow*.

Figure 15-8. *Setting the Fill Color Programmatically using ColorValue()*

Luckily, Power Apps has a *ColorValue()* method just for this purpose. We read the first item of the *CovidStatus* list and then the *Value* of its *Status:Color* column and pass that to *ColorValue()* to convert it to a color[2]:

```
ColorValue(First(CovidStatus).'Status:Color'.Value)
```

We use similar code for the Color property of the label.

```
ColorValue(First(CovidStatus).'Status:TextColor'.Value)
```

Since our *Additional Guidance* is rich text, we need to match that with an HTML text control,[3] as shown in Figure 15-9.

---

[2] We could pass this as a hex color value as well as in "#ffffoo". This would allow us to pick any variation of color we wanted.

[3] We would use *Rich text editor* if we needed to edit the text. But since we only need to display it, *HTML text* is the one we want.

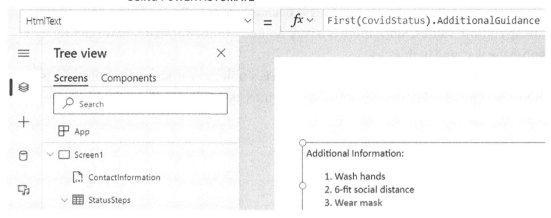

Figure 15-9. *Setting the HtmlText Property for Additional Guidance*

Notice our formatted text comes over fine from SharePoint and that we set the
HtmlText property to our column value.

To display our steps from the *CovidMitigationSteps* list, we use a *Data Table* control.
This allows us to show as many steps as needed and get a scroll bar if the list becomes
longer than the space available. To get the steps associated with our current Covid Status,
we filter such that the *Status:ID* columns match between the two lists:

```
Filter(CovidMitigationSteps, 'Status:ID'.Id =
First(CovidStatus).'Status:ID'.Id)
```

As we have seen, the first parameter is the data source (*CovidMitigationSteps*) and
the second is the logical test. Figure 15-10 shows the results.

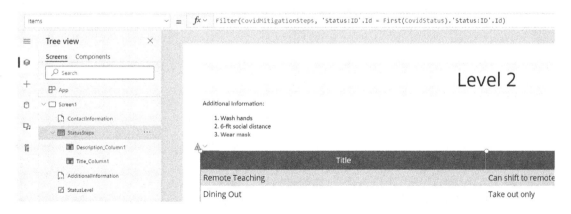

Figure 15-10. *Data Table Showing the Steps for the Current Status*

Notice the delegation warning. This is because we are filtering by the non-primary lookup column values. Since there is a very limited number of statuses, we can safely ignore the warning in this case.

Configuring the columns of the data table is similar to working with galleries. As shown in Figure 15-11, we use the *ThisItem* syntax as in *ThisItem.Text* and *ThisItem. Description*.

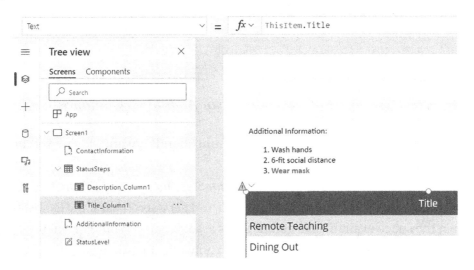

Figure 15-11. *Configuring a Column of a DataTable*

Figure 15-12 shows the complete application with a final HTML text control with the phone number and a link to the Team and channel with additional information.

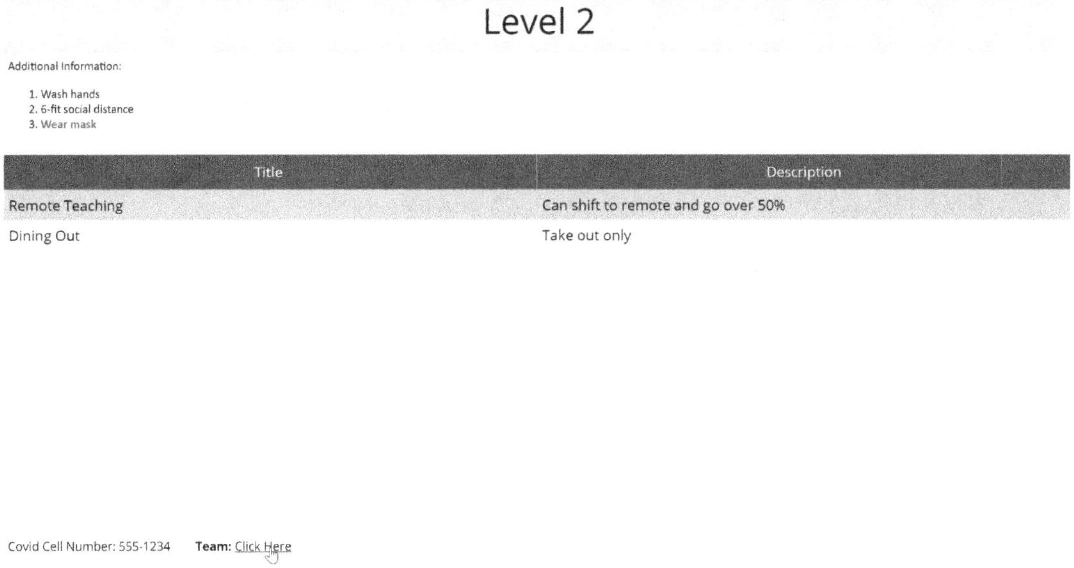

Level 2

Additional Information:

1. Wash hands
2. 6-fit social distance
3. Wear mask

Title	Description
Remote Teaching	Can shift to remote and go over 50%
Dining Out	Take out only

Covid Cell Number: 555-1234   **Team:** Click Here

Figure 15-12. *Covid Status Application including a link to the associated Team*

To get the link, we need to use our knowledge of HTML tags with * * being a space, *<strong>* representing bold text, and the *anchor tag (<a>)* configuring a link.

```
"Covid Cell Number: 555-1234       
<strong>Team:</strong> <a href='https://teams.microsoft.com/l/channe
l/19%3a46aac9c8caf942e0acff73a65f56bb3f%40thread.skype/COVID%2520Response?
groupId=321c7c59-8fd2-4f81-8400-8b7988935ee2&tenantId=314d6fd9-25a2-453f-
b6d5-63f3aa9e355f'>Click Here</a> "
```

Posting to Teams from Power Automate

We are not on our last task for posting to our COVID Response Teams channel whenever the status changes. We accomplish this via Power Automate. We create an automated cloud flow with the trigger being whenever a list item is created or modified, as shown in Figure 15-13.

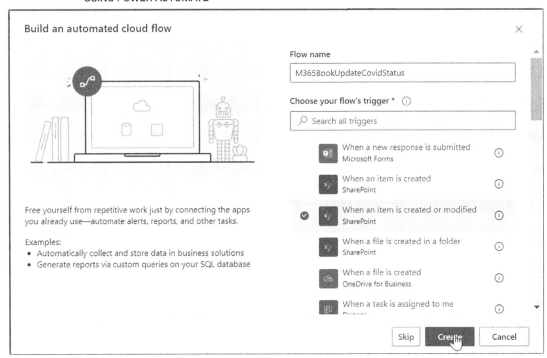

Figure 15-13. *Creating Power Automated Flow with SharePoint List Trigger*

We choose our SharePoint site and the *CovidStatus* list. We then create a *CovidStatus* variable and store the current Status Value in it. More significantly, we research into adaptive cards and realize that the only valid color values in its JavaScript Object Notation (JSON) are "default", "dark", "light", "accent", "good", "warning", or "attention".[4] Because of that, we will need to put one of these values in a new Color variable. Figure 15-14 shows connecting to the list and initializing both variables.

---

[4] Search for color on this page: `https://adaptivecards.io/explorer/TextBlock.html`.

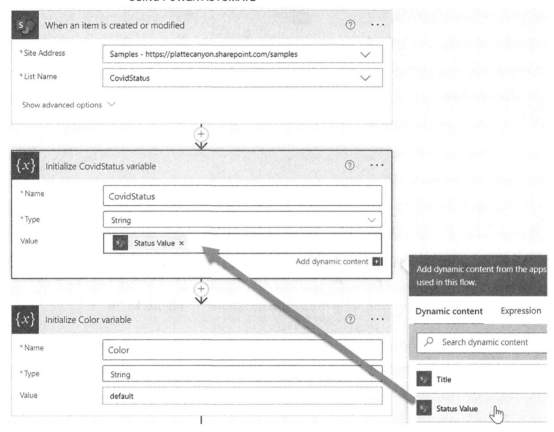

Figure 15-14. *Triggering on SharePoint and Initializing Variables*

Note that we initialize the *Color* variable to one of our valid values – default. From there, we do a Switch condition on the *Status:Color Value* (Green, Yellow, Red, or Black) and set the *Color* variable to the associated string (good, warning, attention, or dark), as shown in Figure 15-15.

Figure 15-15. *Switch on the Color Value in our Flow*

Again thinking ahead to the fact that the adaptive card will want plain rather than
rich text, we add an *Html to text action* for our *AdditionalGuidance* and then the *Post
adaptive card in a chat or channel* action. Both are shown in Figure 15-16.

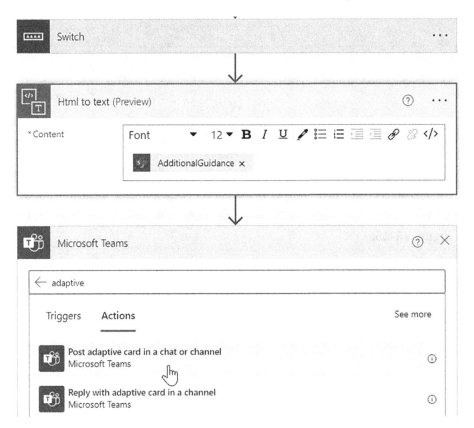

Figure 15-16. *HTML to Text and Post Adaptive Card to Channel*

Before we can configure our adaptive card, we need to look at the available JSON formats.[5] Figure 15-17 gives an example.

Figure 15-17. *Example Adaptive Card JSON*

We can copy this JSON and then adapt it to our purposes. Listing 15-1 shows the edited version,[6] with Figure 15-18 showing how it looks within Power Automate.

Listing 15-1. Adaptive Card JSON Incorporating COVIDStatus, Color, Additional Guidance, and the URL

```
{
    "type": "AdaptiveCard",
    "$schema": "http://adaptivecards.io/schemas/adaptive-card.json",
    "version": "1.2",
    "body": [
        {
            "text": "COVID Status:",
            "type": "TextBlock",
            "size": "Large",
            "separator": true,
            "spacing": "Medium"
        },
```

---

[5] See https://docs.microsoft.com/en-us/power-automate/create-adaptive-cards.
[6] Thanks to my former colleague Anthony Apodaca for doing this edit.

```
        {
            "text": "@{variables('COVIDStatus')}",
            "type": "TextBlock",
            "color": "@{variables('Color')}",
            "weight": "Bolder",
            "size": "ExtraLarge"
        },
        {

            "type": "RichTextBlock",
            "inlines": [
                {
                    "text": "@{outputs('Html_to_text')?['body']}",
                    "type": "TextRun"
                }
            ]
        },
        {

            "type": "ActionSet",
            "actions": [
                {
                    "title": "View Complete Status Information",
                    "type": "Action.OpenUrl",
                    "url": "https://teams.microsoft.com/l/entity/a6b633
                    65-31a4-4f43-92ec-710b71557af9/_djb2_msteams_prefi
                    x_839829755?context=%7B%22subEntityId%22%3Anull%2C%2
                    2channelId%22%3A%2219%3A46aac9c8caf942e0acff73a65f5
                    6bb3f%40thread.skype%22%7D&groupId=321c7c59-8fd2-
                    4f81-8400-8b7988935ee2&tenantId=314d6fd9-25a2-453f-
                    b6d5-63f3aa9e355f"
                }
            ]
        }
    ]
}
```

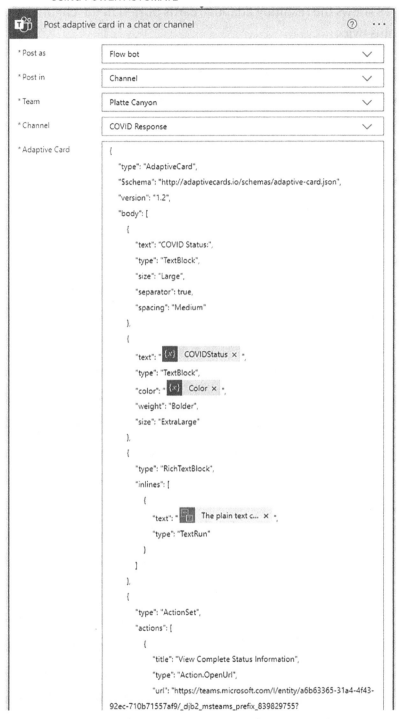

Figure 15-18. *Edited Adaptive Card JSON*

Figure 15-19 shows the resulting adaptive cards posted in the channel when we change the status twice.

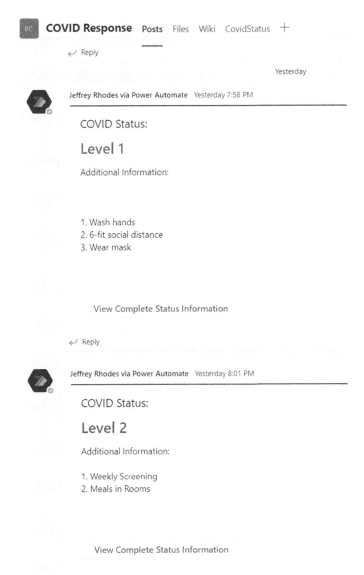

Figure 15-19. *Adaptive Cards Posted in Teams Channel*

Notice that even though we tell Power Automate to use the Flow Bot, it still posts my name as the one who initiated the post (since it is my flow). That is not necessarily totally optimal, but it is good from a security standpoint. At least it has the Flow Bot graphic rather than my picture each time.

Summary

In this chapter, we put many of the key pieces together to build a complete application. We stored some key pieces of data in SharePoint and allowed leadership to edit that information there. Users viewed the data (with color-coding) via Power Apps. They were prompted to do that by Power Automate, triggered by changes to the underlying SharePoint data. The flow sent an adaptive card with a link to the app to the specified Teams channel. This was very effective for pandemic response.

CHAPTER 16

Dynamically Setting Object Properties in Power Apps Based on a SharePoint List

This chapter focuses on some techniques needed to build a "wizard" type of system where the user selects a topic and then is presented with a set of steps to perform the task or submit a request. To make this work effectively, we want to store the Actions and associated steps externally (SharePoint in this case). This keeps us from having to edit and republish our application whenever we add or delete Actions. For this to work, though, we need to be able to dynamically set button text and load each step as we go along. More specifically, we have an indefinite number of Actions that in turn have some number of steps, each with information and possibly attachments. Getting this all working gives us the building blocks that we would need to create the rest of the system.

SharePoint Lists

As is our standard practice by this point, we start with our data source(s) in SharePoint. Figure 16-1 shows the *Actions* list.

© Jeffrey M. Rhodes 2022

J. M. Rhodes, *Creating Business Applications with Microsoft 365*,
https://doi.org/10.1007/978-1-4842-8823-8_16

Actions ☆		
Title ∨	Description ∨	Order ∨
Writing	Use this for performance nd ciappraisals as well as awards.	1
Budget	Submit budget questions or information	2
Pay	Submit Pay Forms	3
Training	Submit training requests or documentation.	4

Figure 16-1. *Actions SharePoint List*

Since we will be filtering on the *Title* later, we tell SharePoint that it must be unique. We will use this as the text of our button and the *Description* as the Tooltip. The *Order* allows us to position the buttons as desired.

Once the user selects the action, we want her to be able to go through its associated steps, which can include attachments as mentioned. Figure 16-2 shows that we add *Action* as a lookup column and bring along its *Description* and *ID*. We will focus on the Budget action in later screens.

Steps ☆

Title ⌄	Action ⌄	Action:Descript... ⌄	Action:ID ⌄	Details ⌄	StepNum ⌄
Create Budget Request	Budget	Submit budget questions	2	Ensure that these items are covered: • Supervisor Approval	1
Submit Request	Budget	Submit budget questions	2	Attachment completed requisition to this form and submit	2
Save Pay Statement	Pay	Submit Pay Forms	3	Some **formatted** info here.	1
Contact Financial Institution	Pay	Submit Pay Forms	3		2

Figure 16-2. *Steps SharePoint List*

We will display the *Title* as well as the *Details*, which we configure as rich text so we can have formatting and images. The *StepNum* column gives us the order of the steps and allows us to insert and reorder down the line as desired. We are now ready to move to Power Apps.

Power Apps: Actions Screen

As with previous examples, we create a blank Canvas app and connect it to our *Actions* (Figure 16-1) and *Steps* (Figure 16-2) lists. Figure 16-3 shows the basic design from there. We have added *Button1* through *Button6*. To make it easier to test, we will click on the button and have it display some text to ensure we have the right button. Once we select the right button, we click the *Begin* button to launch the *StepsScreen* to see our steps.[1]

---

[1] For our real application, we would navigate to the *StepsScreen* when clicking any of the buttons.

Figure 16-3. *Power Apps Design with Buttons 1–6*

Our first challenge is how to set the *Text* and *Tooltip* properties. As we discussed in our opening chapter about programming environments, Power Apps is different in this regard from most other tools in that we can't look though our buttons and directly set these properties. Instead, the best approach I could come up with was to store the reference to each button within our data source. Listing 16-1 shows our code in response to the *OnStart* event.[2]

Listing 16-1. OnStart Code to Create our col Collection

```
ClearCollect(
    col,
    AddColumns(
        Actions,
        "ButtonRef",
        Switch(
            Order,
            1,
            Button1,
```

---

[2] *OnStart* is a good place to initialize code as it runs automatically when you begin the application. Note that you don't want to put non-essential code here though, as this code will run completely before the first screen of your app loads.

```
            2,
            Button2,
            3,
            Button3,
            4,
            Button4,
            5,
            Button5,
            6,
            Button6,
            Button1
        )
    )
)
```

As we have seen previously, *ClearCollect()* creates a new collection (*col* in this case). The second parameter is the record or table to put into *col*. We copy our entire *Actions* list into *col*, but we also want to add a new column named *ButtonRef*.[3] The *AddColumns()* method takes the source (*Actions*), column name (*ButtonRef*), and the values of the column. For the values, we use the *Switch()* statement to decide what we based on the *Order* column of the list. When the *Order* is 1, we want *Button1*, when it is 2, we want *Button2*, and so on.[4]

How does this new *col* collection help us? Figure 16-4 show how we can use it together with the *LookUp()* method to set the *Text* property of each button.

---

[3] We will end up with four columns. *Title*, *Description*, and *Order* come from the *Actions* list. We then add *ButtonRef* from the *AddColumns()* command.

[4] Very importantly, note that these are the object references and NOT the names of the buttons. So we need to create each of these buttons before writing this code.

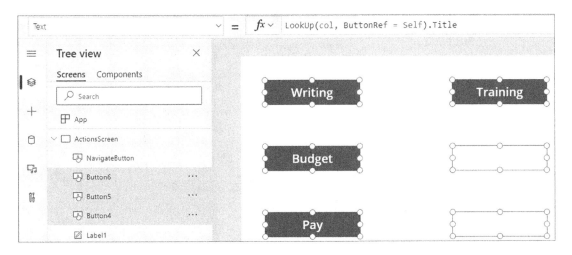

Figure 16-4. *Text Property of the Action Buttons*

```
LookUp(col, ButtonRef = Self).Title
```

To understand this code, we note that the *Self* keyword is the reference to the object (e.g., *Button1* for the first button, *Button2* for the next, etc.). Since we added the reference to each row, we can search for the matching row and then read the *Title* value. We use similar logic for the *Tooltip* property:

```
LookUp(col, ButtonRef = Self).Description
```

Since we have extra buttons (5 and 6 in our example), we can use the fact that the lookup comes back blank to set the *Visible* property:

```
!IsBlank(LookUp(col, ButtonRef = Self))
```

Our next task is to handle on the *OnSelect* event for each button. As discussed earlier, we show the action in a label for debugging purposes and then click the *Begin* button to actually display the steps. This is shown in Figure 16-5.

Figure 16-5. *Clicking on an Action Button*

When the user clicks a button (*Button3* with a *Text* of "Pay" in our example), we set the *selectedAction* variable to *Self.Text*[5]:

```
Set(selectedAction, Self.Text)
```

Our label then has this expression for the Text property:

```
"You clicked on " & selectedAction
```

This will help us ensure we have clicked the right one. Both it and the *NavigateButton* (Begin) have this for the *Visible* property so that they do not show until a button has been clicked:

```
!IsBlank(selectedAction)
```

Our last task on this screen is to control what happens when we click the *NavigateButton*. This is shown in Listing 16-2.

---

[5] We could have used the *LookUp* method to read in the *ID*, but in our case, we know the *Title* is unique.

Listing 16-2. OnSelect Code for the NavigateButton

```
Set(
    selectedActionItem,
    LookUp(
        Actions,
        Title = selectedAction
    )
);
Navigate(StepsScreen)
```

We create a new variable, *selectedActionItem*, which is the entire row of our *Actions* list that corresponds to the selected button. We look it up via the *Title* column matching our *selectedAction* variable. Once this is set, we navigate to the *StepsScreen*. Note that we could put this code in each of our buttons instead for a cleaner experience (e.g., to avoid the *Begin* button).

Power Apps: Steps Screen

Before the Steps screen displays, we need to perform the logic in Listing 16-3. We do that by handling the screen's *OnVisible* event.

Listing 16-3. OnVisible Code for the StepsScreen

```
Set(
    currentStepNum,
    1
);
ClearCollect(
    colSteps,
    Filter(
        Steps,
        'Action:ID'.Id = selectedActionItem.ID
    )
)
```

We initialize a *currentStepNum* variable to be 1 since we will always begin on the first step. We then create a new collection, *colSteps*, that will be just the items in our *Steps* list that match our currently selected action.[6] We will then be able to use *colSteps* for our other controls.

Figure 16-6 shows what displays after we click on the *Budget* button (*Button2*). You might want to refer to the Steps list in Figure 16-2.

Budget: **Create Budget Request**

Ensure that these items are covered:

- Supervisor Approval
- Budget Manager Approval
- Sufficient Funds
- Credit Card

Jeff_Ch01_Programming in the Power Platform.docx

Test 1.txt

<<   >>

Figure 16-6. *Step 1 of 2*

Starting at the top, we have an *Action* label, a *StepTitle* label and a *Home* icon for returning to the *ActionsScreen*. Most of the middle of the screen is our *StepDetails HTML text* control. At the bottom left, we have an *AttachmentsGallery* to display any attachments that have been added in SharePoint. Finally, we have *PrevBtn* and *NextBtn* controls to go backward and forward.

Our *Action* label has this *Text* property:

```
selectedAction & ":"
```

---

[6] Since we are filtering on a non-primary lookup column, we are subject to delegation limits. As long as we increase the limit to 2000 and don't exceed that number of steps, we are OK. If we need more, we can make ID primary or use the technique for avoiding delegation issues from an earlier chapter.

We just use our previously defined *selectedAction* variable (*Budget* in Figure 16-6).

Getting our hands on the information for each step is trickier. Let's say that we had ten steps. Our *currentStepNum* variable will have the current step. But Power Apps collections cannot go to an arbitrary value (2, 3, 4, etc.). However, we can use the *FirstN()* method to limit the number of rows we read. So if we are on step 4, we read four rows. We then use the *Last()* method to read the last one we have (e.g., the fourth row). Using this logic, here is the *Text* for the *StepTitle* label:

```
Last(FirstN(colSteps, currentStepNum)).Title
```

As we go across left to right, here is the *OnSelect* for the *Home* icon:

```
Navigate(ActionsScreen)
```

The *HtmlText* for our *StepDetails* is very similar to what we used for the *StepTitle*:

```
Last(FirstN(colSteps, currentStepNum)).Details
```

We had to do a bit more work to display our attachments. Since there are potentially multiple attachments for each step, we need to use a gallery control. However, our *colSteps* collection does not bring over the attachments. So we need to go back to the *Steps* list for the Items property in our *AttachmentsGallery*:

```
LookUp(Steps, ID = Last(FirstN(colSteps, currentStepNum)).ID).Attachments
```

We match up ideas to find the right item in our list and then find its attachments collection. We have a delegation warning once again as discussed in Footnote 6. Since we want the user to see the file name AND be able to open it, we need to add an *HTML text* control and then set its *HtmlText* property to be:

```
If(
    IsBlank(ThisItem.DisplayName),
    "",
    "<a href='" & ThisItem.AbsoluteUri & "'>" & ThisItem.DisplayName
& "</a>"
)
```

If there is no attachment (*DisplayName* is blank), we don't display anything. Otherwise, we use our handy anchor HTML tag and set its *href* property to the *AbsoluteUri* property and show its *DisplayName*.

Moving to our navigation button, we want to disable the *PrevBtn* if we are on the first step. We do that by using this expression for the *DisplayMode* property:

```
If(
    currentStepNum > 1,
    DisplayMode.Edit,
    DisplayMode.Disabled
)
```

It will be enabled (*Edit*) if we are on a higher step and disabled if on step 1. Notice how this button is disabled back in Figure 16-6. Here is the code for *OnSelect*:

```
If(
    currentStepNum > 1,
    Set(
        currentStepNum,
        (currentStepNum - 1)
    )
)
```

Just to be on the safe side, we check that we are on a step higher than 1. If so, we subtract 1 from the *currentStepNum* variable. As we see from the preceding code, this will immediately cause the *StepTitle*, *StepDetails*, and *AttachmentsGallery* to load the previous step's values.

The *NextBtn* is always enabled, so we don't have to edit its *DisplayMode*. However, we do change its Text to "Submit" if we are on the last step:

```
If(
    currentStepNum < CountRows(colSteps),
    ">>",
    "Submit"
)
```

To figure out if we are on the last step, we use the *CountRows()* method on our *colSteps* collection. This is shown in Figure 16-7. Notice how the *NextBtn* has a text of "Submit" and the *PrevBtn* is enabled.

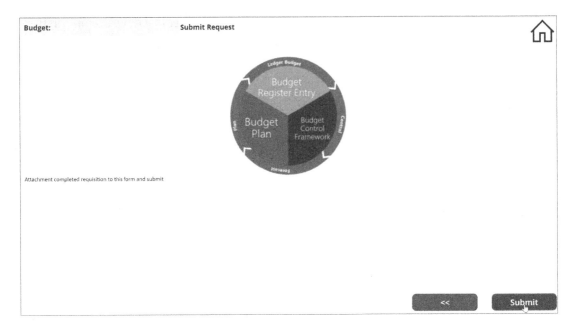

Figure 16-7. *Step 2 of 2*

The *NextBtn OnSelect* code is similar to that of the *PrevBtn*:

```
If(
    currentStepNum < CountRows(colSteps),
    Set(
        currentStepNum,
        (currentStepNum + 1)
    ),
    Notify(
        "Submitting Info Now",
        NotificationType.Information
    )
)
```

If the *currentStepNum* is less than the number of steps, then it adds 1 to *currentStepNum*. Otherwise, it calls the *Notify()* method as a placeholder for more logic such as emailing the information or presenting a screen for filling more data.

Summary

This chapter explored key techniques like dynamically setting button text and keeping track of the current step needed to create a "wizard" with Power Apps. We learned how to make any attachments available via a link in an *HTML text* control and how to control our "next" and "previous" buttons to make the user's experience seamless. We will continue to explore key technologies for this type of system in the next chapter, when we learn how to copy upload user attachments to a SharePoint document library and email links to them.

CHAPTER 17

Uploading Files from Power Apps to SharePoint and Emailing Links using Power Automate

This example follows from our expert system discussed in the last chapter. In the real version of that system, files uploaded to the application could be either saved to a SharePoint list as part of the help ticketing system OR emailed to an individual or group email box. With this latter case, we have a privacy issue with attaching the files directly to the email. These could be forwarded to a third party, the original recipient could change jobs and lose access, etc. Instead, we examine how to combine Power Apps and Power Automate to save the files to a SharePoint document library and email the secured link to the user instead of attaching the file(s).

Techniques for Uploading Files from Power Apps

The first challenge in uploading files from Power Apps is getting our hands on the appropriate control. Since you can't currently add an attachments control directly, you need to create a form and then link it to a SharePoint list or document library, as shown in Figure 17-1.

© Jeffrey M. Rhodes 2022
J. M. Rhodes, *Creating Business Applications with Microsoft 365*,
https://doi.org/10.1007/978-1-4842-8823-8_17

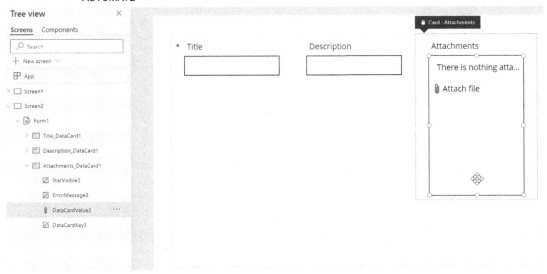

Figure 17-1. *Copying An Attachment Control from a Power Apps Form*

We copy the control and paste it onto our screen. We then fix the various errors since there is no longer a *Parent* control. For example, we change the *BorderColor* property from:

```
If(IsBlank(Parent.Error), Parent.BorderColor, Color.Red)
```

To

```
Color.Black
```

Our next challenge is to figure out the format that Power Automate will want for the files. Thanks for developers like Shane Young[1] and Reza Dorrani,[2] we have something to work with. Their insight is that we need to get to the Base64 representation of the file and doing that requires either an *Image* control directly or one embedded in a gallery. Figure 17-2 shows the technique we will build on.

---

[1] See www.youtube.com/watch?v=3QaiM8SeWfM.

[2] See www.youtube.com/watch?v=UYK7yruBHDM.

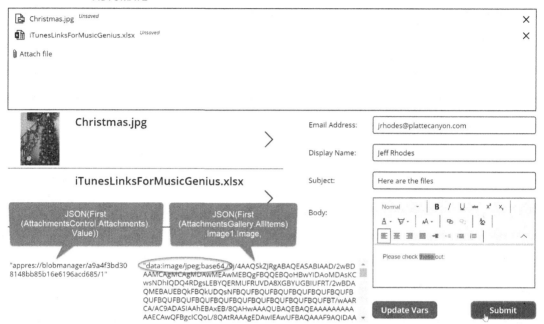

Figure 17-2. *Sample application showing the technique of reading binary data from the image*

We added *AttachmentsControl* using the technique mentioned previously. We update the *colAttachments* collection in response to both the *OnAddFile* and *OnRemoveFile* events with this code:

```
ClearCollect(colAttachments, AttachmentsControl.Attachments)
```

The *AttachmentsGallery* then has *colAttachments* as its *Items* property. Its image has *ThisItem.Value* as its *Image* property. We then display *ThisItem.Name* in the *Text* of the *Title* label.

Clicking the *Update Vars* button populates the two fields shown at the bottom of the screen. Listing 17-1 shows the *OnSelect* code for the *Update Vars* button.

Listing 17-1. OnSelect code for Update Vars button

```
Set(
    jsonValueAttachment,
    JSON(First(AttachmentsControl.Attachments).Value)
);
Set(
```

```
    jsonImage,
    JSON(
        First(AttachmentsGallery.AllItems).Image1.Image,
        JSONFormat.IncludeBinaryData
    )
)
```

The label on the left displays the *jsonValueAttachment* variable, which reads the first attachment in the *Attachments* control and is not useful. The one on the right displays the *jsonImage* variable, which converts the image control within the gallery to JavaScript Object Notation (JSON). Note that *jsonImage* contains the data type (*image/jpeg*) AND the Base64 information. That's what we want.

The rest of the application is for us to test our email functionality. So we have *Email Address*, *Display Name*, *Subject*, and *Body* (HTML format). We will pass all of these onto Power Automate. We can write the first part of our Submit button code (Listing 17-2) before we move over to Power Automate.

Listing 17-2. The first part of the OnSelect code for the Submit button

```
Clear(colAttachmentsFromGallery);
ForAll(
    AttachmentsGallery.AllItems,
    Collect(
        colAttachmentsFromGallery,
        {
            Title: Title1.Text,
            dataStream: Image1.Image
        }
    )
);
// call Power Automate
```

We want to create a *colAttachmentsFromGallery* collection but want to clear it first to start fresh. We once again use *ForAll()* to loop, in this case, through all the items of our *AttachmentsGallery*.[3] The second parameter is the formula we want to run on the first parameter. We want to *Collect()* our *colAttachmentsFromGallery* (which will add onto it for each loop). This collection has two elements: *Title* and *dataStream*. Remember this as we will need to match this with our JSON format when we get to Power Automate. Figure 17-3 shows how it looks if we view this collection within Power Apps. Notice that the *dataStream* displays the image for Christmas.jpg since it can display its Base64 encoding but not for the Excel file. But we will still be fine for both once we get to Power Automate.

Figure 17-3. colAttachmentsFromGallery collection within Power Apps

Saving and Emailing the Files from Power Automate

Most of our heavy lifting is done in Power Automate. As with past example, we create an automated flow. In this case we trigger it using the V2 implementation, as shown in Figure 17-4.

---

[3] Note that we use the gallery and NOT our *AttachmentsControl* since only the gallery has an embedded image control.

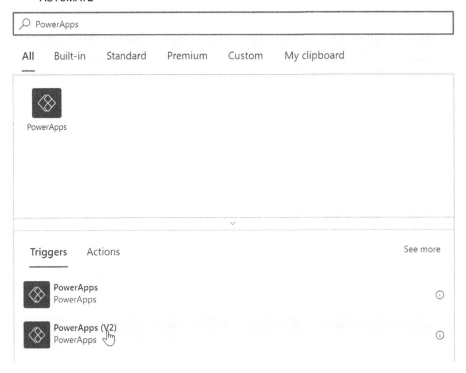

Figure 17-4. *Power Apps Trigger in Power Automate*

The V2 implementation allows us to name our parameters, as shown in Figure 17-5: *fileInfo, emailAddress, displayName, subject,* and *body.*

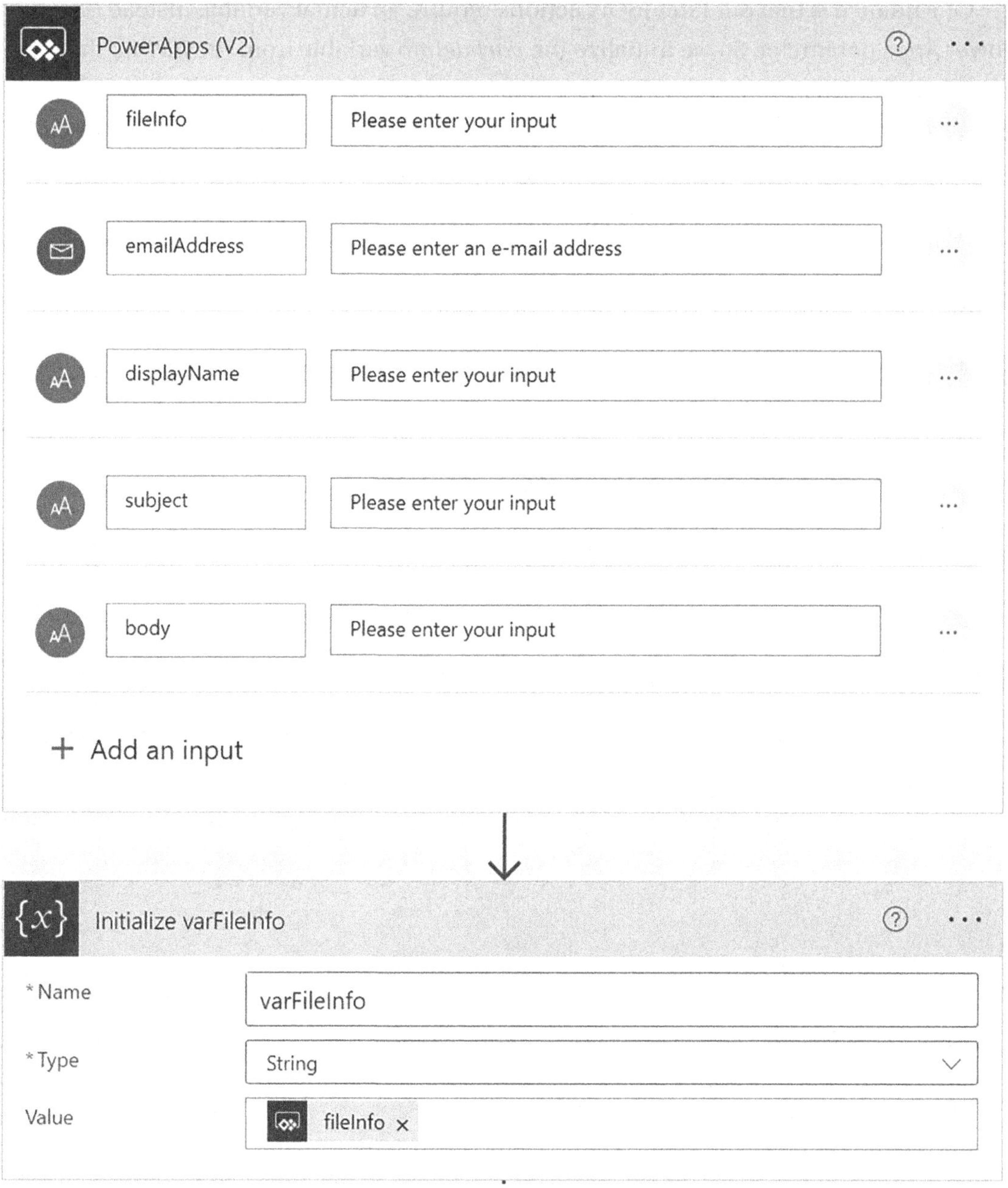

PowerApps (V2)   ⑦   ...

| AA | fileInfo | Please enter your input | ... |

| ✉ | emailAddress | Please enter an e-mail address | ... |

| AA | displayName | Please enter your input | ... |

| AA | subject | Please enter your input | ... |

| AA | body | Please enter your input | ... |

+ Add an input

{x}   Initialize varFileInfo   ⑦   ...

* Name	varFileInfo
* Type	String ∨
Value	⟨◇⟩ fileInfo ×

Figure 17-5.   *Power Apps Parameters and Initializing varFileInfo variable*

One nuance is that our later JSON actions require an actual variable instead of a
Power Apps parameter. So we initialize the *varFileInfo* variable from the *fileInfo* that
we pass in (which is in turn the *Title* and *dataStream* info from Listing 17-2). We also
initialize a *linksList* variable that we will use later to embed the file links inside our email.

Our next task is to convert our *varFileInfo* variable into JSON (it actually already is
but now Power Automate *knows* that it is), as shown in Figure 17-6.

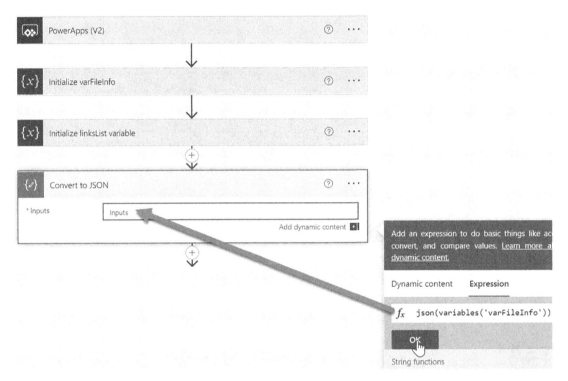

Figure 17-6. *Converting the varFileInfo Variable to JSON*

Notice that we need to switch from *Dynamic content* to *Expression* and then use its
json() function, passing in our *varFileInfo* variable.

```
json(variables('varFileInfo'))
```

Now that we have JSON, we need to parse it. Our first task is to come up with the
schema so Power Automate knows how to interpret it. There are samples online, but my
former colleague, Anthony Apodaca, matched up the schema in Listing 17-3 to what we
will be passing in from Power Apps.

Listing 17-3. JSON schema for our uploaded files

```
{
    "type": "array",
    "items": {
        "type": "object",
        "properties": {
            "Title": {
                "type": "string"
            },
            "dataStream": {
                "type": "string"
            }
        },
        "required": [
            "Title",
            "dataStream"
        ]
    }
}
```

Notice how the *Title* and *dataStream* match up with Listing 17-2. Figure 17-7 shows the results in Power Automate.

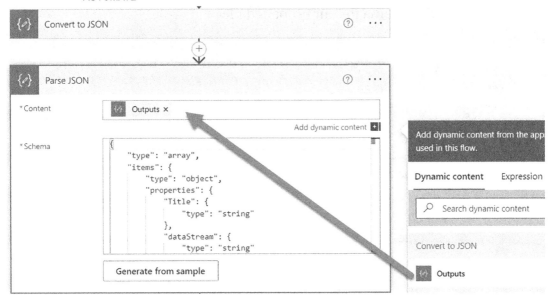

Figure 17-7. Parsing the JSON Output

Notice that the *Content* is the *Outputs* of our previous *Convert to JSON* step.

We add a *Scope* control to keep us organized (and it helps for error management in more complex flow), as shown in Figure 17-8.

240

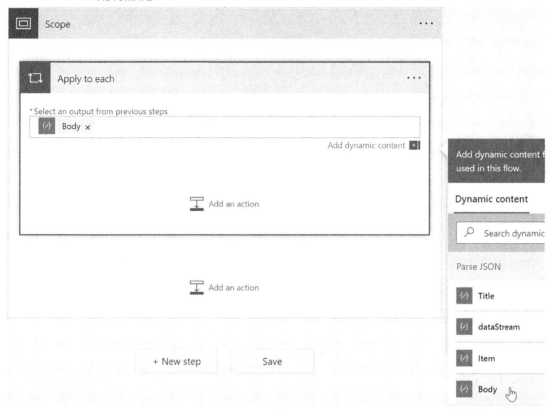

Figure 17-8. *Looping through the Body of the JSON*

Note that the *Apply to each* operates on the *Body*. To understand this better, look at a
section of the output from the *Parse JSON* step (Figure 17-7):

{"body":[{"Title":"Christmas.jpg","dataStream":"data:image/
jpeg;base64,/9j/4AAQSkZJRgABAQEASABIAAD/2wBDAAMCAgMCAgMDAwMEAwMEBQgFBQQ...

So each file (the first being Christmas.jpg) is contained within *Body*. Each loop will
give us a new file. We now use the *Create file* action to write the file to SharePoint. We
select our site and document library, as shown in Figure 17-9.

241

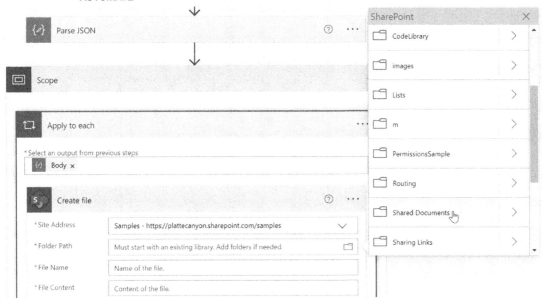

Figure 17-9. *Selecting the Folder Path to be Shared Documents*

We grab the *Title* from our JSON, but then need some manipulation (Figure 17-10) to
get the *File Contents*.

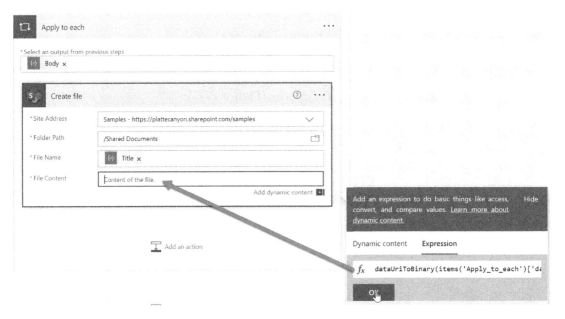

Figure 17-10. *Setting the File Contents*

This is where all our work on Base64 and passing that to Power Automate pays off. We go back to Expression and use this function:

```
dataUriToBinary(items('Apply_to_each')['dataStream'])
```

The *dataUriToBinary()* method takes the *dataStream* as a parameter, which is in turn the Base64 representation of the file we passed to Power Automate. Figure 17-11 show the files successfully written to the SharePoint document library.

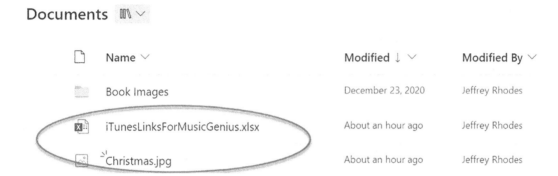

Figure 17-11. *Files Successfully Written to the SharePoint Document Library*

Now that the file exists in SharePoint, we can now *Create sharing link for a file or folder,* as shown in Figure 17-12.

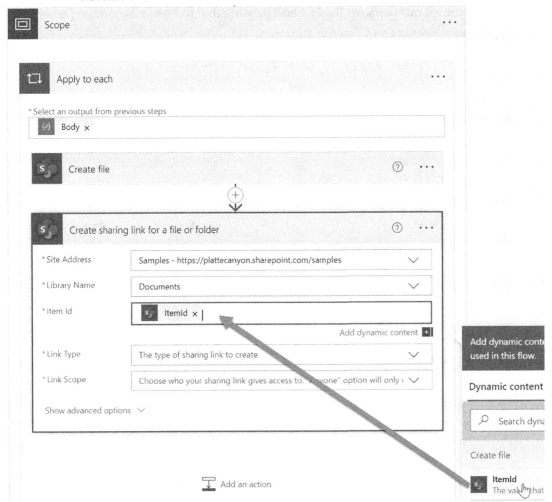

Figure 17-12. *Creating a link to the Uploaded File*

We select the *ItemId* output of our *Create file* action. We set the Link Type to *View and edit* (or just *View*) and our *Link Scope* to be *People in your organization.*[4]

We now have the link but need a way to put it in an email. That is the purpose of our *linksList* variable we initialized earlier. Figure 17-13 shows us the technique.

---

[4]With more work, we could likely find the account associated with the email address (if it's not a group box) and limit access to just that person.

Figure 17-13. *Building the List of Links and File Names*

We *Append to string variable* so that each file gets added onto the variable. For each
one, we use the anchor HTML tag to create a link. Notice how we grab *Sharing Link* from
the *Create sharing link* action and the *Name* from the *Create file* action. We put a *
*
tag at the end of each tag so that each link is on a new line. Listing 17-4 shows how it
looks if you view the source of the resulting email.

Listing 17-4. Example HTML of the links to the uploaded files

```
<a href="https://plattecanyon.sharepoint.com/:i:/g/samples/ERVOmy57ZvpHvklc
Rj9P9uoByHamMMLN2RigzCfwZgDa5A">Christmas.jpg</a><br>
<a href="https://plattecanyon.sharepoint.com/:x:/g/samples/ETVAFpO-jWxEiGES
WmRLmogBS1ADq9ZfZ-7dP9ZrVQIunw">iTunesLinksForMusicGenius.xlsx</a>
```

We get a little fancier by using the Compose action to add a style to our links, as
shown in Figure 17-14.

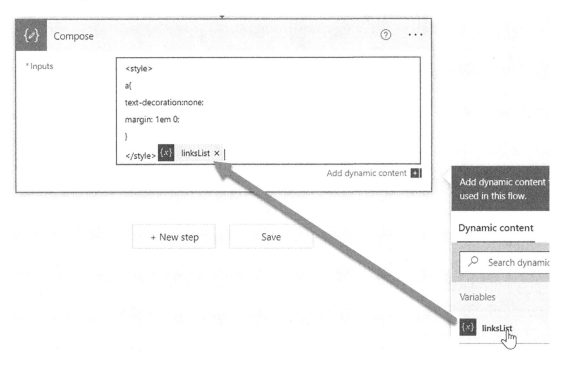

Figure 17-14. *Styling the Links*

This style changes the anchor tags so that they are not underlined and have a
slight margin:

```
<style>
a{
text-decoration:none;
margin: 1em 0;
}
</style>@{variables('linksList')}
```

Our last task is to send the email. As with other examples, we use the *Office 365 Outlook* connector and the Send an email (V2) action, as shown in Figure 17-15.

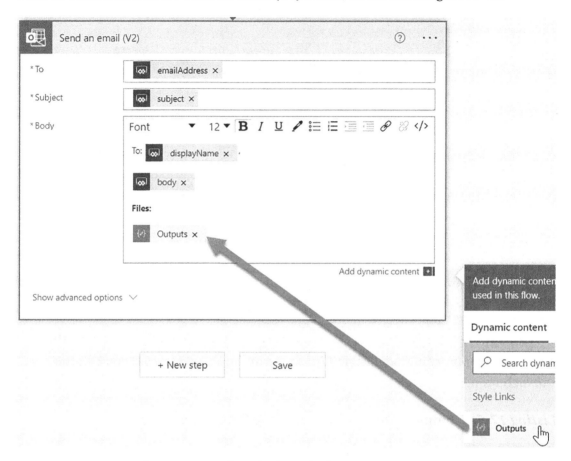

Figure 17-15. *Sending an Email with the Info from Power Apps and File Links*

We use our parameters from Power Apps as well as the *Outputs* from our *Compose* (Style Links) action.

The flow is ready and we can now return to Power Apps to finish up.

Completing Power Apps Application

To avoid overwriting our existing *OnSelect* code, we create a new button and link it to our Power Automate flow (Figure 17-16).

Figure 17-16. *Adding the Power Automate Flow to Power Apps*

We copy the *M365Book_ShareFilesFromPowerApps.Run* part of the code and then
delete our temporary button. Listing 17-5 shows our updated *OnSelect* code for the
Submit button.

Listing 17-5. Complete OnSelect code for the Submit button

```
Clear(colAttachmentsFromGallery);
ForAll(
    AttachmentsGallery.AllItems,
    Collect(
        colAttachmentsFromGallery,
        {
            Title: Title1.Text,
            dataStream: Image1.Image
        }
    )
);
```

```
// call Power Automate
M365Book_ShareFilesFromPowerApps.Run(
    JSON(
        colAttachmentsFromGallery,
        JSONFormat.IncludeBinaryData
    ),
    EmailAddressBox.Text,
    DisplayNameBox.Text,
    SubjectBox.Text,
    BodyBox.HtmlText
);
Notify(
    "Submitted Successfully",
    NotificationType.Success,
    3000
)
```

Starting with the call to our Power Automate flow, we pass in our *colAttachmentsFromGallery* collection in JSON format:

```
JSON(
        colAttachmentsFromGallery,
        JSONFormat.IncludeBinaryData

    )
```

This is the key and allows us to successfully write the files to our SharePoint document library. The rest is straightforward and a matter of passing in the email address, display name, subject, and body. Although we can get a return value back from Power Automate, that is not currently reliable. Instead, we assume success and use our *Notify()* method to tell the user.

Figure 17-17 shows us the resulting email.

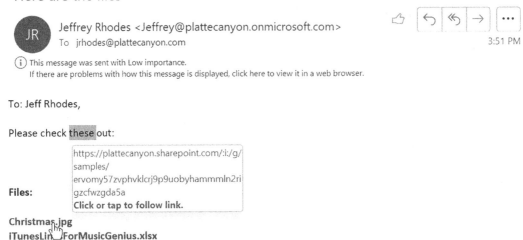

Here are the files

Figure 17-17. *Resulting Email with Links to Files Stored in SharePoint*

You might compare this to the form in Figure 17-2 and the HTML in Listing 17-4.
Whew – that was some effort.

Summary

In this chapter, we learned how to encode a file attached to a Power Apps application
and then pass that and other relevant information to Power Automate, which in turn
uploads the file to a SharePoint document library and emails the link to the recipient.
This is much more secure than attaching the file directly to an email, since the user
clicking the link must still be authenticated before gaining access to the file. Along
the way, we learned quite a bit about JSON, encoding, styles, and passing information
between Power Apps and Power Automate.

CHAPTER 18

Using Power BI to Find Inconsistent Data Between Excel Spreadsheets

This example solves a challenge that confronted my wife, Sue, in her job in human resources. She had to reconcile large spreadsheets taken from different systems that had conflicting data. Since these had hundreds of rows and dozens of columns, trying to eyeball the differences was time-consuming and prone to errors. Since she has to listen to me drone on about how great Power BI and the rest of the Power Platform is ☺, the least I could do is try to help.

A Microsoft Access Solution

The key to a solution is to have a common data element in both spreadsheets and then "join" on that element. In our example, here I use a *Position Number* column. Before tackling the problem in Power BI, I first wanted to try a Microsoft Access solution. Figure 18-1 shows the first step of importing both spreadsheets as tables.

© Jeffrey M. Rhodes 2022
J. M. Rhodes, *Creating Business Applications with Microsoft 365*,
https://doi.org/10.1007/978-1-4842-8823-8_18

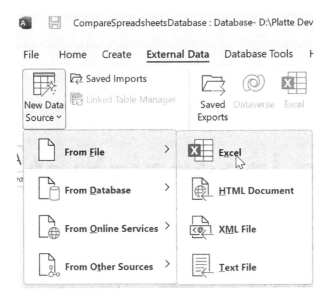

Figure 18-1. *Importing Excel spreadsheets into Access tables*

We use the Import Spreadsheet Wizard and choose to use the first row as headers, as shown in Figure 18-2.

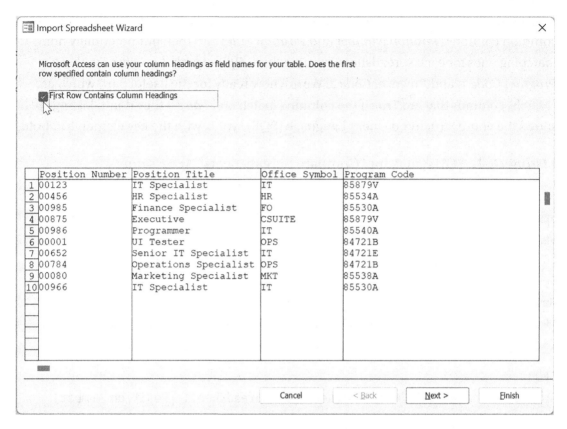

Figure 18-2. *Import Spreadsheet Wizard using first row as headers*

Once we get our tables imported, we create a query, as shown in Figure 18-3.

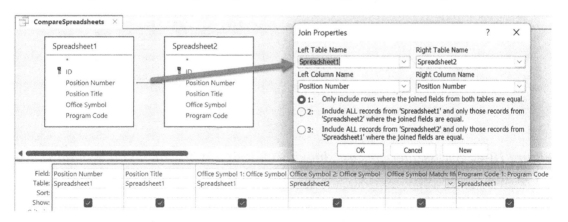

Figure 18-3. *Access Query Design View*

The key is to do a join[1] on our common column, *Position Number*. We then add our common columns (*Position Number* and *Position Title*) and then our potentially non-matching ones for each spreadsheet, naming them *Office Symbol 1*, *Office Symbol 2*, *Program Code 1*, and *Program Code 2*. We are now ready for the useful part, which are "Match" columns that are *True* if the columns match and *False* if they don't. Listing 18-1 shows the entire Structured Query Language (SQL) syntax with the key elements in **bold**.

Listing 18-1. SQL syntax for "Compare Spreadsheets" Access query

```
SELECT
Spreadsheet1.[Position Number], Spreadsheet1.[Position Title],
Spreadsheet1.[Office Symbol] AS [Office Symbol 1], Spreadsheet2.
[Office Symbol] AS [Office Symbol 2], IIf([Spreadsheet1].[Office
Symbol]=[Spreadsheet2].[Office Symbol],True,False) AS [Office Symbol
Match], Spreadsheet1.[Program Code] AS [Program Code 1], Spreadsheet2.
[Program Code] AS [Program Code 2], IIf([Spreadsheet1].[Program
Code]=[Spreadsheet2].[Program Code],True,False) AS [Program Code Match]

FROM
Spreadsheet1 INNER JOIN Spreadsheet2 ON Spreadsheet1.[Position Number] =
Spreadsheet2.[Position Number];
```

We use the *IIf* function to show *True* if the two *Office Symbol* or *Program Code* columns match and *False* otherwise. Figure 18-4 shows the results.

Position Number	Position Title	Office Symbol 1	Office Symbol 2	Office Symbol Match	Program Code 1	Program Code 2	Program Code Match
00123	IT Specialist	IT	HR	0	85879V	85879V	-1
00456	HR Specialist	HR	HR	-1	85534A	84721B	0
00985	Finance Specialist	FO	FO	-1	85530A	85530A	-1
00875	Executive	CSUITE	CSUITE	-1	85879V	85879V	-1
00986	Programmer	IT	IT	-1	85540A	85540A	-1
00001	UI Tester	OPS	OPS	-1	84721B	85534A	0
00652	Senior IT Specialist	IT	IT	-1	84721E	84721E	-1
00784	Operations Specialist	OPS	OPS	-1	84721B	84721B	-1
00080	Marketing Specialist	MKT	OPS	0	85538A	85538A	-1
00966	IT Specialist	IT	IT	-1	85530A	85530A	-1

Figure 18-4. *Access query results showing Office Symbol Match and Program Office Match columns*

---

[1] We do an *inner join* here where we "only include rows where the joined filed from both tables are equal." But we could choose one of the other *outer join* options if one spreadsheet is primary and we want to include all of its data and just the rows from the other spreadsheet where there is matching data.

Notice that *True* shows up as *-1* while *False* shows up as *0*. We would then export this query back out to Excel and then filter on these values to find our problem rows.

While this solution works, it is not very scalable in that the user needs to import new spreadsheets each month (or create a linked table, which is itself fairly complicated) and then redo the query. Worse, there is no good way to share this data with other team members without them having to be able to open and understand an Access database.

Configuring Our Data in Power BI

In Power BI, we link to both spreadsheets as data sources in the normal way and then *Transform data*. The only change we need to make in the original data is to *Change Type* for *Position Number* to *Text* so that we don't lose the leading 0's, as shown in Figure 18-5.

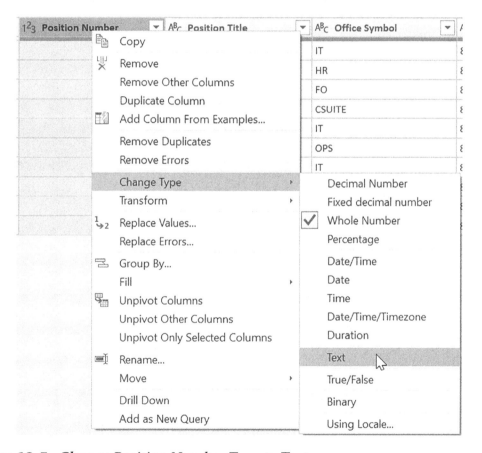

Figure 18-5.   *Change Position Number Type to Text*

We now have to figure out the best way to join our data. Going to the model screen as in a previous chapter will not work in this case as we want to do more than just show both tables in one visualization. We actually need our new "Match" columns in the same data source. For that, we need a new Merge Queries as New, as shown in Figure 18-6.

Figure 18-6. *Merge Queries as New*

This gives us the dialog shown in Figure 18-7.

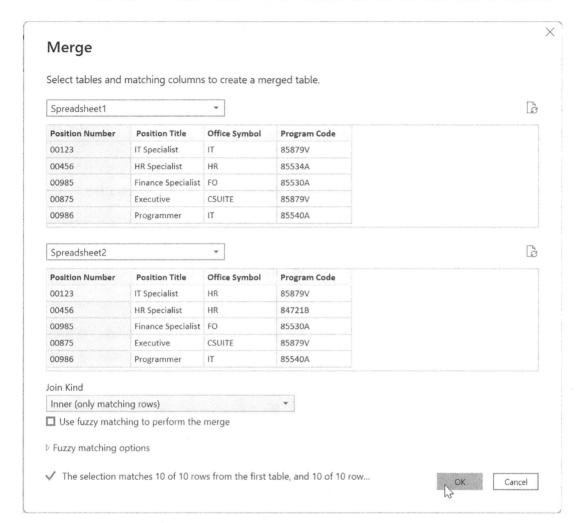

Figure 18-7. *Inner Join merge on Position Number column*

We choose our two data sources and select that the *Position Number* column is the one that matches in each. We perform an inner join as in our Access implementation. This gives us the result shown in Figure 18-8 after we have renamed *Office Symbol* to *Office Symbol 1* and *Program Code* to *Program Code 1*.

	ABC Position Number	▼ ABC Position Title	▼ ABC Office Symbol 1	▼ ABC Program Code 1	▼ Spreadsheet2	↔
1	00123	IT Specialist	IT	85879V	Table	
2	00456	HR Specialist	HR	85534A	Table	
3	00985	Finance Specialist	FO	85530A	Table	
4	00875	Executive	CSUITE	85879V	Table	
5	00986	Programmer	IT	85540A	Table	
6	00001	UI Tester	OPS	84721B	Table	
7	00652	Senior IT Specialist	IT	84721E	Table	
8	00784	Operations Specialist	OPS	84721B	Table	
9	00080	Marketing Specialist	MKT	85538A	Table	
10	00966	IT Specialist	IT	85530A	Table	

Queries [3]
- Spreadsheet1
- Spreadsheet2
- MergedData

fx = Table.RenameColumns(Source,{{"Office Symbol", "Office Symbol 1"}, {"Program Code", "Program Code 1"}})

Figure 18-8. *Merged Data After Renaming Spreadsheet 1 columns with Spreadsheet 2 data as a Table*

Notice how all of *Spreadsheet2* is shown as a *Table*. We expand that to add its Office Symbol and Program Code columns, as shown in Figure 18-9.

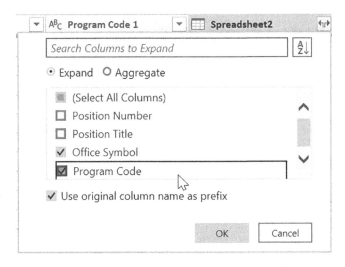

Figure 18-9. *Selecting desired Spreadsheet2 columns - Office Symbol and Program Code*

Since we check the box to "Use original column name as prefix," that gives us columns like *Spreadsheet2.Office Symbol*. We rename them and reorder to get to Figure 18-10.

	ABC Position Number	ABC Position Title	ABC Office Symbol 1	ABC Office Symbol 2	ABC Program Code 1	ABC Program Code 2
1	00123	IT Specialist	IT	HR	85879V	85879V
2	00456	HR Specialist	HR	HR	85534A	84721B
3	00985	Finance Specialist	FO	FO	85530A	85530A
4	00875	Executive	CSUITE	CSUITE	85879V	85879V
5	00986	Programmer	IT	IT	85540A	85540A
6	00001	UI Tester	OPS	OPS	84721B	85534A
7	00652	Senior IT Specialist	IT	IT	84721E	84721E
8	00784	Operations Specialist	OPS	OPS	84721B	84721B
9	00080	Marketing Specialist	MKT	OPS	85538A	85538A
10	00966	IT Specialist	IT	IT	85530A	85530A

Figure 18-10. *Merged Data with both spreadsheets displayed and columns renamed*

We are now ready to implement our "Match" columns. These are a good use of Conditional Columns. Rather than comparing the value as is the default, however, we want to compare *Office Symbol 1* to another column (*Office Symbol 2*), as shown in Figure 18-11.

Figure 18-11. *Match Column Values in Conditional Column*

If these match, we put in *True* and otherwise *False,* as shown in Figure 18-12.

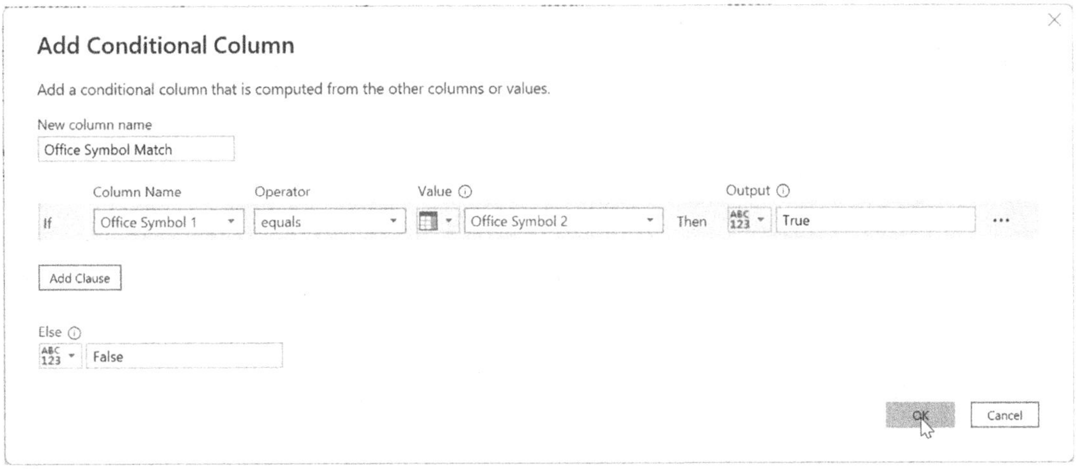

Figure 18-12.   *Office Symbol Match Conditional Column*

We do the same thing for a *Program Code Match* column.

Thinking forward to our desire to color-code our entries (e.g., show *True* in green and *False* in red), it turns out that we need a numeric conditional column as well. Figure 18-13 shows how we can set that up.

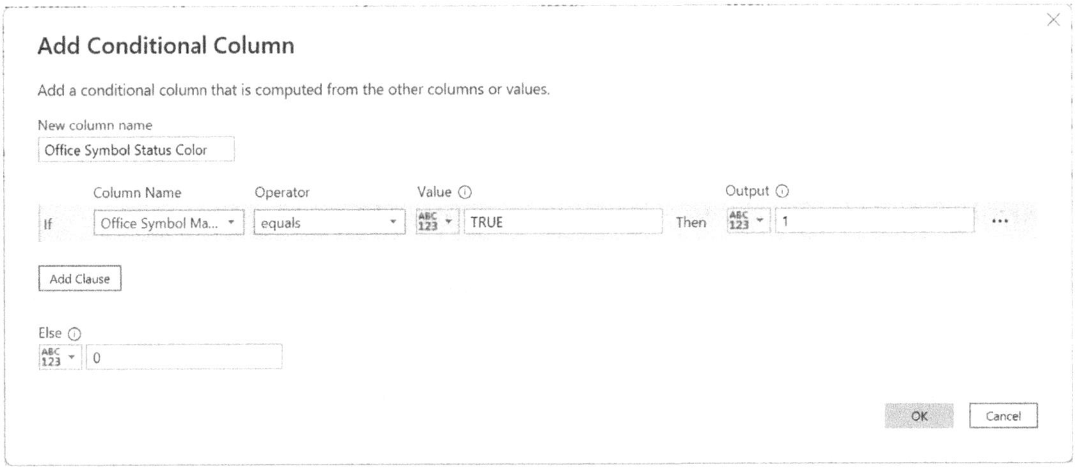

Figure 18-13.   *Conditional Column for Setting Color*

We won't display this column in our visualization, but rather just use it in our conditional formatting. We are now ready to *Close and Apply* and start on the report.

Visualizing Our Data in Power BI

We are now ready to display our data. We start with a Table control to show the values from our original spreadsheet. The users can then filter to show non-matches and then export that data if desired. We create slicers for *Office Symbol Match* (Figure 18-14) and *Program Code Match* as well as card to show the number of positions affected.

Figure 18-14. *Office Symbol Match Slicer*

Our last objective is to color code our "Match" columns so that *True* values show as green and *False* ones show as red. To do that, we select our column in the table and apply *Conditional formatting,* as shown in Figure 18-15.

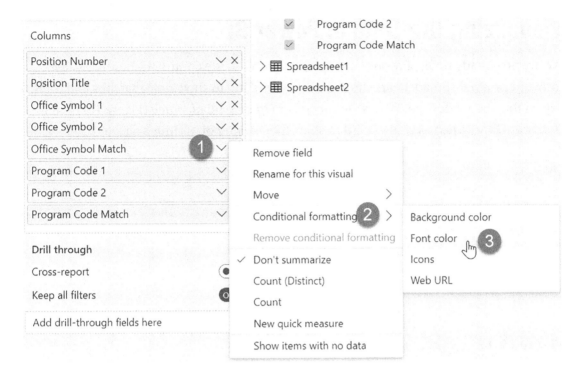

Figure 18-15. *Conditional formatting in Power BI Table visualization*

Power BI conditional formatting is not yet as flexible as Excel's and thus we can't apply formatting with non-numeric data. That's why we created the additional conditional column back in Figure 18-13. As we see in Figure 18-16, we change the *Format style* to *Rules*, leave the *Apply to* as *Values only*, and then choose our *What field should we base this on?* to be our *Office Symbol Status Color* column. We leave it as *Sum*, but *Average, Minimum,* or *Maximum* would all have worked the same.

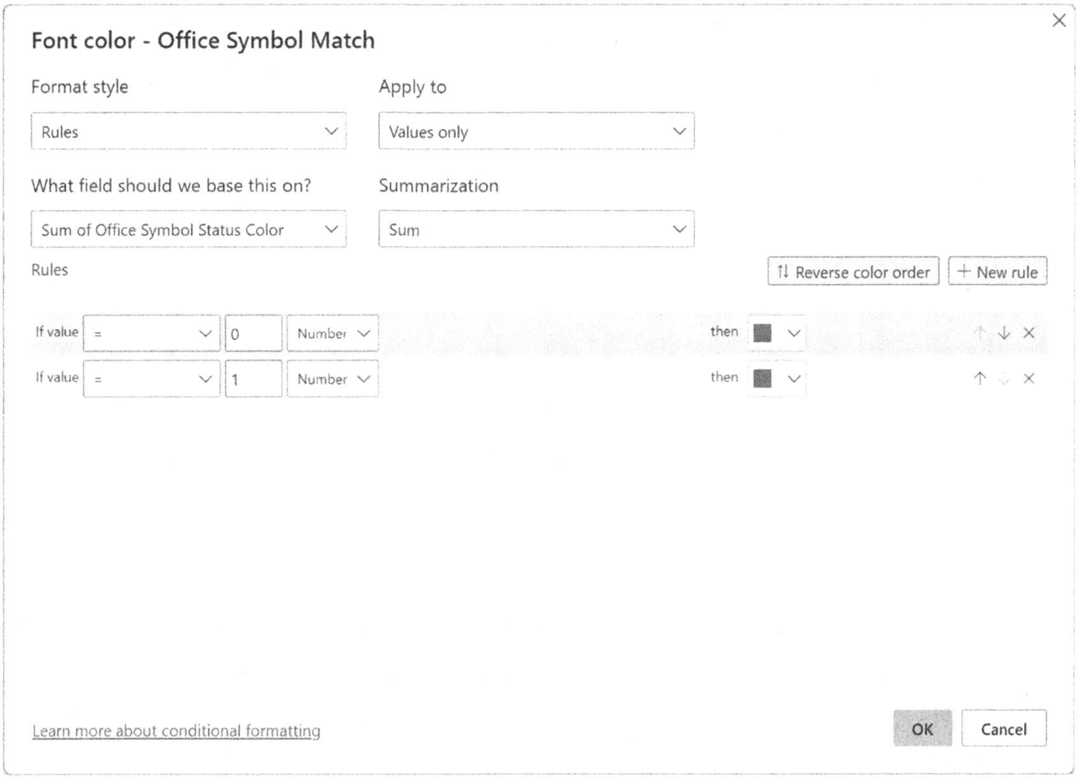

Figure 18-16. *Setting Conditional Access Font Color*

We edit the first rule to be = *0* as a *Number* and then choose red as the color. We add a *New rule* and use = *1* as a *Number*. We choose a variation of green (*#039703* hex value) for its color. Figure 18-17 shows the final result.

Office Symbol Match		Program Code Match ⌄						
☐ False		☐ False						
☐ True		☐ True					**10**		
						# of Positions		

Position Number	Position Title	Office Symbol 1	Office Symbol 2	Office Symbol Match	Program Code 1	Program Code 2	Program Code Match
00001	UI Tester	OPS	OPS	True	84721B	85534A	False
00080	Marketing Specialist	MKT	OPS	False	85538A	85538A	True
00123	IT Specialist	IT	HR	False	85879V	85879V	True
00456	HR Specialist	HR	HR	True	85534A	84721B	False
00652	Senior IT Specialist	IT	IT	True	84721E	84721E	True
00784	Operations Specialist	OPS	OPS	True	84721B	84721B	True
00875	Executive	CSUITE	CSUITE	True	85879V	85879V	True
00966	IT Specialist	IT	IT	True	85530A	85530A	True
00985	Finance Specialist	FO	FO	True	85530A	85530A	True
00986	Programmer	IT	IT	True	85540A	85540A	True

Figure 18-17. *Visualization with slicers and conditional color formatting*

While this is a comparable amount of work to the Access solution, the big advantage is that updated feeds could be uploaded to Teams or another location and processed via Power BI's scheduled refresh. The report can easily be shared with other staff. They just use the two slicers and, if needed, export the problem data. This is MUCH easier and less prone to error than the Access solution.

Summary

In this chapter, we took a common example of needing to determine if data from multiple systems was consistent. We first looked at a "legacy" technique of using Microsoft Access queries to do the job. We then examined how to create a reusable solution in Power BI via Merged Queries. We added slicers and conditional formatting to easily see unmatched data. Powerful indeed!

CHAPTER 19

Linking Power BI to Microsoft Forms Responses and Showing the Most Current Submission

This chapter stems from some real-world examples where we wanted to use Microsoft Forms but needed a mechanism for users to submit updated information, either because they changed their mind or had new data. We will examine how to address that in Power BI so we only see the most recent submission. We will also look at how to address multiple answers in our form and incorporate a map control.

How to Decide between Forms and Power Apps

When I help organizations design a Microsoft 365 solution to meet their data entry and storage requirements, here are the main things I look at:

1. Do users need to edit their data later? If so, that argues toward a Power Apps or SharePoint front end. If not, Forms becomes a strong candidate.

2. Is it appropriate for users to see ALL of the data? If so, the easiest thing is the built-in SharePoint form that goes with a list. Next

© Jeffrey M. Rhodes 2022
J. M. Rhodes, *Creating Business Applications with Microsoft 365*,
https://doi.org/10.1007/978-1-4842-8823-8_19

is the standard Power Apps template form that mirrors the
SharePoint list. If not, then either Forms (no editing) or Power
Apps (editing) would be optimal. The Help Ticketing system we
looked at earlier is a good example. Users only needed to enter a
few items to open the ticket. The rest of the data (category, notes,
assigned technician, etc.) was in the SharePoint list, but only
editable in the Technician's application. If there is only limited
information such as status and notes that needs to be edited (and
there are only a few people with editing rights), I will often just
stick with the standard SharePoint form, with the column order
edited to put the data to be changed at the top of the form.

3. As much as I love Power Apps, Forms is much easier. This is
    particularly true for non-technical users. So if Forms can meet the
    needs, I go with it.

A permutation of the preceding #1 is the situation where a user doesn't need to
edit their data but perhaps needs the opportunity to submit a new version. If we can
use Power BI to only show the most recent submission, we have a whole category of
applications that can be accomplished in Forms instead of Power Apps. Plus, we get a
good version history of a user's submissions.

Sample Microsoft Form

Figure 19-1 shows our sample form. We ask for users' zip code, what they think
of cicada's,[1] their favorite sport (including an *Other* choice), and what Office 365
applications they have used so far.

---

[1] You might guess that I created this form in 2021, which was a year of cicada emergence.

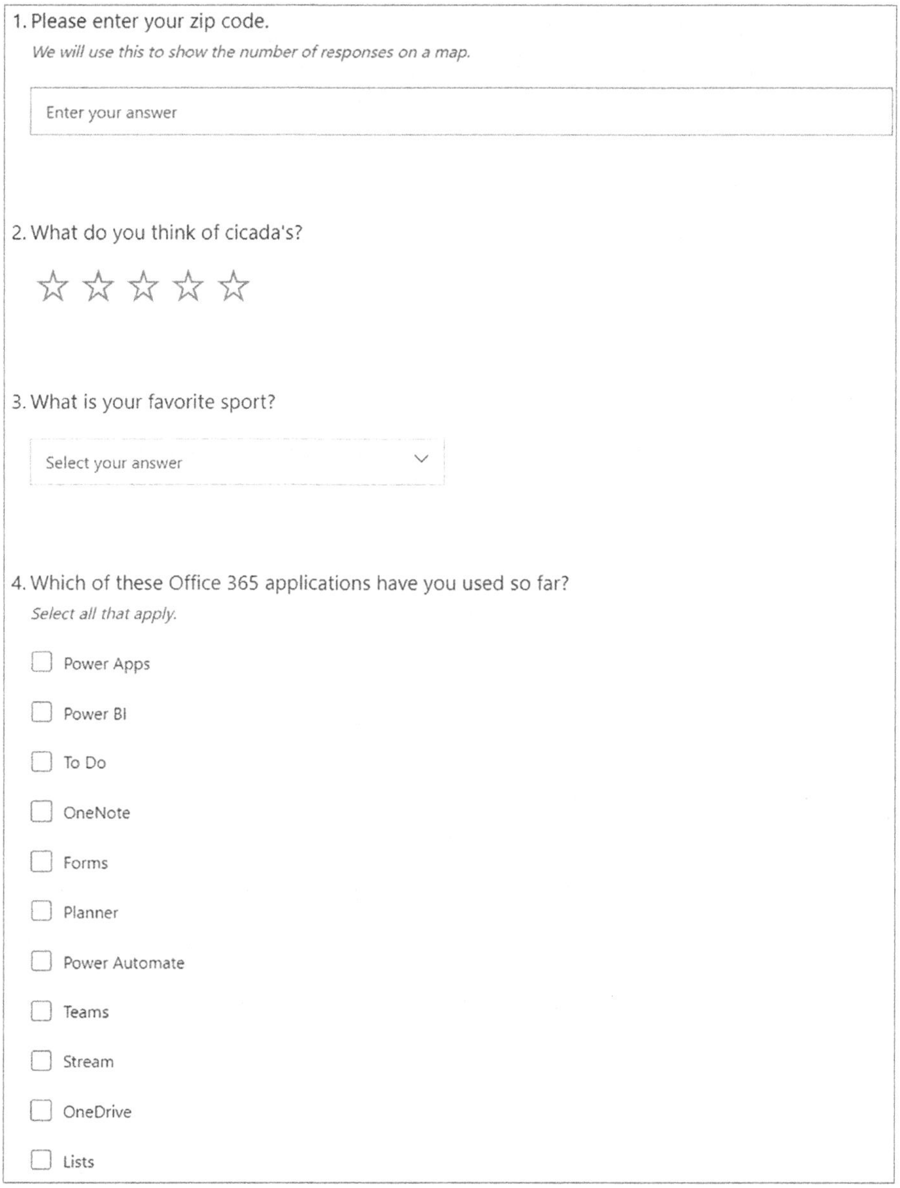

1. Please enter your zip code.

   We will use this to show the number of responses on a map.

   Enter your answer

2. What do you think of cicada's?

   ☆ ☆ ☆ ☆ ☆

3. What is your favorite sport?

   Select your answer ⌄

4. Which of these Office 365 applications have you used so far?

   Select all that apply.

   ☐ Power Apps

   ☐ Power BI

   ☐ To Do

   ☐ OneNote

   ☐ Forms

   ☐ Planner

   ☐ Power Automate

   ☐ Teams

   ☐ Stream

   ☐ OneDrive

   ☐ Lists

Figure 19-1. *Sample Form*

In real life, I made the form anonymous, but for our purposes, I put in musical users so that we can get the most recent response per user. The results spreadsheet is shown in Figure 19-2.

ID	Start time	Completion time	Email	Name	Please ent	What	What is your favorit	Which of these Office 365 applications have you used so far?
2	6/1/21 17:08:56	6/1/21 17:09:29	john@lennon.com	John Lennon	80920	2	Basketball	Forms;Planner;Teams;Power Apps;Stream;OneDrive;Power BI;Power Automate;OneNote;
3	6/1/21 17:10:23	6/1/21 17:10:37	paul@mccartney.com	Paul McCartney	86326	4	Soccer	Planner;Forms;Teams;Stream;
4	6/2/21 8:30:05	6/2/21 8:30:35	george@harrison.com	George Harrison	80501	2	Cycling	OneNote;Planner;Teams;OneDrive;Stream;
5	6/3/21 8:07:39	6/3/21 8:08:23	ringo@starr.com	Ringo Starr	20775	1	Track and Field	Teams;Forms;OneDrive;Power BI;OneNote;
6	6/3/21 13:10:26	6/3/21 13:10:57	shawn@mullins.com	Shawn Mullins	80487	1	Cycling	Lists;To Do;Forms;OneNote;Stream;Planner;Power BI;OneDrive;Teams;
7	6/3/21 13:10:15	6/3/21 13:10:59	peter@himmelman.co	Peter Himmelman	64089	2	Football	OneDrive;Teams;
8	6/3/21 13:10:44	6/3/21 13:11:02	sammy@hagar.com	Sammy Hagar	22033	1	Golf	Teams;OneDrive;
9	6/3/21 13:10:41	6/3/21 13:11:02	ed@roland.com	Ed Roland	20774	1	Swimming	Teams;
10	6/3/21 13:10:43	6/3/21 13:11:04	amy@ray.com	Amy Ray	08054	2	Baseball	Teams;OneDrive;OneNote;Stream;
11	6/3/21 13:10:36	6/3/21 13:11:04	emily@saliers.com	Emily Saliers	80203	5	Basketball	Teams;OneDrive;OneNote;Planner;Lists;
12	6/3/21 13:10:38	6/3/21 13:11:05	bear@rinehart.com	Bear Rinehart	20003	1	Soccer	OneNote;Teams;OneDrive;
13	6/3/21 13:10:42	6/3/21 13:11:20	jimmy@buffett.com	Jimmy Buffett	20017	3	Soccer	Teams;OneDrive;
14	6/3/21 13:11:06	6/3/21 13:11:33	stephen@stills.com	Stephen Stills	94901	5	Underwater Shuffleboa	OneNote;Teams;
15	6/3/21 13:11:24	6/3/21 13:11:49	zac@brown.com	Zac Brown	10075	1	Tennis	OneDrive;Teams;
16	6/3/21 13:10:33	6/3/21 13:12:09	john@lennon.com	John Lennon	20001	3	Formula 1	Lists;OneNote;Teams;OneDrive;Power BI;
17	6/3/21 13:11:36	6/3/21 13:12:32	paul@mccartney.com	Paul McCartney	90210	5	eSports like Software S	Power Automate;Teams;OneNote;Lists;Stream;Power Apps;Forms;Power BI;To Do;OneDrive;Planner;
18	6/3/21 13:12:07	6/3/21 13:12:42	george@harrison.com	George Harrison	80214	3	Running	OneNote;OneDrive;Teams;
19	6/3/21 13:23:29	6/3/21 13:24:26	ringo@starr.com	Ringo Starr	20743	2	Baseball	OneDrive;OneNote;
20	6/10/21 13:27:46	6/10/21 13:34:11	shawn@mullins.com	Shawn Mullins	22030	5	Running	Teams;OneNote;OneDrive;Forms;
21	6/11/21 7:31:39	6/11/21 7:32:09	peter@himmelman.co	Peter Himmelman	27974	1	Baseball	Power BI;OneDrive;Teams;
22	6/11/21 7:32:46	6/11/21 7:34:18	sammy@hagar.com	Sammy Hagar	22033	1	Golf	OneDrive;Teams;Forms;Planner;
23	6/11/21 7:34:35	6/11/21 7:35:05	ed@roland.com	Ed Roland	11746	1	Basketball	Lists;Teams;Forms;OneNote;OneDrive;
24	6/11/21 7:36:43	6/11/21 7:37:08	amy@ray.com	Amy Ray	80504	2	Cycling	OneNote;Planner;Lists;Teams;Stream;OneDrive;

Figure 19-2. Form Responses Spreadsheet

Notice how the *Which of these Office 365 applications have you used so far?* responses are formatted:

```
Forms;Planner;Teams;Power Apps;Stream;OneDrive;Power BI;Power
Automate;OneNote;
```

We will have to deal with this once we get to Power BI.

Getting the Path in OneDrive

I would normally use Power Automate to copy each response to a SharePoint list and then connect to it instead, but that's not necessary for this example and allows me to cover how to connect to a file in OneDrive[2] as well. Our first challenge is to get the path. Figure 19-3 shows how we get started by clicking the ... next to the file and then select *Details*.

---

[2] I normally prefer Teams/SharePoint instead of OneDrive so that important data is not lost when a user leaves the organization. OneDrive is OK for demonstrations or while under development but needs to be changed for production.

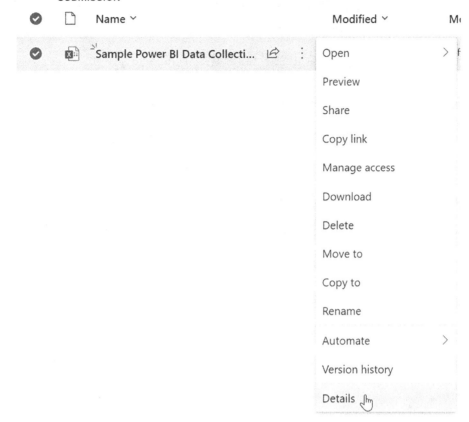

Figure 19-3. *Details in OneDrive*

We then go to *More details,* as shown in Figure 19-4.

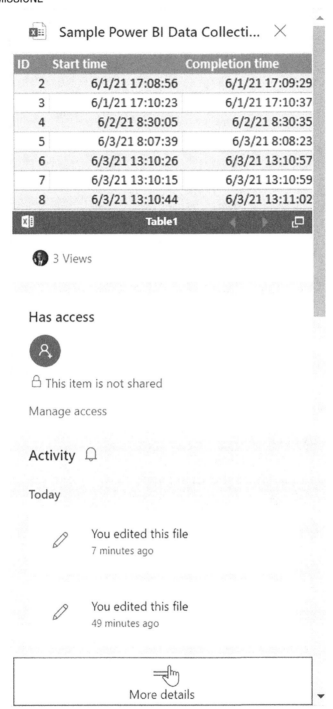

Figure 19-4. *More details in OneDrive*

We now can copy the path (Figure 19-5).

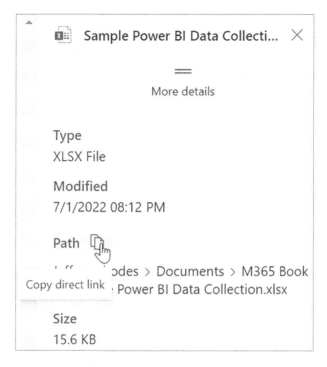

Figure 19-5. *Copying the path in OneDrive*

Here is how it looks in my case:

```
https://plattecanyon-my.sharepoint.com/personal/jeffrey_plattecanyon_
onmicrosoft_com/
Documents/M365%20Book/Sample%20Power%20BI%20Data%20Collection.xlsx
```

We are now ready for Power BI.

Configuring Our Data in Power BI

Also, you might reasonably expect that we use the Excel workbook data source, I've had better luck with the Web source, as shown in Figure 19-6.

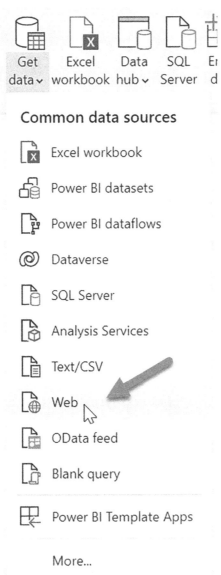

Figure 19-6. *Web data source in Power BI Desktop*

We then paste in the path we copied back in Figure 19-5. Figure 19-7 shows how
it looks.

Figure 19-7. *Pasting in the OneDrive path*

If we haven't logged into Microsoft 365 recently in Power BI Desktop, we need to switch to *Organizational account* and sign in, as shown in Figure 19-8.

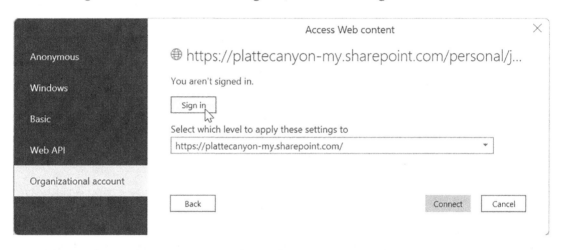

Figure 19-8. *Validating M365 credentials*

We take advantage of the fact that Microsoft Forms saves its response data as an Excel table and thus choose *Table1*, as shown in Figure 19-9.

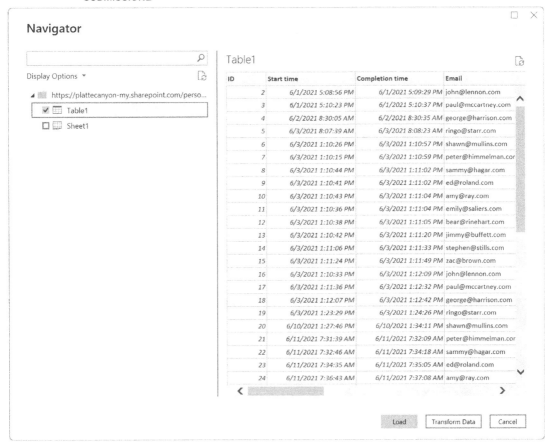

Figure 19-9. *Choosing the form responses table*

We immediate Transform Data. We change the *Please enter your zip code* column
to be *Text* instead of Whole Number since otherwise leading zeros are lost, as shown in
Figure 19-10.

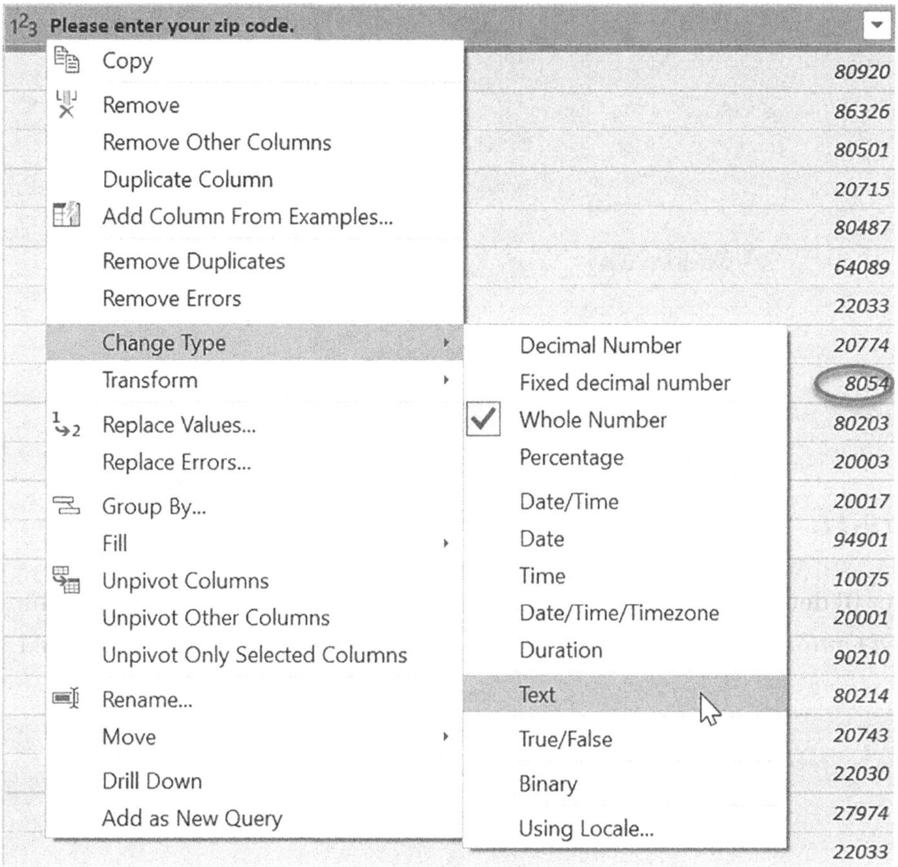

Figure 19-10. *Changing zip code data type to Text*

Our next challenge is with our *Which of these Office 365 applications have you used so far?* column. As we discussed before, this type of data is a challenge and needs to be split out so that we are not counting *combinations* of responses rather than the responses themselves. One interesting difference between using Power Automate to copy Forms results to SharePoint is that SharePoint puts the data in JSON format like this:

```
["Planner","Forms","Teams","Stream"]
```

Leaving the data in Excel makes it values delimited by a semicolon:

```
Planner;Forms;Teams;Stream;
```

To handle this, we *Split Column* and choose *By Delimiter* (Figure 19-11).

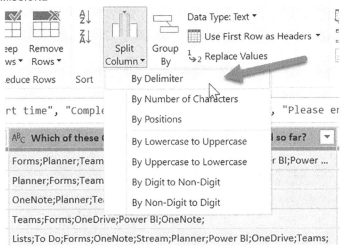

Figure 19-11. Splitting the column by a delimiter

Power BI detects our semicolon. We tell it to use each occurrence and go into
Advanced Options to split into rows[3] and not have a quote character (Figure 19-12).

---

[3] Note that this relies on having an index or ID column that is unique. We will do a *Count
(Distinct)* on this column so we get accurate data with the new rows.

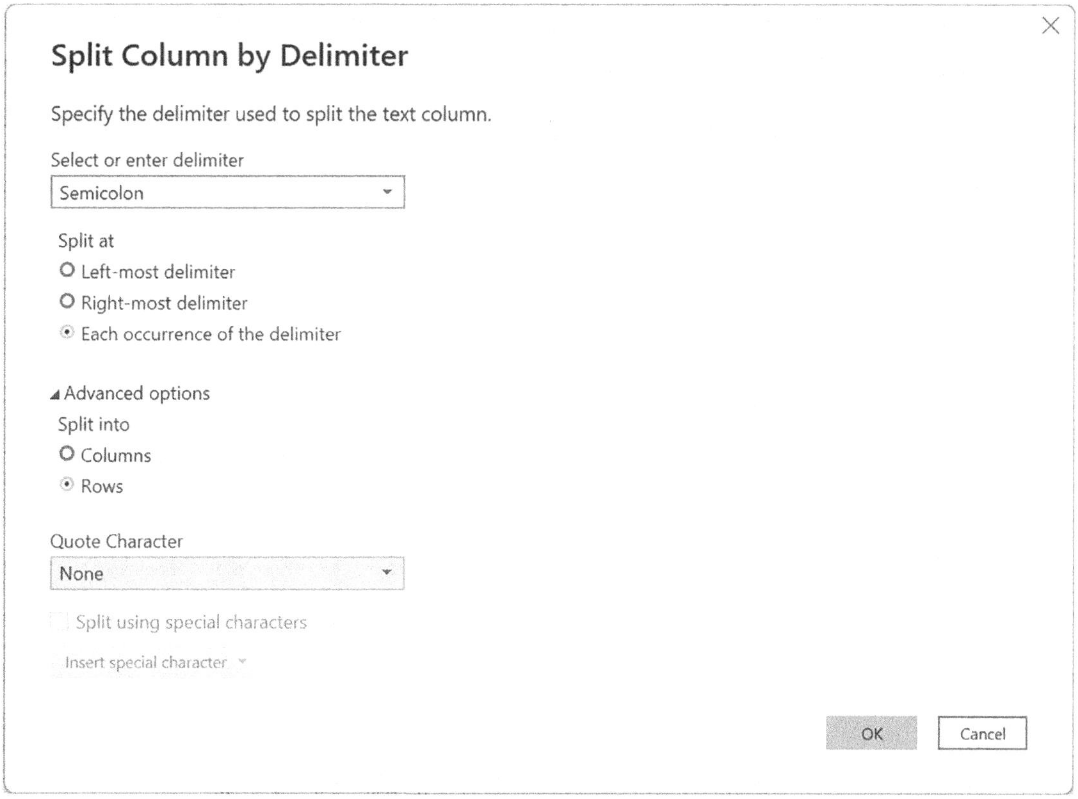

Figure 19-12. *Delimiter options to include splitting into Rows and no Quote Character*

We are almost there, but you may have noticed that there is a semicolon at the *end* of the data as well. That gives us a blank row for each response. Luckily, Power BI has a *Remove Empty* option. The blank rows and selecting *Remove Empty* are shown in Figure 19-13.

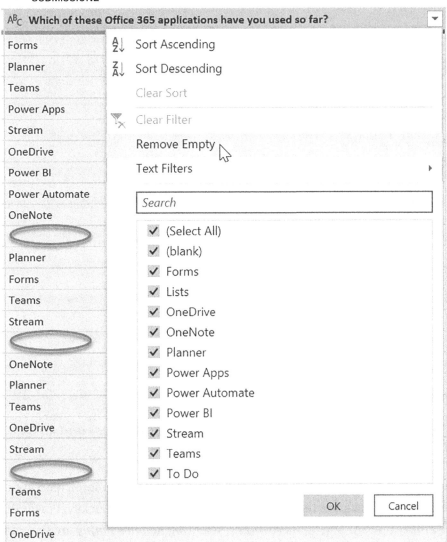

Figure 19-13. *Removing empty rows*

Our last transformation is to add a custom *Days Since Response* column
(Figure 19-14). This allows us to easily show "responses in the last 30 days" and similar
time frames. This is also a major advantage of using Power BI over the built-in response
summary in Forms (which visualizes all data).

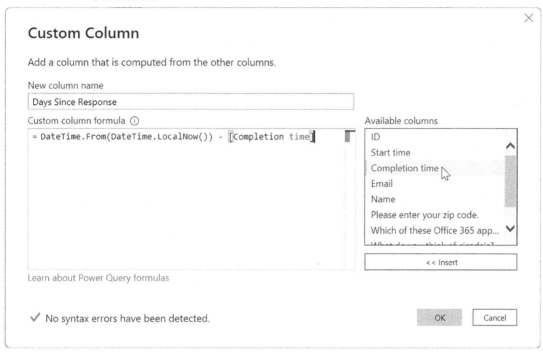

Figure 19-14. *Days Since Response custom column*

We change the data type to *Whole Number* and are now ready to tackle limiting the
data to just to the most recent submission for each user. For that, we go to *Transform* tab
and choose *Group By,* as shown in Figure 19-15.

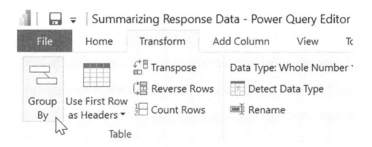

Figure 19-15. *Selecting Group By on the Transform tab*

Figure 19-16 shows the resulting dialog box.

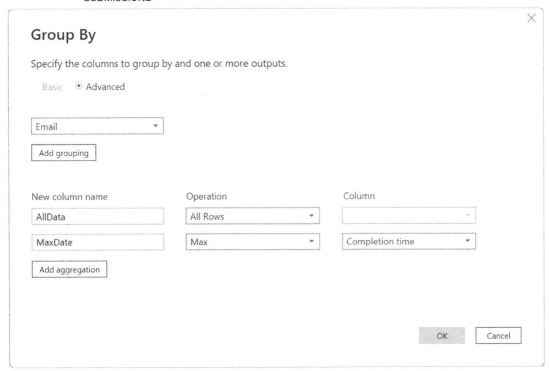

Figure 19-16. *Group By Email with AllData and MaxDate columns*

We pick our unique column, which is *Email*[4] in this case. We add an *AllData* column
with the corresponding *AllRows* operation. That will put *all* of our existing data into a
new column. We add one more column, *MaxDate*, which we define as the latest (Max)
of the *Completion time* column. Very importantly, then, *MaxDate* will hold the latest
completion time of all the rows with that particular email address.

Figure 19-17 shows the result.

---

[4] *Email* is better than *Name* since *Email* will be unique and *Name* possibly not.

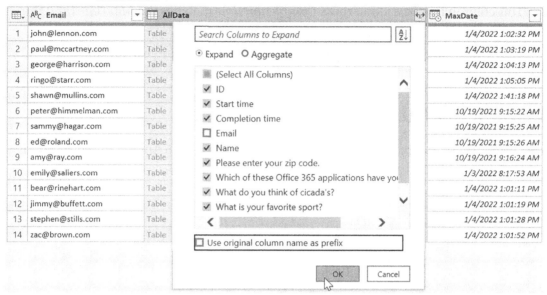

Figure 19-17. *Expanding the AllData table*

Notice how there are now only 14 rows (one per email address). We expand the *AllData* column (each row of which contains a *Table*) and choose all our previous columns except *Email* (since we already grouped on that).

Our last step is to create an *isMostRecentSubmission* conditional column, as shown in Figure 19-18.

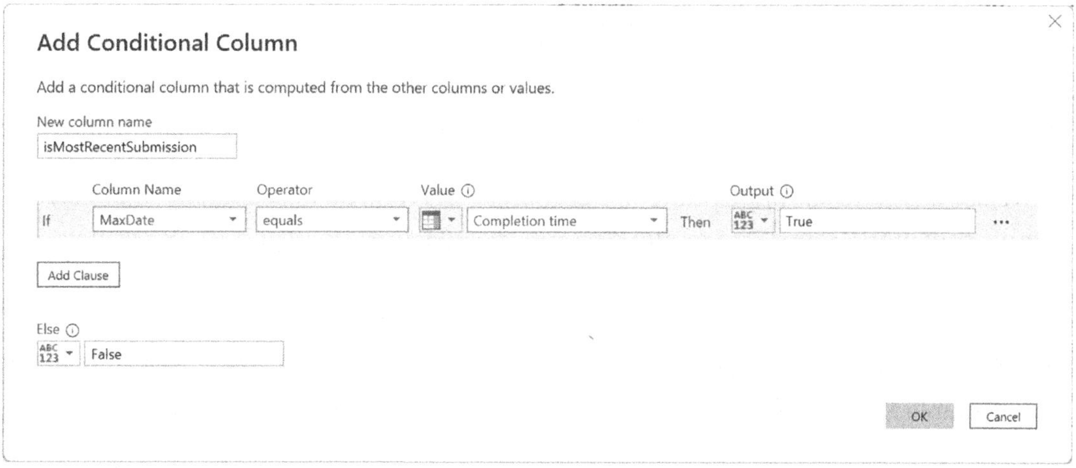

Figure 19-18. *IsMostRecentSubmission Conditional Column*

This column has *True* if that row's *Completion time* matches the *MaxDate* (and thus is the most recent submission) and *False* otherwise.

That's it. We select *Close and Apply* and then move onto our visualizations.

Visualizing Our Data in Power BI

We create pages/tabs for Cicadas, Favorite Sport, Microsoft 365 Apps, and Word Cloud, as shown in Figure 19-19. We are initially showing all responses but will limit to the most recent shortly.

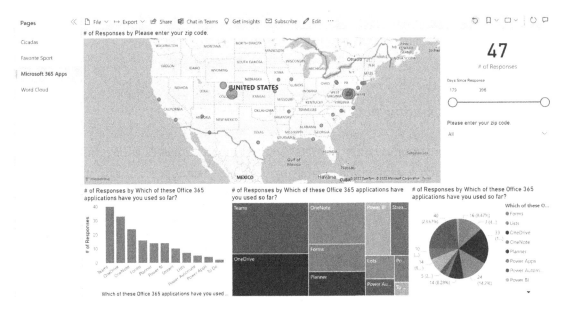

Figure 19-19. *Visualization showing all responses*

We use a *Card* to show the number of responses. It is critical to use *Count (Distinct)* since we split the 365 apps into multiple rows back in Figures 19-12 and 19-13. We have slicers for *Days Since Response* and zip code. We show the number of responses per product in a bar chart, treemap, and pie chart. Our zip code data allows us to add the Map control. If you get a warning message and want to use that control, a Power BI Admin will need to enable Map and filled map visuals, as shown in Figure 19-20.

◢ Map and filled map visuals
Disabled for the entire organization

Allow people in your org to use the map and filled map visualizations in their reports.

  Disabled

ⓘ By selecting "Enabled", you agree that map and filled map visuals may use Bing
services located outside of your Power BI tenant's geographic region, compliance
boundary, or national cloud instance. This feature uses mapping capabilities that
are powered in part by third parties, TomTom and SK Telecom, and operate
outside your tenant's geographic region, compliance boundary, or national cloud
instance. Microsoft shares the address and location queries with these third
parties, but not the name of the customer or end user who entered the query.
This feature is non-regional and the queries you provide may be stored and
processed in the United States or any other country in which Microsoft or its
subprocessors operate. Use of map and filled map is subject to the following
terms.

Apply   Cancel

ⓘ This setting applies to the entire organization

***Figure 19-20.** Enabling Map and Filled Visuals in the Power BI Admin portal*

From there, Figure 19-21 shows how we put the zip code in the *Location* field and use
the *Count (Distinct)* [*# of Responses*] as the *Bubble size.*

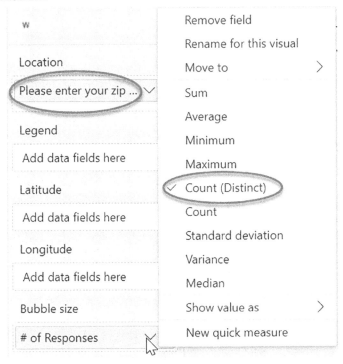

Figure 19-21. *Configuration of the Map control showing Count (Distinct)*

We are now ready to limit our responses to the most recent per person. To do that,
we add the *isMostRecentSubmission* column to *Filters on all pages*. We select only
True, as shown in Figure 19-22. Note how the number of rows matches our number in
Figure 19-17 before we expanded the *AllData* table.

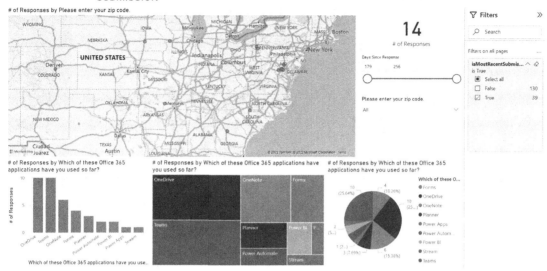

Figure 19-22. *Limiting to the most recent response per person*

The 39 *True* values shown correspond to all the split-out rows for Office 365 products but there are only 14 unique responses.

Since the favorite sport and product names are conducive to a word cloud, we choose to add more visuals and search for the free Word Cloud control, as shown in Figure 19-23.

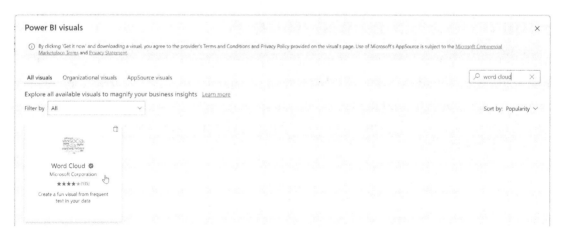

Figure 19-23. *Adding the Word Cloud visualization*

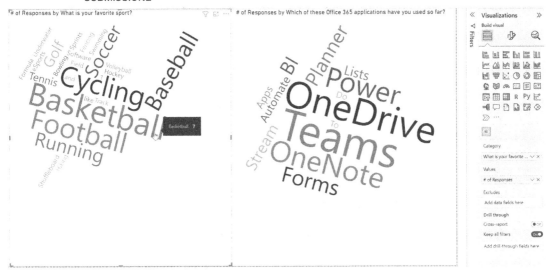

Figure 19-24. *Setting up the Wordcloud visualization*

Figure 19-23 shows how we configure it with the *Category* (Favorite Sport or Office Product) and *Values* (# of Responses).

Notice how each word gets visualized separate, so *Power* and *BI* show up as two different words.

Setting Up a Scheduled Refresh

To complete the job, we need to publish our visualization to the Power BI Service and then configure a scheduled refresh. That will allow changes to our OneDrive spreadsheet to automatically be reflected in our visualization. To get started, we go to *Data hub* on the left side of the Power BI screen, find out dataset, and then go to *Settings*. This is shown in Figure 19-25.

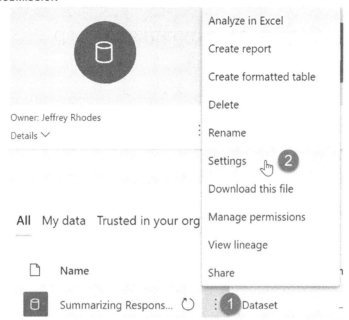

Figure 19-25. *Going to the Settings for the dataset*

You will normally have to configure your Data source credentials, as shown in
Figure 19-26, before you can schedule a refresh. Until you do, that option will be
disabled.

Figure 19-26. *Editing data source credentials*

You will normally select the *OAuth2* Authentication method and the *Organizational*
privacy level, as shown in Figure 19-27.

Figure 19-27. *Setting the OAuth2 authentication method*

This will then prompt you for your normal Microsoft 365 email/credentials.

At this point, you are able to configure one or more scheduled refreshes, as shown in Figure 19-28.

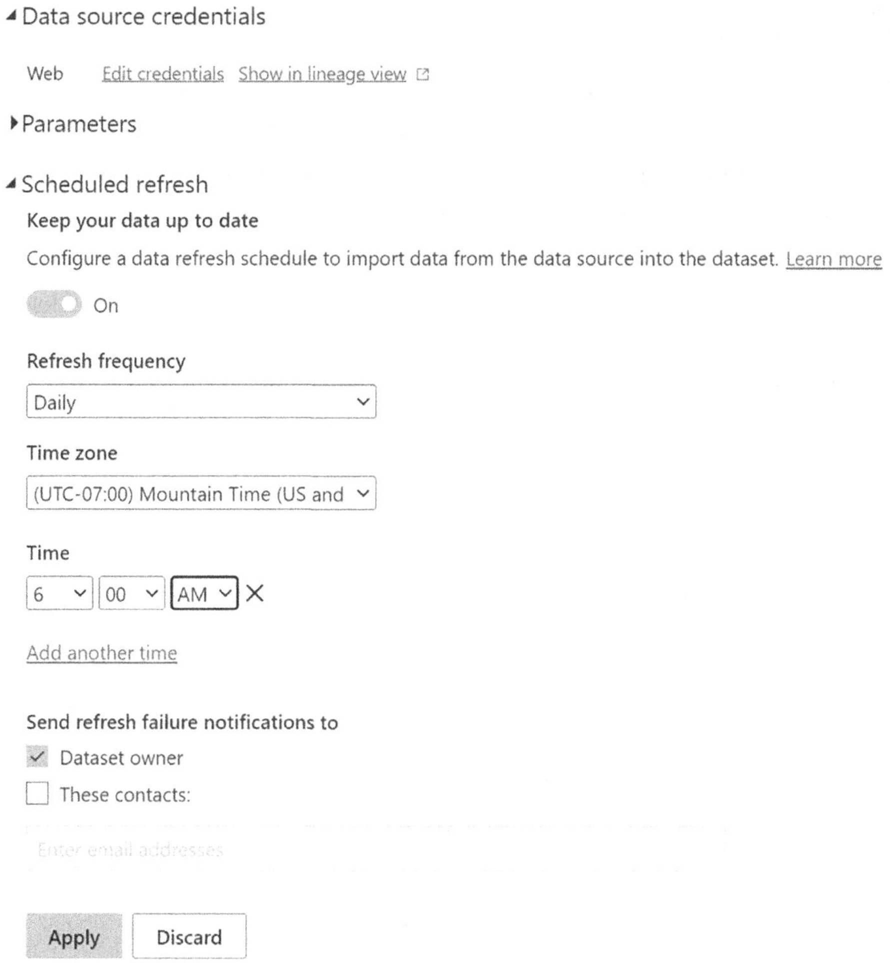

◢ Data source credentials

Web   Edit credentials   Show in lineage view ⬈

▶ Parameters

◢ Scheduled refresh

Keep your data up to date

Configure a data refresh schedule to import data from the data source into the dataset. Learn more

⬤◯ On

Refresh frequency

| Daily   ⌄ |

Time zone

| (UTC-07:00) Mountain Time (US and ⌄ |

Time

| 6   ⌄ || 00   ⌄ || AM ⌄ | ✕

Add another time

Send refresh failure notifications to

✓ Dataset owner

☐ These contacts:

Enter email addresses

Apply   **Discard**

Figure 19-28. *Adding a scheduled refresh*

You can set the frequency, time zone, and time of day. It is a good idea to add
additional contacts for refresh failures if this is an important visualization.

Summary

In this chapter, we learned how to connect to a OneDrive Excel file and split our multiple responses by their delimiter into multiple rows, removing the resulting empty rows caused by the ; at the end of each set of multiple responses. We explored using the *Group By* feature to only use the most recent submission from each user. We saw how to use the Map control with our zip code data and enable it if needed in our environment. Another key point was authenticating our data source after publishing to the Power BI service, which then allowed us to schedule automatic refreshes of our data. In our next chapter, we will examine another key challenge of working with Microsoft Forms data – how to get our hands on their attachments and copy them to SharePoint.

CHAPTER 20

Copying Microsoft Forms Attachments to a SharePoint List Item Using Power Automate

Following up last chapter's discussion of whether to use Microsoft Forms or Power Apps, this chapter covers the situation where Forms is appropriate, but we need to copy the results AND the uploaded attachments to a SharePoint list. It builds on a solution by Norm Young[1] from Canada.

Configuring the Form and List

A personal form in Microsoft Forms will store its attachments in that user's OneDrive. Since it is typically the organization's data, I prefer to use group forms, which store their data and attachments in the SharePoint site associated with the group/team. Figure 20-1 shows how to scroll down to *My groups* and then select the one you want.

---

[1] See https://normyoung.ca/2020/09/12/add-attachments-from-forms-to-microsoft-lists-using-power-automate.

© Jeffrey M. Rhodes 2022
J. M. Rhodes, *Creating Business Applications with Microsoft 365*,
https://doi.org/10.1007/978-1-4842-8823-8_20

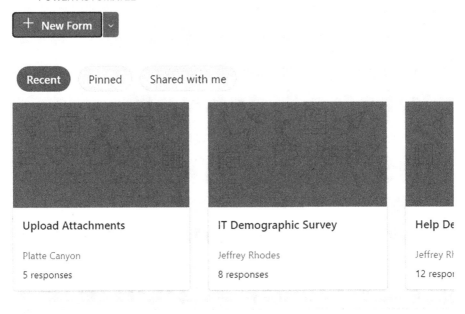

Figure 20-1. *Going to My groups in Microsoft Forms*

We click on *New Group Form,* as shown in Figure 20-2.

Figure 20-2. *Creating a New Group Form*

We add as many questions as we want. In our case, we add a text question and then
choose *Upload File*[2] (Figure 20-3).

---

[2] Note that *Upload file* is only available if you choose *Only people in my organization can respond*
under the form settings. Anonymous/non-authenticated forms do not allow file attachments for
security reasons.

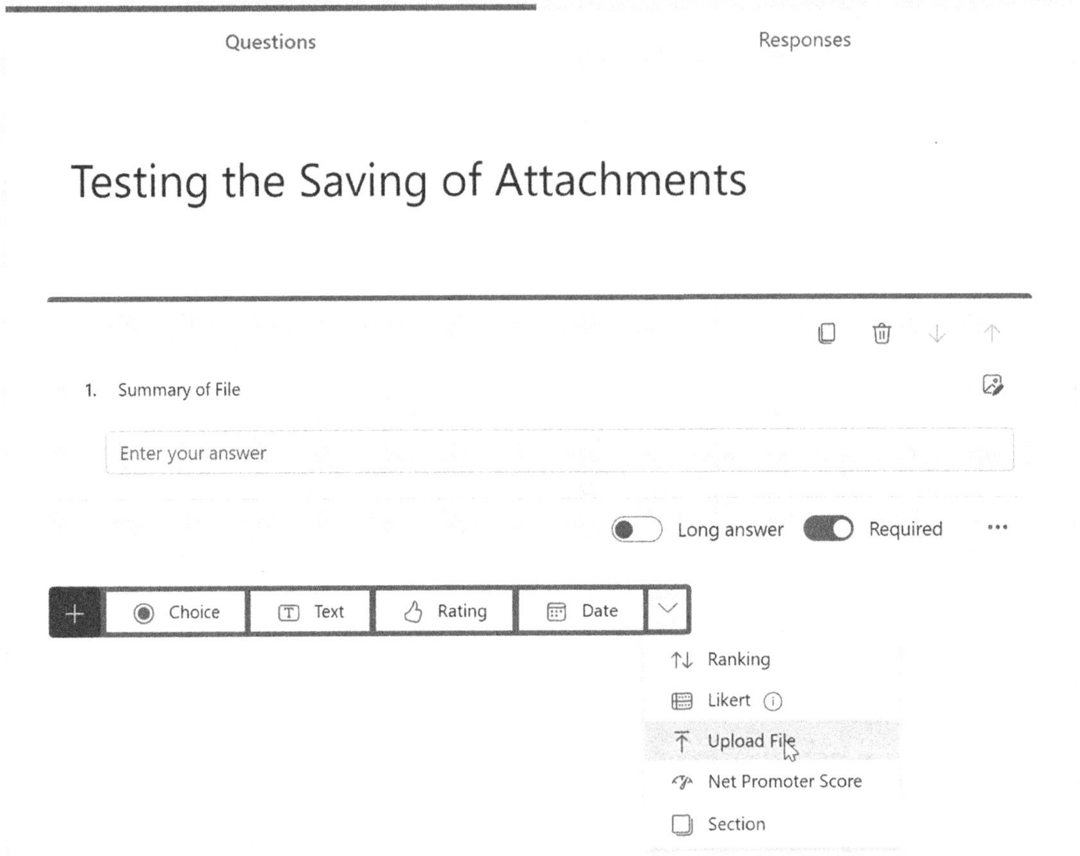

Questions   Responses

Testing the Saving of Attachments

Figure 20-3. *Addng an Upload File question*

We can allow up to ten files with the maximum size per file of 1 GB, as shown in Figure 20-4.

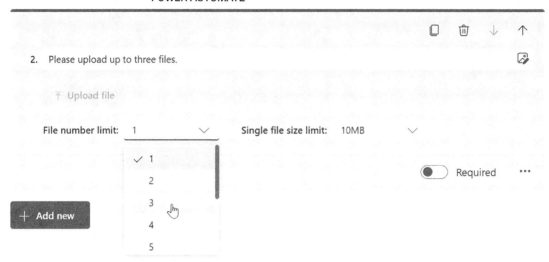

Figure 20-4. *Configuring the upload question*

Figure 20-5 shows how the form looks to the end user.

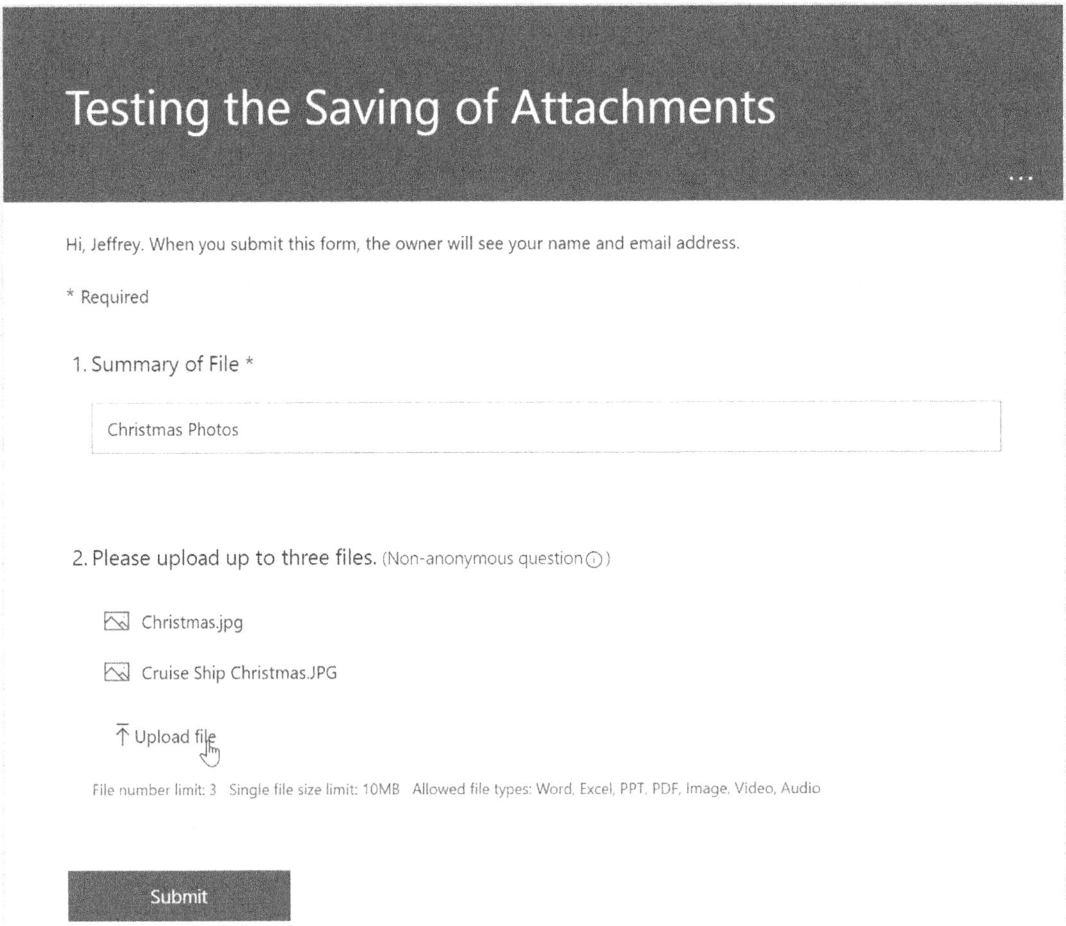

Figure 20-5. *Testing form with up to three attachments*

As I mentioned before, the implication of making this a Group form is that the responses and, most importantly for us, the attachments, are stored in the SharePoint site for the group. Figure 20-6 shows this location. Note that it is in this format:

```
Documents/Apps/Microsoft Forms/<Name of the Form>/Question
```

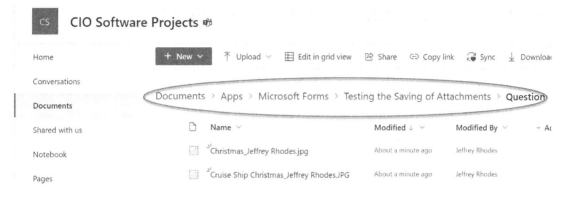

Figure 20-6. *Attachments location in SharePoint*

Our last setup task is to create our list for storing the responses and attachments. We thought long and hard 😊 to come up with the *AttachmentsList* name, as shown in Figure 20-7.

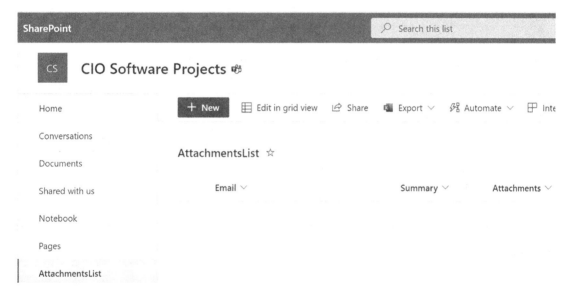

Figure 20-7. *Attachments List for storing form responses*

Note that we are showing the *Attachments* column to make it easier to see if our Power Automate flow is working.

Setting Up the Flow in Power Automate

The heavy lifting for this solution is within Power Automate. As we have done previously, we create an *automated cloud flow* with the trigger being *When a new response is submitted* from Microsoft Forms (Figure 20-8).

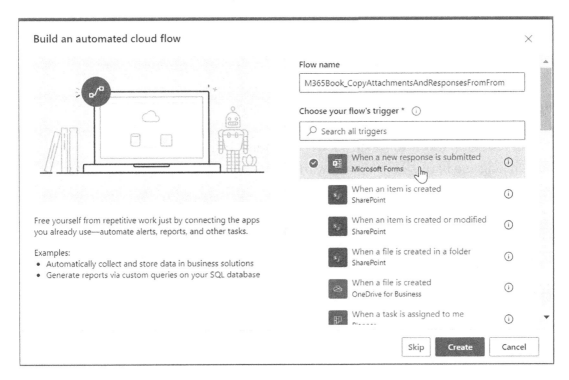

Figure 20-8. *Configuring the automated cloud flow*

A current challenge of group forms is that they don't show up in the form list. Instead, we need to *Enter custom value,* as shown in Figure 20-9.

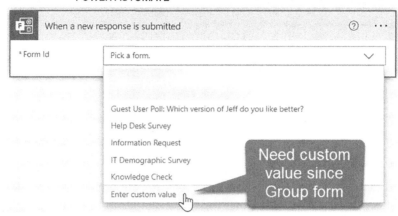

Figure 20-9. *Choosing custom value since using Group form*

We get this value by previewing the form and copying the info after "id=", as shown in
Figure 20-10.

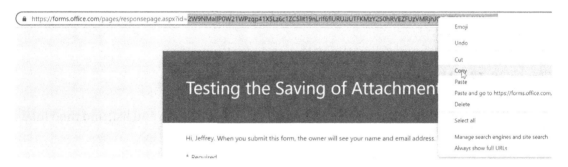

Figure 20-10. *Copying Form Id from Form URL*

We use this value twice ("When a response is submitted" and "Get response details").
The latter action uses the *Response Id* from the former, as shown in Figure 20-11.

Figure 20-11. *Also using the Form Id for response details*

We then use the SharePoint *Create item* action, select our site and list, and then load
the *Email* and *Summary* information from the form (Figure 20-12).

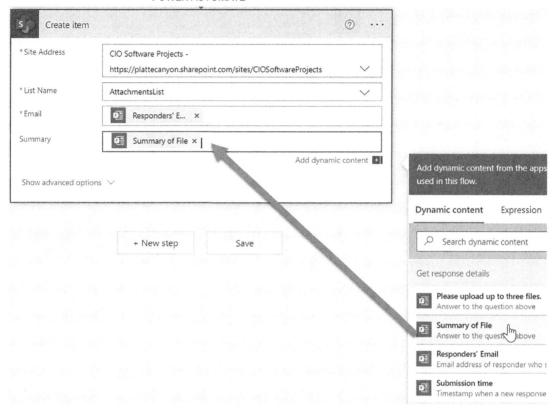

Figure 20-12. *Copying the form responses to SharePoint*

We now need to check to see if the form has any attachments. We do that with a
Condition action and check if the *Please upload up to three files* question *is not equal to*
<blank>. If the answer is yes, we use the *Compose* action and use this same question as
the *Inputs* (Figure 20-13).

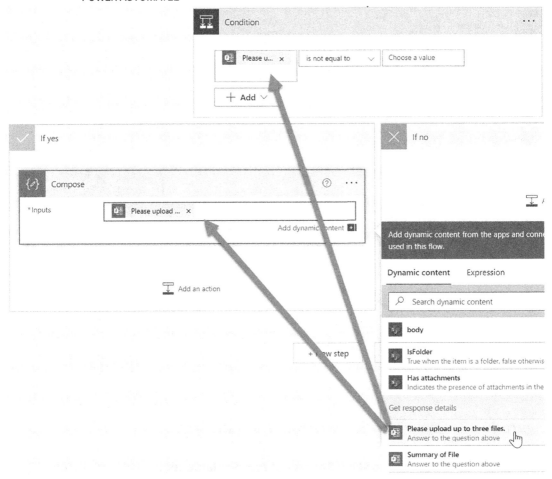

Figure 20-13. *Using the form attachment in the Condition and Compose actions*

At this point, we save the flow and test the form (being sure to include at least one attachment). We go to Power Automate's run history and click the one run showing (that hopefully has a status of *Succeeded*). As shown in Figure 20-14, we go into the *Compose* action and copy the JSON shown in the *Outputs*. This will help us complete our flow.

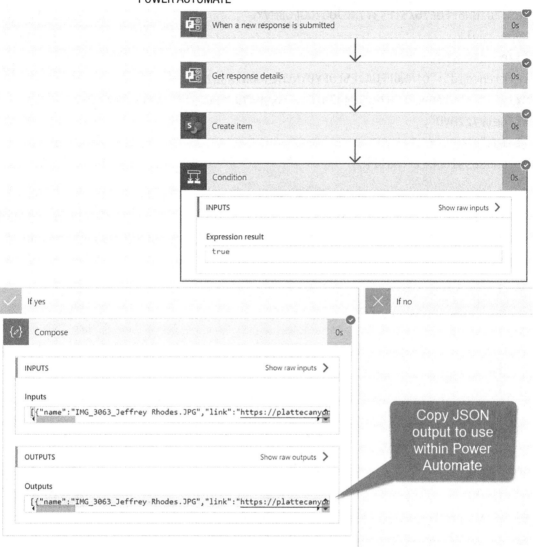

Figure 20-14. *Copy JSON Output from Power Automate run history*

Listing 20-1 shows what this JSON looks like.

Listing 20-1. JSON Output to be used as a Sample.

[{"name":"IMG_3063_Jeffrey Rhodes.JPG","link":"https://plattecanyon.
sharepoint.com/sites/CIOSoftwareProjects/Shared%20Documents/Apps/
Microsoft%20Forms/Testing%20the%20Saving%20of%20Attachments/Question/
IMG_3063_Jeffrey%20Rhodes.JPG",

"id":"01NW6LEUE76ZSTE53Y7NCJUG7OGLGBMVYC",

"type":null,

"size":2440764,

"referenceId":"01NW6LEUA4ESLOFYBYNVHL5UDNLA3W2UFH",

"driveId":"b!obmEHFCH7ky3Q4qJa1btFD8x9HA7JPFFuC5fXa2KrIKD2RNm8o
LRR7uelV7z2HVD",

"status":1,

"uploadSessionUrl":null}]

Power Automate doesn't care about the specific data but instead wants the schema (format): name, id, type, size, etc. We edit our flow and add a *Parse JSON* action and load the *Outputs* from the *Compose* action into the *Parse JSON's Content*. This is shown in Figure 20-15.

Figure 20-15. *Parse the JSON and Generate the schema from a sample*

We click the *Generate from Sample* button and paste in the JSON from the clipboard (Listing 20-1). The top part of Figure 20-16 shows the resulting schema.

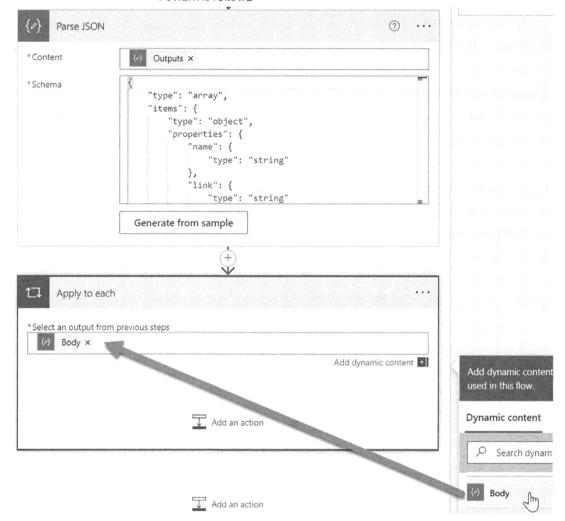

Figure 20-16. *Looping through the attachments from the JSON Body*

Since there can be multiple attachments, we use the *Apply to each* action on the *Body* from our *Parse JSON* action (Figure 20-16).

We now need to read each attachment so we can copy it to our SharePoint list item. Since the files are in a SharePoint document library (see Figure 20-6), we use SharePoint's *Get file content using path* action, as shown in Figure 20-17.

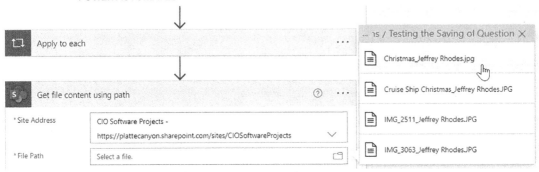

Figure 20-17. *Selecting the path and name of one of the attachments*

We select our site and then navigate through its document libraries and folders to
pick one of the attachments (*Christmas_Jeffrey Rhodes.jpg* in this case). This allows us
to get the path right. We then load in the actual file name from the JSON, which we are
looping through to get each file attached for a particular form response. This is shown in
Figure 20-18.

Figure 20-18. *Replacing the hard-coded file name with the dynamic name from
the JSON*

We are almost done. We just need to attach the file to our SharePoint list item. For that, we use SharePoint *Add attachment* action, as shown in Figure 20-19.

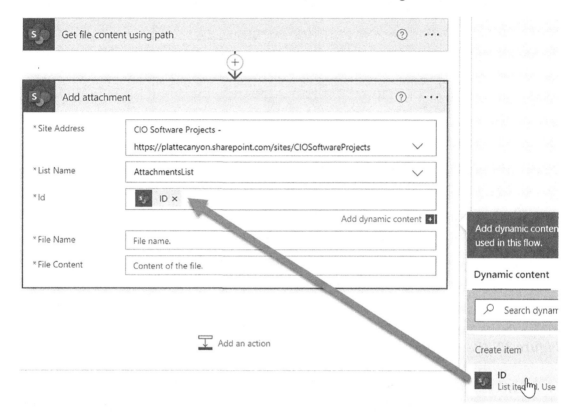

Figure 20-19. *Adding the list item attachment and setting the Id*

We go all the way back to our *Create item* action (Figure 20-12) to get the ID of the list item we created. From there, we are ready to add the *File Name* and *File Content,* as shown in Figure 20-20.

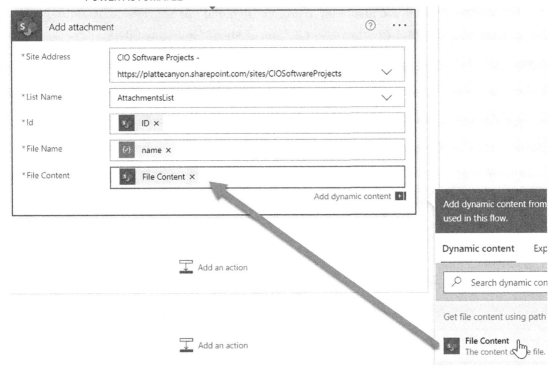

Figure 20-20. *Adding the File Name and File Content of the attachment*

We get the *File Name* from our *Parse JSON* action (Figure 20-15) and the *File Content* from our *Get file content using path* action (Figure 20-18).

Viewing our Results in SharePoint

We are now ready to test. We complete a response with the maximum of three attachments, as shown in Figure 20-21.

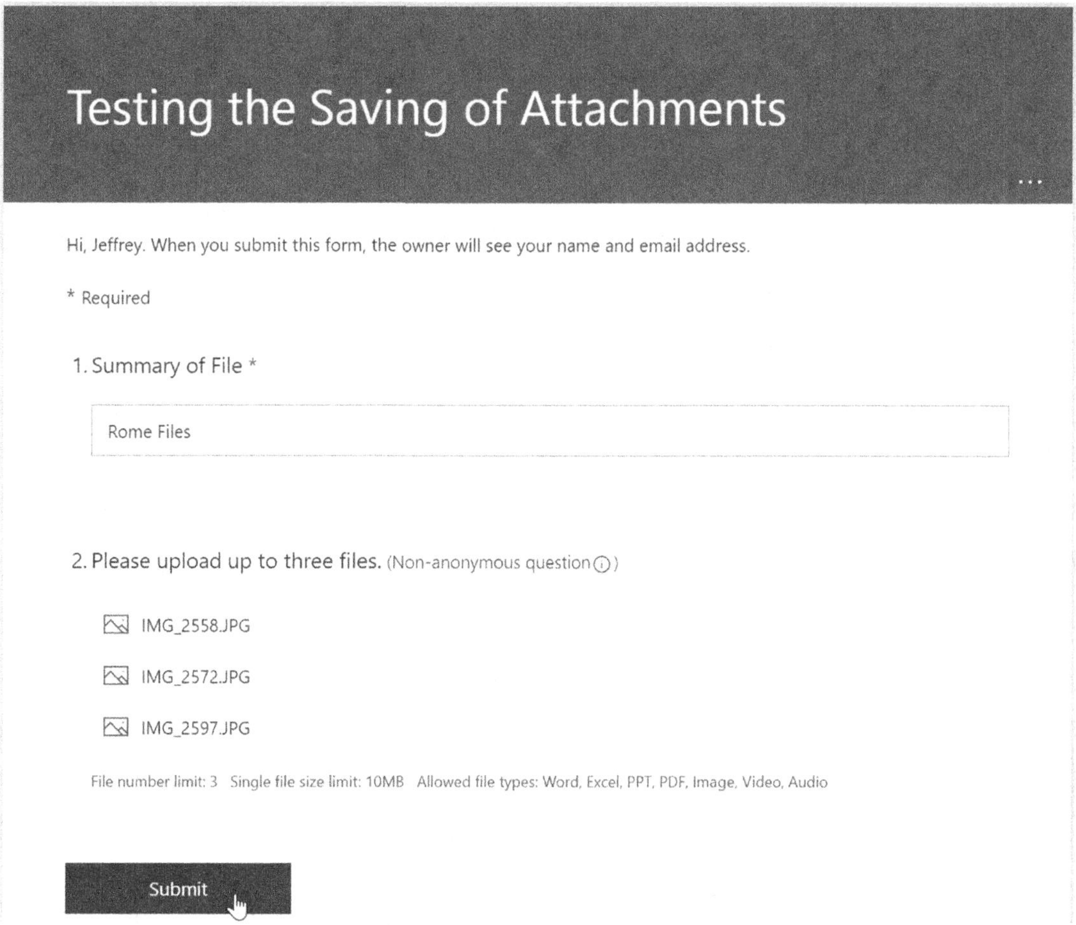

Figure 20-21. *Testing the form and flow*

Note the names of the uploaded files. We expect the name to be the same but with the user added.[3] So *IMG_2558_Jeffrey Rhodes.jpg,* for example. We will, of course, also want to click on the files from the SharePoint list item to ensure they open correctly and are the same files. Figure 20-22 shows the results in our SharePoint list.

---

[3] Forms does this to distinguish files of the same name uploaded by different users. It will also rename files as needed to make them unique. So if I uploaded the same file again, it would be *IMG_2558_Jeffrey Rhodes 1.jpg.*

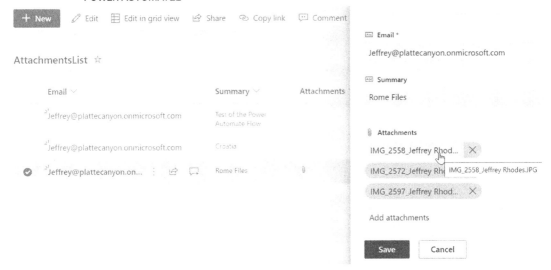

Figure 20-22. *Viewing the attachments from SharePoint*

Notice that all three attachments have been added to the list item. They are also in
the original document library. So we have backups, if needed. Success!

Summary

In this chapter, we learned how to use Power Automate connected to Microsoft Forms
to check if there are any attachments and, if so, use the *Compose* action and then Power
Automate's run history to copy the JSON output. We then returned to the development
view and used this output to Generate from sample and then parsed the JSON
containing the attachments. We used SharePoint's *Get file content using path* action
and to get our hands on the file and then its *Add attachment* action to write it to our list
item. We are now ready to put all this knowledge together and build some complete
applications.

CHAPTER 21

Creating an Employee Recognition App in Power Apps, Power Automate, Power BI, Teams, and SharePoint

This example is based on a prototype I created to replace a previous process where the organization emailed a PDF form to everyone where they could select what value(s) other members displayed, add some optional text, and then either attach the form to an email to that member or send it to a central location for where the person filling out the form would stay anonymous. It predates Microsoft's Praise app[1] and in fact we have moved to that solution as it was already built into Teams. But this example gives us an opportunity to put all the pieces together: SharePoint, Power Apps, Power Automate, and Power BI.

---

[1] See https://support.microsoft.com/en-us/office/send-praise-to-people-50f26b47-565f-40fe-8642-5ca2a5ed261e.

© Jeffrey M. Rhodes 2022
J. M. Rhodes, *Creating Business Applications with Microsoft 365*,
https://doi.org/10.1007/978-1-4842-8823-8_21

Configuring the SharePoint List

As with other examples, we store our data in a SharePoint list. It is not strictly necessary in this case, as the core functionality is an email, post, and/or chat to the recipient. But storing the data allows us to visualize what values are being displayed over time, which organizations are displaying them, and top recipients. It also gives documentation of what messages were sent in case there were any harassment or similar complaints.

For our example, I used the Air Force core values of *Integrity First, Service Before Self,* and *Excellence in All We Do.*[2] It can easily be adjusted to more or fewer values. As shown in Figure 21-1, we store whether the recipient demonstrated these values in *Yes/No* columns.

Columns	
A column stores information about each item in the list. The following columns are currently available in this list:	
Column (click to edit)	Type
Office	Single line of text
Details	Multiple lines of text
Recipient	Person or Group
Integrity First	Yes/No
Service Before Self	Yes/No
Excellence in All We Do	Yes/No
Share Submitter Name with Recipient	Yes/No
Share to Teams	Yes/No
Share via Chat	Yes/No
Share via Email	Yes/No
Modified	Date and Time
Created	Date and Time
Created By	Person or Group
Modified By	Person or Group

Figure 21-1. *SharePoint List Columns*

We also store the user's *Office,* any optional *Details* the submitter entered, and the *Recipient.* Notice that this is a *Person* column and thus we don't have any issues with similar names and don't need to separately store an email address. We have another Yes/No column to store the *Share Submitter Name with Recipient* choice. Finally,

---

[2] See www.airforce.com/mission/vision.

we store whether the submitter wanted to *Share to Teams*, *Share via Chat*, and/or *Share via Email*. Note that the *Created By* column will store the submitter, so we don't need an extra column for that purpose.

We are now ready to move to Power Apps.

Creating Our Application in Power Apps

Figure 21-2 shows our completed application.

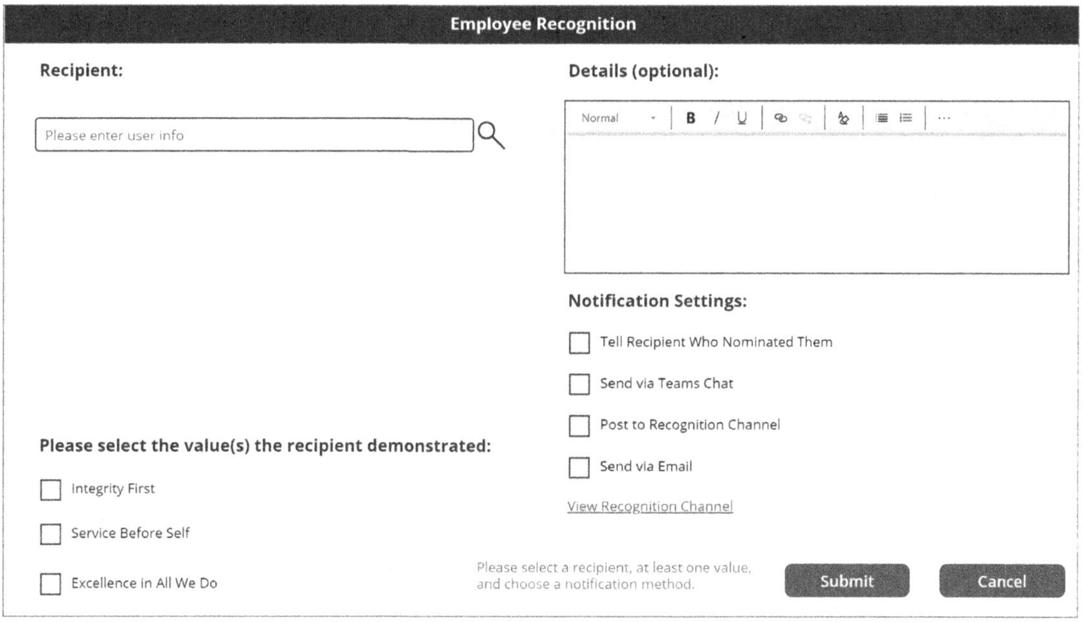

Figure 21-2. *Employee Recognition application*

As with past applications, we create a *Blank canvas app* with a *Tablet* format. We connect to *Office365Users* in order for us to look up recipients and to our SharePoint list we created in the last section. The Power Automate flow we create in the next section shows up as well once we connect to it. These connections are shown in Figure 21-3.

313

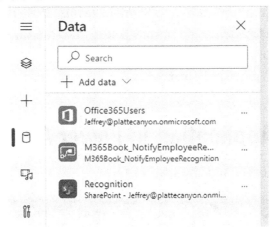

Figure 21-3. *Application data – Office365Users, Power Automate flow, and
SharePoint list*

Our first task is to pick a recipient. For that, we have a Search *Text input* control and a
Gallery (Figure 21-4).

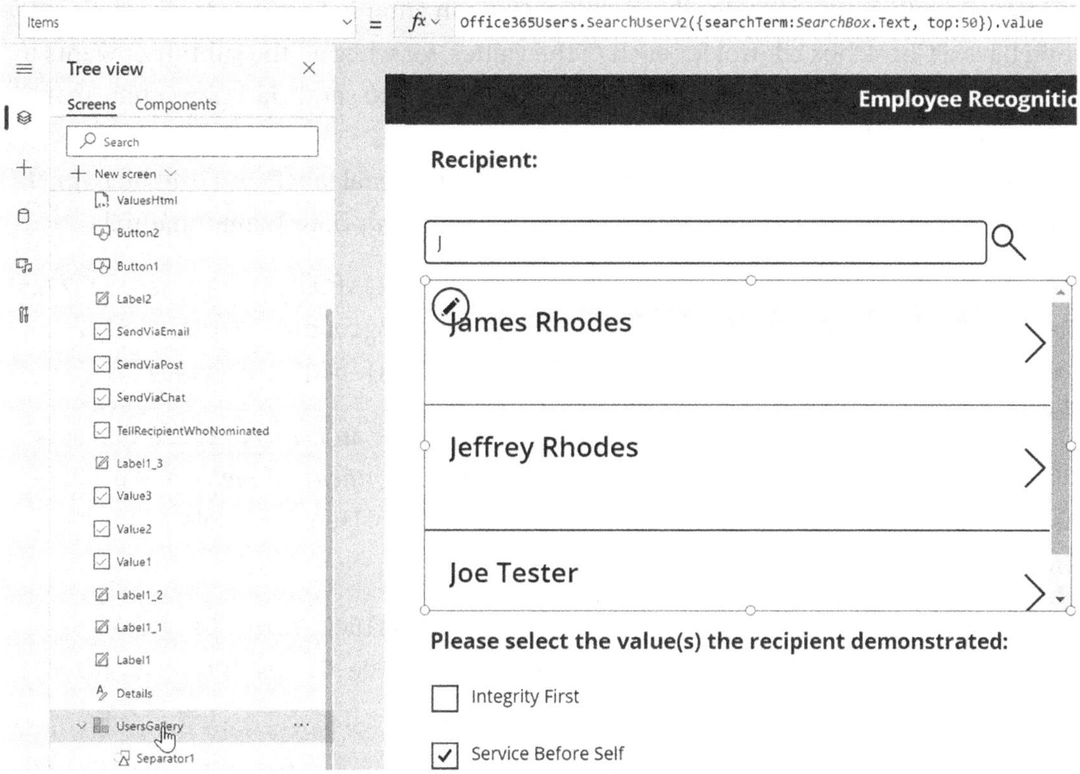

Figure 21-4. *Configuring the Users Gallery*

We used the *Office365User SearchUserV2()* function again to search for recipients:

```
Office365Users.SearchUserV2({searchTerm:SearchBox.Text, top:50}).value
```

We set the *varRecipient* variable in response to the *OnSelect* event:

```
Set(varRecipient, UsersGallery.Selected)
```

We use this variable to set the *Visible* property:

```
!IsBlank(varRecipient) Or SearchBox.Text <> ""
```

This is why the gallery is not shown in Figure 21-2. We also use this variable in customizing the *Text* of our title label at the top of the screen:

```
If(IsBlank(varRecipient), "Employee Recognition", "Employee Recognition for "
& varRecipient.DisplayName)
```

Skip forward to Figure 21-5 to see how this looks once the submitter selects a user.

315

We add a *Rich text editor* for the *Details* so we can enter in formatted information. We then have a Check box control for each of the values, for whether the submitter wants to *Tell Recipient Who Nominated Them*, and for the choices to send via Teams chat, Teams post, and/or email.

For the *View Recognition Channel* link, we have a normal label[3] and use the *Launch()* method in response to its *OnSelect* event to go to the appropriate Teams channel.

```
Launch("https://teams.microsoft.com/l/channel/19%3af98d381f13c34a51879272f3
9b3e7697%40thread.skype/Employee%2520Recognition?groupId=321c7c59-8fd2-
4f81-8400-8b7988935ee2&tenantId=314d6fd9-25a2-453f-b6d5-63f3aa9e355f")
```

If you look at the bottom of Figure 21-2, you will notice an *ErrorLabel* text that says: *Please select a recipient, at least one value, and choose a notification method*. We will use the visibility of this label in the *Patch()* code as follows. Here is the label's *Visible* property:

```
If(!IsBlank(varRecipient) And (Value1.Value Or Value2.Value Or Value3.
Value) And (SendViaChat.Value Or SendViaEmail.Value Or SendViaPost.Value),
false, true)
```

Since the logic is fairly complicated, we use the *If()* function. We make sure that the *varRecipient* is not blank, at least one value is checked, and at least one output (chat, post, or email) is checked in order to hide the label.

Once it comes time to send the recognition via Teams or email, it will be nice to have a list of all the selected values. For that, we add an *HTML text* control, name it *ValuesHtml*, and use this code in its *HtmlText* property:

```
Concatenate("<ul>", If(Value1.Value, "<li>" & Value1.Text & "</li>", ""),
If(Value2.Value, "<li>" & Value2.Text & "</li>", ""), If(Value3.Value,
"<li>" & Value3.Text & "</li>", ""), "</ul>")
```

This used the *Concatenate()* method, to build an unordered list (*ul*) of list items (*li*), which is displayed as bullets. If a value is checked, its *Text* is wrapped up in a list item as in *<li>Service Before Self</li>*. We normally hide the control as it is only used programmatically in the *Submit* button, but Figure 21-5 shows how it looks when we show it for testing.

---

[3] As you've seen in other examples, we could have used an HTML text control and then put in the anchor tags: *<a href="url here">View Recognition Channel</a>*.

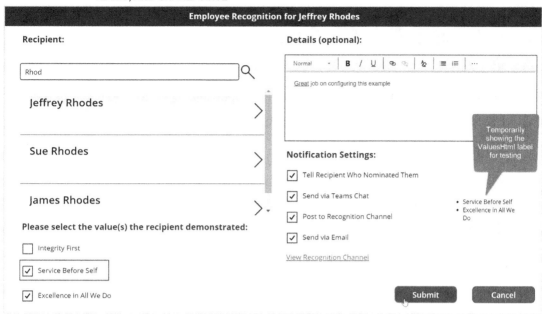

Figure 21-5. *Testing the Employee Recognition application*

The rest of the action is in the *Submit* button. Listing 21-1 shows the first part of the *OnSelect* code, where we set variables we need.

Listing 21-1. Variable Setting part of OnSelect code

```
Set(
    varBody,
    "Congratulations!<br/><br/>You have exemplified the qualities of these
values:<br/><br/>" & ValuesHtml.HtmlText
);
If(
    IsEmpty(Details.HtmlText),
    "",
    Set(
        varBody,
        varBody & "<br /><br />" & Details.HtmlText
    )
);
```

```
If(
    TellRecipientWhoNominated.Value,
    Set(
        varBody,
        varBody & "<br />You have been recognized by " & User().FullName
    );
    Set(
        varSubmitter,
        User().FullName
    ),
    Set(
        varSubmitter,
        ""
    )
);
```

We start by creating a *varBody* variable that puts a congratulations message and combines it with the selected values (*ValuesHtml.HtmlText*). Notice how we use the HTML line break (<br />) to get hard returns. Here is how it looks in a later chat, post, or email:

Congratulations!

You have exemplified the qualities of these values:

- Service Before Self

- Excellence in All We Do

If the submitter typed in *Details*, we add that below the values. We then check to see if the *Tell Recipient Who Nominated Them* box is checked and, if so, add on the name using *User().FullName* to get the name of the person using the format. We also set to *varSubmitter* variable either to this name or to blank.

Our next task is to write the information back to our SharePoint list using the *Patch()* method, as shown in Listing 21-2.

Listing 21-2. Patch portion of the OnSelect code

```
If(
    ErrorLabel.Visible,
    false,
    Patch(
        Recognition,
        Defaults(Recognition),
        {
            Recipient: {
                '@odata.type': "#Microsoft.Azure.Connectors.SharePoint.
SPListExpandedUser",
                ODataType: Blank(),
                Claims: Concatenate(
                    "i:0#.f|membership|",
                    varRecipient.Mail
                ),
                DisplayName: varRecipient.DisplayName,
                Email: varRecipient.Mail,
                Department: varRecipient.Department,
                JobTitle: varRecipient.JobTitle,
                Picture: ""
            },
            Office: varRecipient.Department,
            'Integrity First': Value1.Value,
            'Service Before Self': Value2.Value,
            'Excellence in All We Do': Value3.Value,
            Details: Details.HtmlText,
            'Share Submitter Name with Recipient':
TellRecipientWhoNominated.Value,
            'Share to Teams': SendViaPost.Value,
            'Share via Chat': SendViaChat.Value,
            'Share via Email': SendViaEmail.Value
        }
    )
);
```

We've seen this pattern before. We check if our *ErrorLabel* is visible and, if so, just return false. This avoids lots of error checking for a valid recipient, values, and output. We've covered how to write the data for a *Person* column in earlier chapters. Note how we use the *varRecipient* variable heavily to get the email address, display name, department, and job title. From there, we set the values to be written to each column (you might want to refer to Figure 21-1). We use the *Department* value of the user for the *Office* column and the *Details Rich text control* for the *Details* column. We then set the various *Yes/No* columns with the corresponding check boxes on the form.

Before we can finish this code, we need to go to Power Automate and create our flow.

Setting Up the Flow in Power Automate

Within Power Automate, we set up an automated cloud flow and trigger it from Power Apps (Figure 21-6).

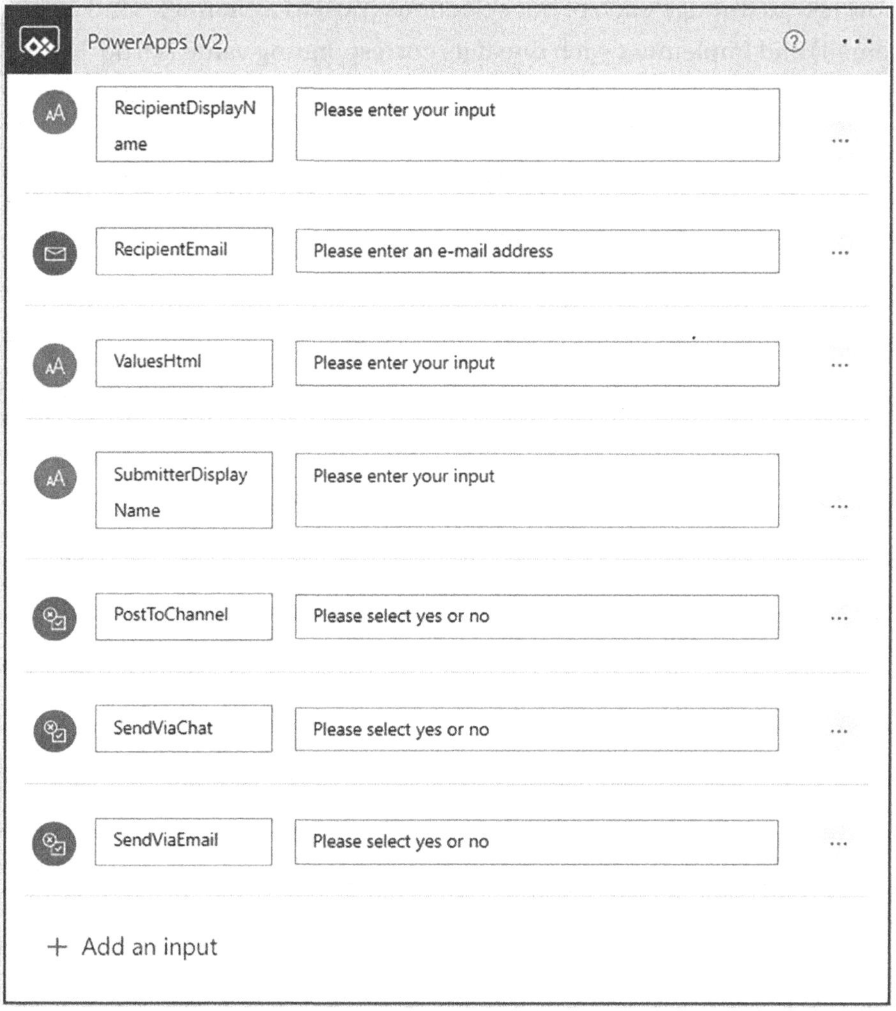

Figure 21-6. *Power Apps Inputs in Power Automate*

We plan to pass in these parameters from Power Apps: *RecipientDisplayName, RecipientEmail, ValuesHtml, SubmitterDisplayName, PostToChannel, SendViaChat,* and *SendViaEmail.* These latter three are *Boolean* (Yes/No) values, while the rest are *Text.* You might recall from Listing 21-1 that *varSubmitter* will be blank if the *Tell Recipient Who Nominated Them* box is not checked. Since that variable will be passed into the *SubmitterDisplayName* parameter, we will be able to check if it is blank in order to determine whether to try to send anonymously.

We now just go through each of our selections (post to a channel, send a chat, and send an email) and implement each one if its corresponding value is true. Figure 21-7 shows how we use the *Condition* action and select the *PostToChannel* parameter.

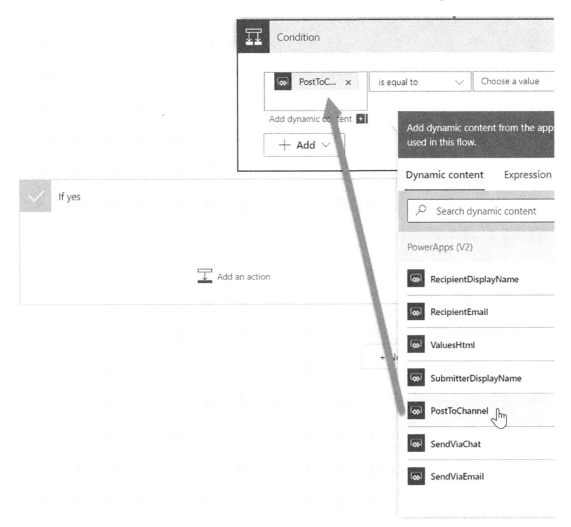

Figure 21-7. *Configuring the PostToChannel condition*

Actually, comparing this value can be challenging. I've found the most reliable way is to use the true dynamic expression, as shown in Figure 21-8.

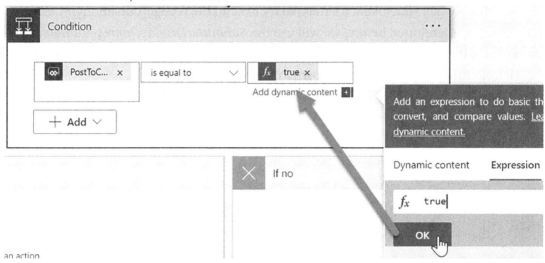

Figure 21-8. *Setting the true dynamic expression*

Note that you select the *Expression* tab, type in *true*, select it from the popup list, and then click the OK button.

Since we will want to @mention the user so that the recognition shows up in their activity feed, our next step is to create the token from the *RecipientEmail,* as shown in Figure 21-9.

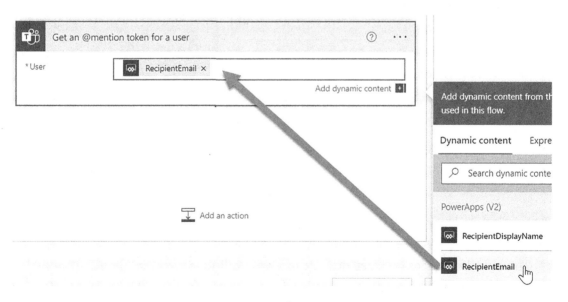

Figure 21-9. *Generating an @mention token*

323

Now that we have the token, we need to try to send the recognition anonymously if possible.[4] As mentioned before, we will use the *SubmitterDisplayName* parameter to check this. If it is not equal to blank, then send the post from the *User*. Otherwise, we send it from the *Flow bot*. Both are shown in Figure 21-10.

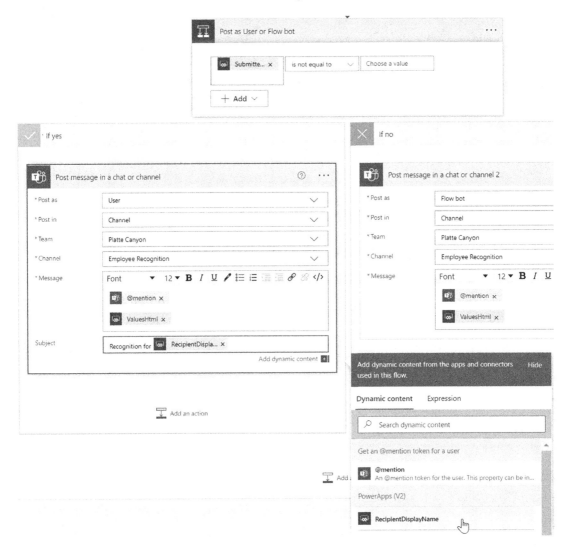

Figure 21-10. *Posting as a User or Flow bot*

The only differences between our *Yes* and *No* conditions are 1) sending as *User* or *Flow bot* and 2) whether we get to include a *Subject*. You might recall from Listing 21-1

---

[4] We will see that Microsoft has taken this ability away, likely for security reasons.

that the *ValuesHtml* parameter will also include the name of the submitter if appropriate. Notice how we select our *@mention* token, the *ValuesHtml* parameter, and, for the *Yes* case, *RecipientDisplayName* from the Dynamic content. If you want to skip ahead to Figure 21-15, you will see that this is only partially successful. The *No* case uses the *Flow bot* picture rather than the user's picture/icon, but it still says "<User> via Power Automate." This is likely for security reasons.

For chats, it turns out we can't do anything other than a *Flow bot* (unless we want to add to an existing group chat). So we don't bother checking the *SubmitterDisplayName* parameter. Figure 21-11 shows the resulting *Conditions* block.

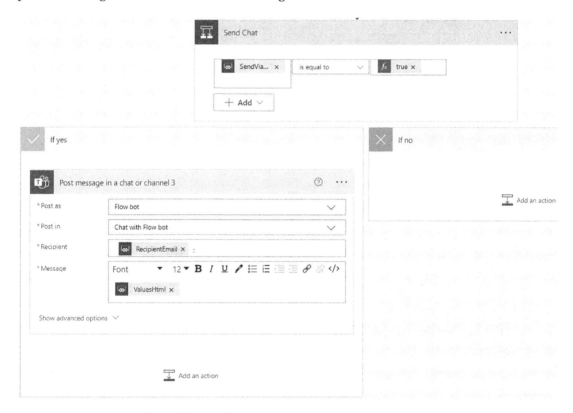

Figure 21-11. *Sending chat with no check of Submitter since sent as Flow bot*

We use the same technique as before to check if *SendViaChat* is true. If so, we chat with the *Flow bot* to the *RecipientEmail* with our *ValuesHtml* as the *Message*. Skipping ahead again to Figure 21-16, you can see the "<User> via Power Automate" is there again regardless of whether our *ValuesHtml* has who has done the recognizing.

We try again to send anonymously when we get to email, as shown in Figure 21-12.

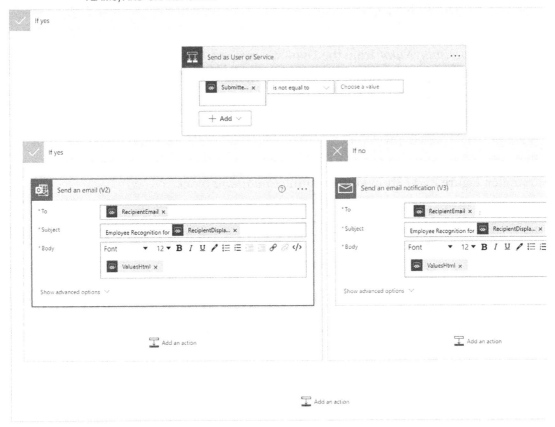

Figure 21-12. *Configuring email from user or anonymously*

We again check *SubmitterDisplayName* to see if we want to list the Submitter. If
so, we use the standing *Send an email (V2)* action from *Office 365 Outlook*. We use the
RecipientEmail, RecipientDisplayName, and *ValuesHtml* parameters. This sends an
email from the submitter to the recipient. See Figure 21-17 for an example. If not, we
try the *Send an email notification (V3)* action.[5] This sends the email from microsoft@
powerapps.com rather than from the submitter. Other than that, the configuration is
the same as the Outlook action. While this has worked for me in the past, this connector
is apparently a magnet for spam and is not only throttled but currently showing as
unauthorized for me (Figure 21-18).

---

[5] See https://docs.microsoft.com/en-us/connectors/sendmail/#send-an-email-
notification-(v3).

One thing that bothers me with the default emails from both Power Apps and Power Automate is they show up as "Low Importance." Figure 21-13 shows how to change that in our Outlook action.

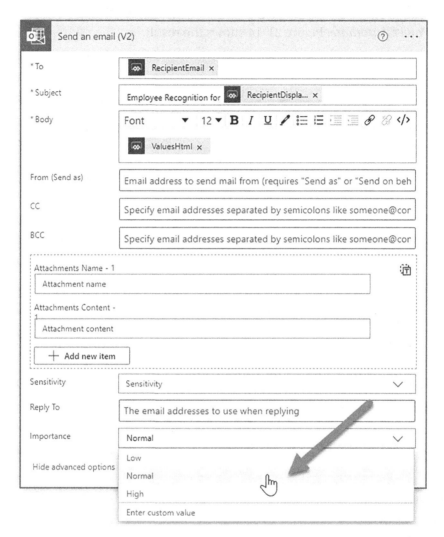

Figure 21-13. *Setting Normal importance for email in Office 365 Outlook*

That completes our logic. We save our flow and go back to Power Apps.

Completing the Application in Power Apps

We are now ready to complete our app. Returning to Power Apps, we create a new button (so that we don't overwrite our existing *OnSelect* script), select it, go to the *Action* tab, and select *Power Automate*. Figure 21-14 shows the result.

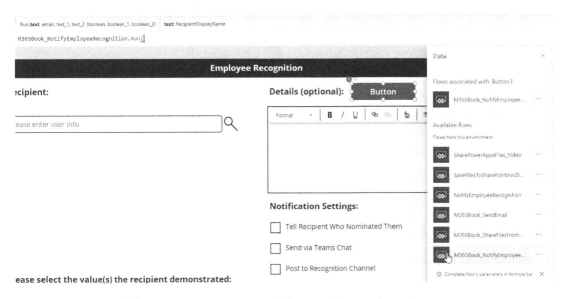

Figure 21-14. *Adding Power Automate Flow to Power Apps button*

We copy this code and add it to the existing *OnSelect* script for our *Submit* button. Listing 21-3 shows the remaining code.

Listing 21-3. Remainder of OnSelect code

```
If(
    ErrorLabel.Visible,
    false,
    M365Book_NotifyEmployeeRecognition.Run(
        varRecipient.DisplayName,
        varRecipient.Mail,
        varBody,
        varSubmitter,
        SendViaPost.Value,
        SendViaChat.Value,
        SendViaEmail.Value
```

```
);
Notify(
    "Recognition Submitted.",
    NotificationType.Success
);
Reset(Details);
Reset(TellRecipientWhoNominated);
Reset(SendViaPost);
Reset(SearchBox);
Reset(SendViaChat);
Reset(SendViaEmail);
Reset(UsersGallery);
Reset(Value1);
Reset(Value2);
Reset(Value3);
Set(
    varRecipient,
    Blank()
)
)
```

If our *ErrorLabel* is visible, we just return *false* and don't launch Power Automate. Otherwise, we pass in the parameters in the same order as we defined them in Power Automate (Figure 21-6). We then use the *Notify()* method with the text we want to display along with the *Success* parameter to tell the user all is OK. Since we don't specify a timeout, it will display for the default of 10 seconds. We then *Reset()* each of the controls so that all our data is cleared out and the user could create a new recognition if desired. To make sure we are starting over, we also set the *varRecipient* variable to *Blank()*.

Let's look at each of our outputs in turn. Figure 21-15 shows the results of *Post to Recognition Channel*.

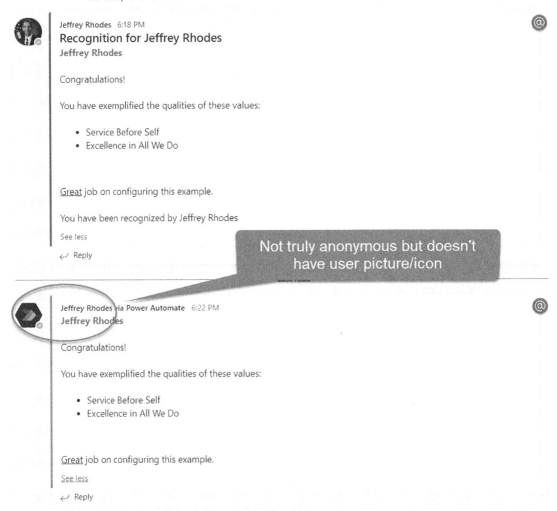

Figure 21-15. *Teams post by user compared with Flow bot*

The top post shows what happens if we check *Tell Recipient Who Nominated Them.* Notice that it has my picture and says that the post comes from me. Our logic to add "You have been recognized by <user>" from Listing 21-1 means that this is at the end of the post as well. The bottom post shows what happens if we don't check that box. The picture is for the *Flow bot* but says *Jeffrey Rhodes via Power Automate* for who made the post. So it is not anonymous. But it does give some idea that it was not a normal user post.

Figure 21-16 shows the *Send via Teams Chat* option.

Jeffrey Rhodes via Power Automate   6:19 PM
Congratulations!

You have exemplified the qualities of these values:

- Service Before Self
- Excellence in All We Do

Great job on configuring this example.

You have been recognized by Jeffrey Rhodes

Congratulations!

You have exemplified the qualities of these values:

- Service Before Self
- Excellence in All We Do

Great job on configuring this example.

Figure 21-16. *Teams Chat is via Flow bot, but not anonymous*

As discussed in the previous section, we send the chat as Flow bot either way. So both chats have that picture and are from *Jeffrey Rhodes via Power Automate*. The only effect of the *Tell Recipient Who Nominated Them* box is the recognition line at the end of the top chat.

Figure 21-17 shows the results with *Send via Email* and with the *Tell Recipient Who Nominated Them* box checked.

Employee Recognition for Jeffrey Rhodes

Jeffrey Rhodes
To   Jeffrey Rhodes

Congratulations!

You have exemplified the qualities of these values:

- Service Before Self
- Excellence in All We Do

Great job on configuring this example.

You have been recognized by Jeffrey Rhodes

Figure 21-17. *Email when Tell Recipient Who Nominated checked*

The email comes from me and actually shows up in my *Sent Items* in Outlook. It shows up as normal importance due to our change in Figure 21-13.

When I don't check the *Tell Recipient Who Nominated Them* box, there is no email, however. To troubleshoot, we go back to Power Automate and look at our *Run History*. We see that runs where we try to send email with that box unchecked all fail. We click on one of the runs and see there is a white exclamation point inside a red circle for the *Send Email* condition. Figure 21-18 shows what it looks like when we expand the condition.

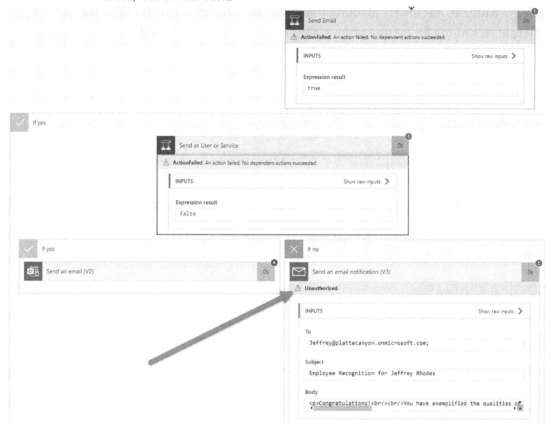

Figure 21-18. *Unauthorized error in sending anonymous email*

Even though this has worked for me in the past, I consistently get this error now. As I mentioned earlier, this is likely due to spam being sent using this connector.

If I were updating this app, I would remove the *Tell Recipient Who Nominated Them* box completely as it didn't do much for the post and chat cases and failed with email. Otherwise, we have a pretty functional application.

Reporting on Employee Recognition in Power BI

The last piece of the puzzle is visualizing the recognition data we shared to our SharePoint list. As we've discussed earlier, we can choose either the 1.0 or 2.0 implementation when connecting to *SharePoint Online Lists*. I tried it both ways in this case since I like retrieving the plain text by expanding *FieldValuesAsText*, which you only get with 1.0. But the Unpivoting that we need gives errors with 1.0, so we use a different technique for getting plain text and use 2.0. Figure 21-19 shows us selecting the Recognition list.

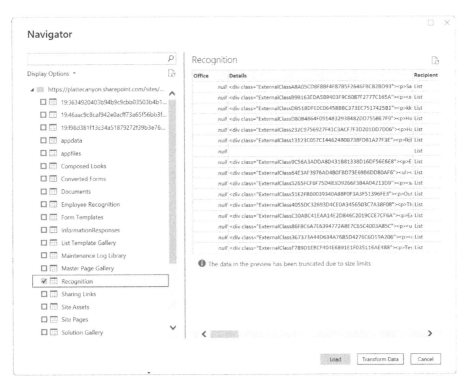

Figure 21-19. *Selecting our SharePoint List Data Source*

Notice how the *Details* column shows HTML rather than the plain text we want.[6] We *Transform data* and do our normal task of renaming columns and ensuring the data types are correct. Since the Recipient column displays as a *Record,* we expand its *title* and *email* columns, as shown in Figure 21-20.

---

[6] There are HTML controls available, but I typically want to display longer text in a *Table* or *Matrix* control rather than have to slice or drill-down into a particular record.

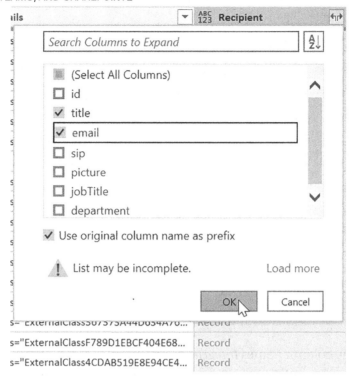

Figure 21-20. *Expanding Recipient into title and email*

We then rename them to *Recipient* and *Recipient Email*. We similarly expand *Created By* into *title* and then rename that column to *Submitter*.

Dealing with our True/False data for our *Values* is more challenging. We want to be able to count the number of recognitions by value and also slice and drill down by value shown. Another way to look at this is that we care about the True values, but not the False ones. To get the data how we want it, we again *unpivot* the data, as shown in Figure 21-21.

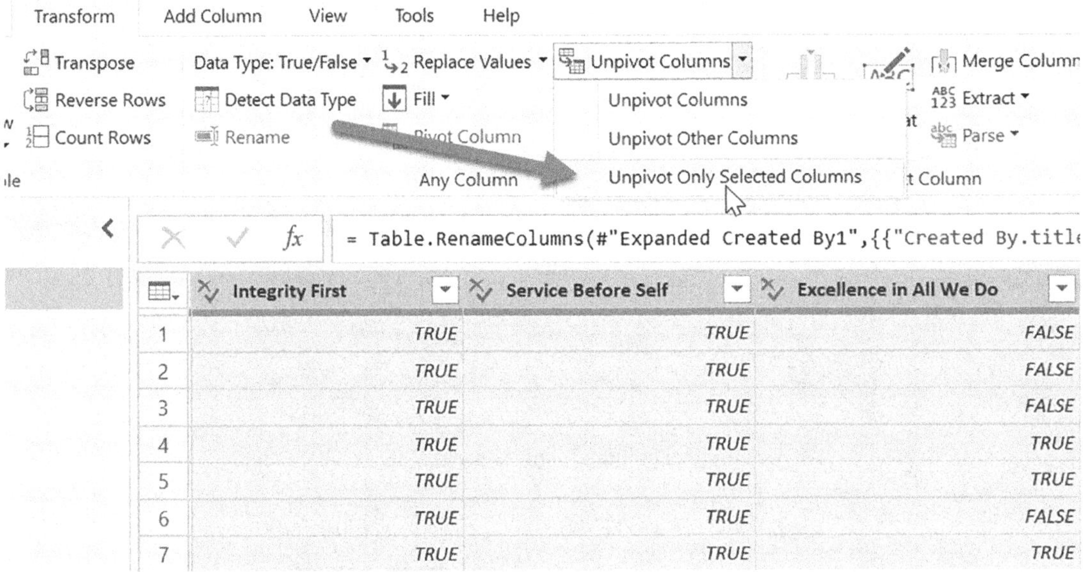

Figure 21-21. *Unpivot Value Columns*

This copies the column name (*Integrity First, Service Before Self,* and *Excellence in All We Do*) to the *Attribute* and then the True or False to the *Value* (Figure 21-22).

ᴬᴮC Attribute		✕⧸ Value	
Integrity First			TRUE
Service Before Self			TRUE
Excellence in All We Do			FALSE
Integrity First			TRUE
Service Before Self			TRUE
Excellence in All We Do			FALSE
Integrity First			TRUE
Service Before Self			TRUE
Excellence in All We Do			FALSE

Figure 21-22. *Attribute and Value columns*

Notice that this expands the number of rows and thus we will need to use *Count (Distinct)* when we get to our visualization. We then rename *Attribute* to *Value* and *Value* to *HasValue*. Since we only care about the True values, we create an *Exemplified Value* conditional column that is True if *HasValue* is True and is otherwise null. Figure 21-23 show the screen for doing this.

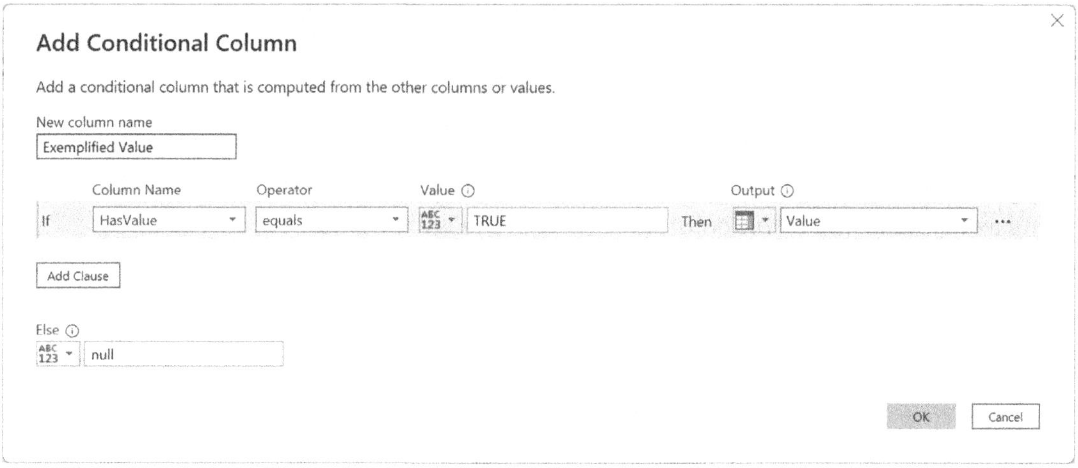

Figure 21-23. *Exemplified Value Conditional Column*

We now can filter out all the null rows,[7] as shown in Figure 21-24.

Figure 21-24. *Filtering out null Exemplified Value rows*

It will likely be useful to compare recognitions over particular time frames like the last 7 or 30 days. So we create a custom *Days Since Submitted* column with this formula:

```
DateTime.From(DateTime.LocalNow()) - [Created]
```

---

[7] We could have skipped the conditional column by renaming *HasValue* to *Exemplified Value* and filtering out False instead of null. But I think the conditional column is easier to understand and test.

337

As with past similar columns, we change the data type to *Whole Number* as we don't care about partial days.

Our last challenge is that our *Details* column still contains HTML (you might want to refer back to Figure 21-19). We start by renaming the column to *Details - HTML*. That will allow us to eventually get to a new column we will call *Details*. Before that, we need to create a custom *DetailsTable* column, as shown in Figure 21-25.

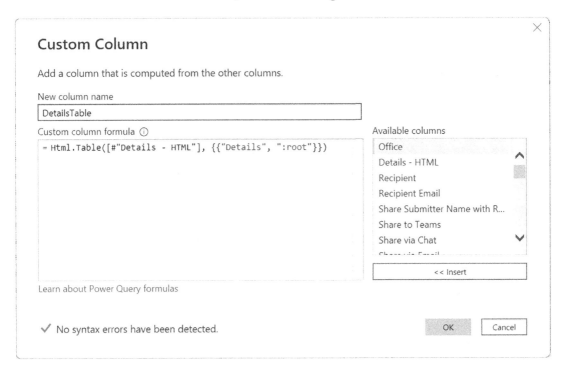

Figure 21-25. *DetailsTable Custom Column*

This uses the powerful *Html.Table()* method and the technique I learned from Dhruvin Shah's video.[8] The first parameter is the HTML itself (our *Details - HTML* column). The second parameter is called *columnNameSelectorPairs*. Since it is a list, we enclose it in {} with each item also in {}. We call the name of the table we will create "Details," which is why that is what we will select in Figure 21-26. Since we want all the text in all the HTML, we use ":root" for the second parameter. If we wanted sections of

---

[8] See www.youtube.com/watch?v=4UDynnPQpG4.

our HTML, we could use specific selectors.[9] Looking again at Figure 21-26, we see that there is a *Table* in each row of our custom column.

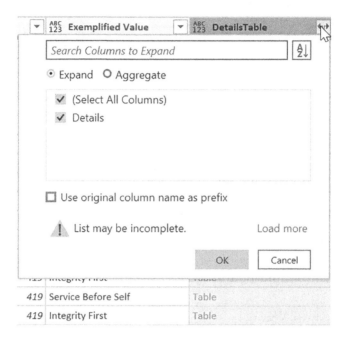

Figure 21-26. *Expanding the Details table*

We expand it and select our *Details* table. This creates a *Details* column that contains the plain text we want.

We are now ready to visualize our data. Our first challenge stems from unpivoting our Values data (see Figure 21-21). Since there are multiple rows now for each value exemplified by the recipient, a *Table* control would have excess data. Instead, we want to use a *Matrix* control, as shown in Figure 21-27.

---

[9] Those of you who use jQuery are likely very familiar with selectors. See the previous edition of this book for more on using jQuery together with SharePoint.

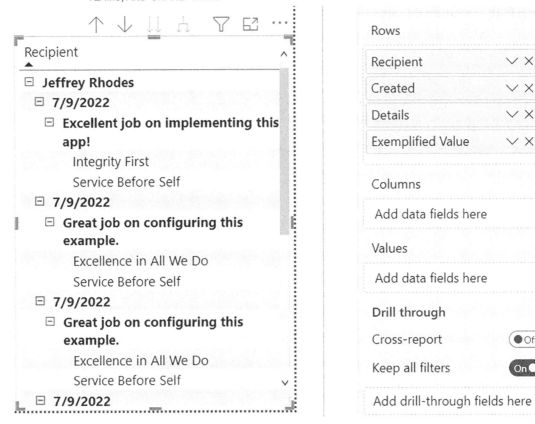

Figure 21-27. *Configuring the Matrix control*

We include *Recipient, Created* (Date), *Details,* and *Exemplified Value.* The order is important since *Exemplified Value* is the one that can have multiple values per submission and thus needs to be last. We expand the *Matrix* to its lowest level so all four columns are displayed. Note that we don't include the *Submitter* in this example, but could easily add this to the control and also create a slicer for it and the Recipient if desired.

Figure 21-28 shows why we unpivoted, filtered, and created our *Exemplified Value* column. We can have a slicer that shows our three possible values as well as both a pie and bar chart that (distinctly) counts number of recognitions for each value.

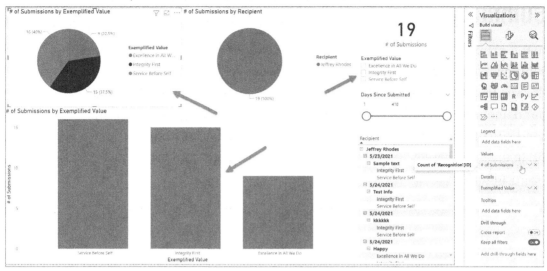

Figure 21-28. *Using Exemplified Value in the visualizations*

Although we have a *Days Since Submitted* slicer, we can duplicate this page and then add a page-level filter to create a *Previous 7 Days* page, as shown in Figure 21-29.

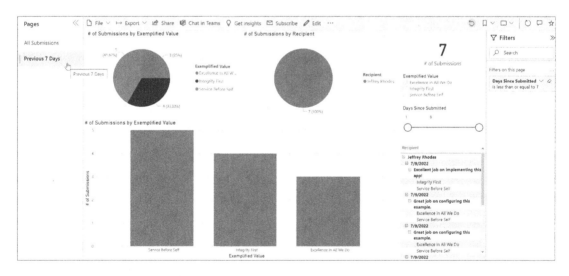

Figure 21-29. *Viewing the previous 7 days of recognition*

Summary

In this chapter, we put all the pieces together to create an Employee Recognition solution. We stored our information in SharePoint, created the user interface and saved the info back to SharePoint in Power Apps (with some special sleight of hand to format our demonstrated values), called a Power Automate flow to post to a Teams channel, send a Teams chat, or and/or send an email, and then visualized the results in Power BI. In the next chapter, we will some of these same pieces and techniques to create a reservations solution.

CHAPTER 22

Creating a Reservations Booking Solution in Power Apps, SharePoint, and Power Automate

This chapter continues our objective of putting multiple pieces of the Microsoft 365 environment together into cohesive solutions. It stemmed from a customer wanting to try the Microsoft Bookings application but that not being approved for use. I suggested using our familiar combination of SharePoint and Power Apps. For our sample here, I added the automatic scheduling of an associated Teams meeting via Power Automate. It has a few advantages over Bookings, such as being able to schedule on behalf of another user and the ability to offer multiple appointments at the same time.

Configuring the SharePoint List

Figure 22-1 shows the SharePoint list where we store our data.

© Jeffrey M. Rhodes 2022
J. M. Rhodes, *Creating Business Applications with Microsoft 365*,
https://doi.org/10.1007/978-1-4842-8823-8_22

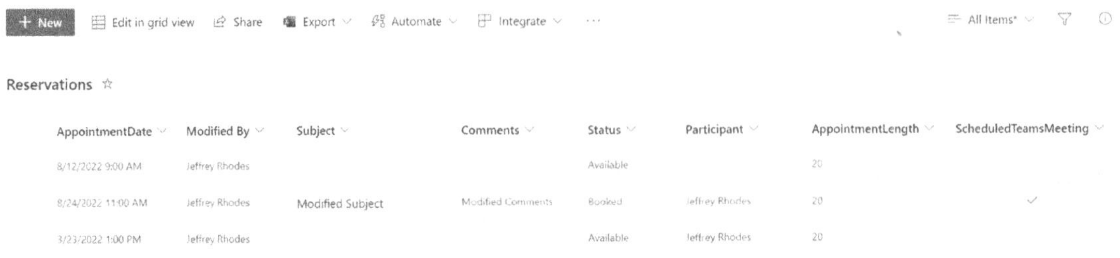

Figure 22-1. *SharePoint list storing reserviation information*

Importantly, we include the time component in our *AppointmentDate* column since the user will be picking from available dates and times. We include *Modified By* in our view since we are going to allow either the person who created the appointment[1] OR the person for whom it was scheduled edit the appointment. We include a Subject and Comments for the user to give some additional detail on what they want to discuss in the reservation. *Status* is a choice column with the default value of *Available*. Our Power App will change it to *Booked* when the appointment is scheduled. If the user cancels, it will put it back to *Available* and clear the *Subject* and *Comments*. We store the *Participant* (Person column) separately so a user can schedule for someone else as mentioned before[2]. We default *AppointmentLength* to 20 (minutes) but preserve the ability to change this value if desired. Finally, we have a *ScheduledTeamsMeeting* Yes/No column. We will use that later with our scheduled Power Automate flow. We will query for all the *Booked* reservations where *ScheduledTeamsMeeting* is *No*. The flow will then schedule the meeting and set this value to *Yes*.

Next on the docket is Power Apps.

Creating our Application in Power Apps

Our first task is to set a variable in during the application's *OnStart* event, as shown in Listing 22-1.

---

[1] You might think this would be the *Created By* column, but the actual list items are created in advance by the person adding all the appointments. So the one who modified the list item is the one who scheduled it.

[2] We'd like to clear the *Participant* as well if an appointment is cancelled, but that is not currently possible from Power Apps. So we just don't show a *Participant* if the *Status* is *Available* and then update the value when the appointment is booked by someone else.

Listing 22-1. OnStart to set initial variables

```
Set(
    varUserEmail,
    User().Email
);
Set(
    varParticipant,
    Blank()
)
```

We will use *varUserEmail* later in determining if there are existing reservations the current user can edit. *varParticipant* is useful in updating the participant as well as showing or hiding our error label. We initialize it to be *Blank()*.

Figure 22-2 shows the *Home* screen of our application.

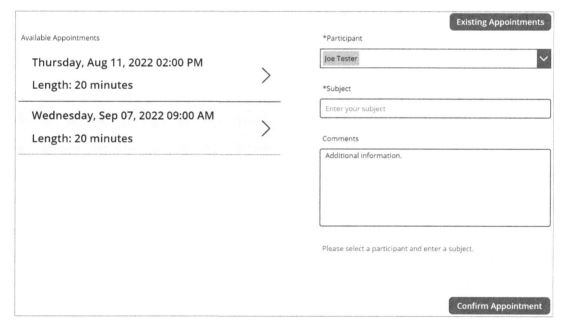

Figure 22-2. *Adding an appointment*

As we have seen in other examples, we use a Gallery control to view and select the available records. In this case, it shows the available appointments. We filter our *Reservations* list to only show available ones in the future by setting the *Items* property:

```
Filter(Reservations, Status.Value = "Available" && AppointmentDate > Now())
```

Note that we need to say *Status.Value* because *Status* is a *Choice* column. We use *Now()* rather than *Today()*, since only the former includes the current time as well as the current date. We display the appointment date and time in the "long" date format we want by using the *DateTimeValue()* method together with the *Text()* method, which has a second parameter to format the date and time in the *Wednesday, Sep 07, 2022 09:00 AM* format. Here is the label's *Text* property:

```
Text(DateTimeValue(ThisItem.AppointmentDate), "dddd, mmm dd, yyyy
hh:mm AM/PM")
```

To give the appointment length value a context, we concatenate it with a label and units in the second label's *Text* property:

```
"Length: " & ThisItem.AppointmentLength & " minutes"
```

To set the entire selected item to yellow, we set the gallery's *TemplateFill* property to:

```
If(ThisItem.IsSelected, Yellow, RGBA(0, 0, 0, 0))
```

When the user selects an appointment slot, we store it in our *varSelectedApt* variable in the gallery's *OnSelect* event:

```
Set(varSelectedApt, Gallery1.Selected)
```

Since we want to reserve our screen real estate for our appointments and for comments, we use a combo box for our participant. We set its *Items* to be:

```
Office365Users.SearchUserV2({searchTerm: ParticipantBox.SearchText,
top:50}).value
```

We call the *SearchUserV2()* method from *Office365Users*, passing in the *SearchText* of the combo box. That method returns a record, but its value is the table that the box wants. We set the *DisplayFields* and *SearchFields* properties to both be *["DisplayName"]* so the user's name displays and searches correctly. We also set *isSearchable* to *true* and *SelectMultiple* to *false*. It will be useful to have the selected user stored in the *varParticipant* variable, which we set in both the combo box's *OnSelect* and *OnChange* events[3]:

```
Set(varParticipant, ParticipantBox.Selected)
```

---

[3] We need *OnChange* as well since it fires when the user removes a user who has already been selected.

We have an *ErrorLabel* to remind the user what they need to do before confirming the appointment. Since we need a participant and a *Subject* as a minimum, we set its *Visible* property to:

```
IsBlank(varParticipant) Or SubjectBox.Text = ""
```

To write our reservation back to the SharePoint list, we use our old friend the *Patch()* method, as shown in Listing 22-2.

Listing 22-2. OnSelect code for the Confirm Appointment button

```
Patch(
    Reservations,
    LookUp(
        Reservations,
        ID = varSelectedApt.ID
    ),
    {
        Subject: SubjectBox.Text,
        Comments: CommentsBox.Text,
        Status: {Value: "Booked"},
        Participant: {
                '@odata.type': "#Microsoft.Azure.Connectors.SharePoint.
                SPListExpandedUser",
                ODataType: Blank(),
                Claims: Concatenate(
                    "i:0#.f|membership|",
                    varParticipant.Mail
                ),
                DisplayName: varParticipant.DisplayName,
                Email: varParticipant.Mail,
                Department: varParticipant.Department,
                JobTitle: varParticipant.JobTitle,
                Picture: ""} ,
                ScheduledTeamsMeeting: false
    }
);
Reset(ParticipantBox);
```

```
Reset(SubjectBox);
Reset(CommentsBox);
Set(
    varParticipant,
    Blank()
)
```

This is less complicated than some of our other examples as we don't need to create any new records. Instead, we use the *LookUp()* method to find the correct SharePoint list item. We then set the *Subject* and *Comments* to the values entered in their respective controls. Setting the *Status* is non-trivial, though, since it is a *Choice* column in SharePoint. We normally just match it to a drop-down box, but in this case we always want to always set it to *Booked*. I originally tried to create a variable from a hidden drop-down box, but that was strangely unreliable. Luckily, a quick search found the proper *{Value: "Booked"}* syntax. We've covered how to update a SharePoint *Person* column, so we won't cover it again here other than to note how we took advantage of our *varParticipant* variable. The *ScheduledTeamsMeeting* column should already be false, but we set it that way to be on the safe side. We don't set *AppointmentLength* since that is part of the appointment and not set in our design by the person scheduling. We *Reset()* our controls so they are empty if the user selects another appointment or returns after editing an appointment. We also set our *varParticipant* to *Blank()* to be sure that it doesn't persist now that we have cleared the combo box where we set it.

Our design is to only show the *Existing Appointments* button if the user has a future appointment. So we set its *Visible* property, as shown in Listing 22-3.

Listing 22-3. Visible property for the Existing Appointment button

```
With(
    {
        ds: Filter(
            Reservations,
            ((Participant.Email = varUserEmail || 'Modified By'.
            Email = varUserEmail) && Status.Value = "Booked" &&
            AppointmentDate > Now())
        )
    },
    CountRows(ds) > 0
)
```

This is a bit different than our normal syntax, but my original formulation[4] was subject to delegation issues. Instead, we use the *With()* function to evaluate our filter and treat it as a single record. As we described in the last section, we want for either the participant or the person who made the reservation to be able to edit it. Since both *Participant* and *Modified By* are *Person* columns, we can get their *Email* property and compare it to the current user's email. We also wanted our *Status* to be *Booked* and for the appointment to be in the future.

When the user clicks the *Existing Appointments* button, we want to go to the *ModifyAppointment* screen and thus have this in its *OnSelect* event:

```
Navigate(ModifyAppointment)
```

Figure 22-3 shows the resulting screen.

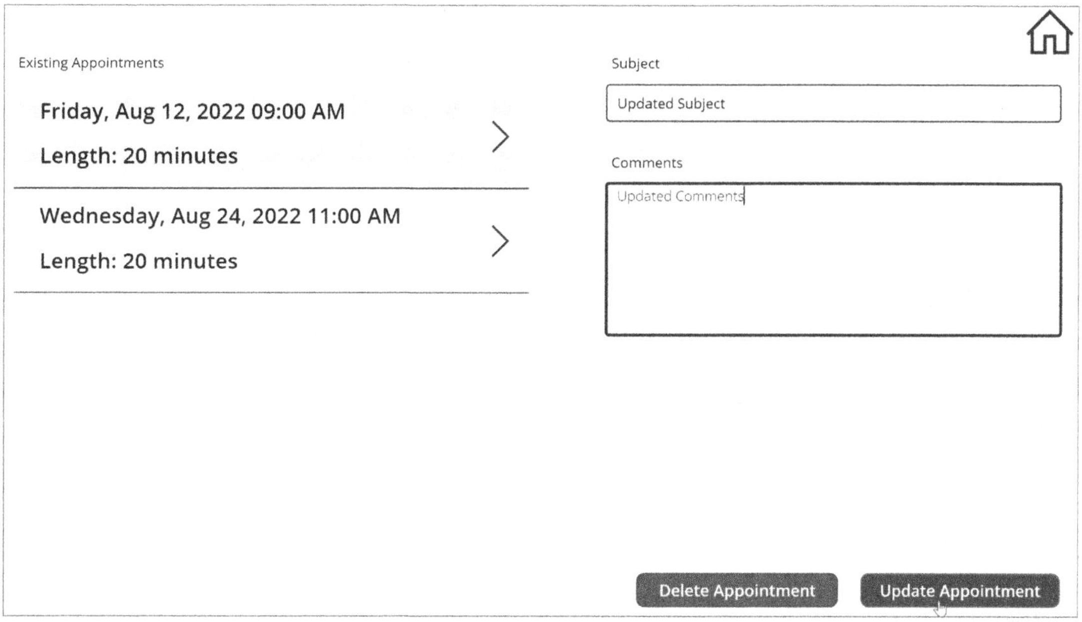

Figure 22-3. *Updating or deleting an appointment*

---

[4] I originally used the *CountIf()* method:

```
CountIf(
    Reservations,
    ((Participant.Email = varUserEmail || 'Modified By'.Email = varUserEmail)
&& Status.Value = "Booked" && AppointmentDate Now())
)>0
```

Our gallery's *Items* property uses the same *Filter()* as our *Existing Appointments*
button to get future appointments for which the user is either the participant or the one
to set up the appointment:

```
Filter(
    Reservations,
    (Participant.Email = varUserEmail || 'Modified By'.Email =
varUserEmail) && Status.Value = "Booked" && AppointmentDate > Now()
)
```

As is our standard practice, we set a variable[5] in the *OnSelect* event when the user
picks an appointment:

```
Set(varSelectedModifiedApt, ExistingAptsGallery.Selected)
```

Since the user can edit the existing *Subject* or *Comments*, we link their *Default*
properties to the selected appointment:

```
varSelectedModifiedApt.Subject
```

and

```
varSelectedModifiedApt.Comments
```

This will display the existing values that the user can then edit if desired. This is
helpful as we will write the contents of these boxes back to the appointment (even if they
haven't changed).

The rest of the logic is in the two buttons. Listing 22-4 shows the *OnSelect* code for
the *Delete Appointment* button.

Listing 22-4. OnSelect code for the Delete Appointment button

```
Patch(
    Reservations,
    LookUp(
        Reservations,
        ID = varSelectedModifiedApt.ID
```

---

[5] Be sure this is a different variable than the one used on the *Home* screen and that you use this
new variable in our *Delete Appointment* and *Update Appointment* buttons. Otherwise, this will
cause hard-to-find errors.

```
    ),
    {
        Subject: "",
        Comments: "",
        Status: {Value: "Available"},
        ScheduledTeamsMeeting: false
    }
);
Navigate(Home)
```

We want to *Patch()* the selected appointment by clearing its *Subject* and *Comments*, setting its *Status* back to *Available*, and setting *ScheduledTeamsMeeting* to false. We'd like to clear the *Participant* as well, but that is not currently possible. But since we will write a new *Participant* when the appointment is rescheduled, we should be fine.[6] We then navigate back to the *Home* screen.

The logic for the *Update Appointment* button is similar, as shown in Listing 22-5.

Listing 22-5. OnSelect code for the Update Appointment button

```
Patch(
    Reservations,
    LookUp(
        Reservations,
        ID = varSelectedModifiedApt.ID
    ),
    {
        Subject: UpdatedSubjectBox.Text,
        Comments: UpdatedCommentsBox.Text
    }
);
Navigate(Home)
```

We update both the *Subject* and the *Comments* and then return to the *Home* screen.

---

[6] We just need to be careful in our Power BI reporting to only display *Participant* if the *Status* of an appointment is *Booked*.

We are now ready to go to Power Automate to schedule a Teams meeting for each booked appointment.

Adding a Scheduled Flow in Power Automate

While we could have launched Power Automate from within our application, in this case, it makes more sense to have a scheduled flow, as shown in Figure 22-4, perhaps every day at 5 AM.

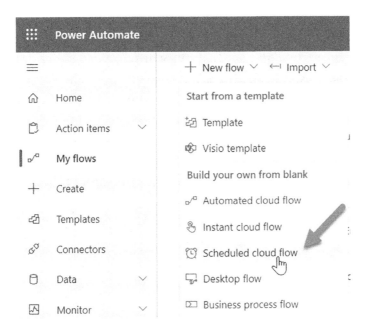

Figure 22-4. *Creating a Scheduled cloud flow*

That will minimize the rework if the user cancels or changes the appointment the same day. While we will schedule a Teams meeting for each future appointment, we could add additional logic to only schedule meetings one week or some other time frame before the appointment. Figure 22-5 shows how we set the frequency and the time for the flow to run.

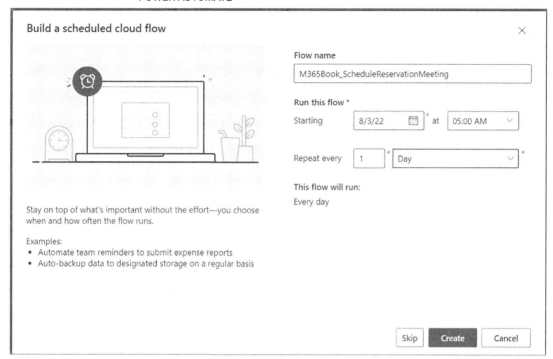

Figure 22-5. *Scheduled cloud flow settings*

After setting up this recurrence, we go to the SharePoint connector and configure the *Get items* action, as shown in Figure 22-6.

Figure 22-6. *Calling the Get items SharePoint action*

We configure the *Site Address* and *List Name* to match our connection in Power
Apps. We then need to click *Show advanced options* in order to choose which items we
want. We do that by entering an Open Data Protocol (OData) filter query, as shown in
Figure 22-7.

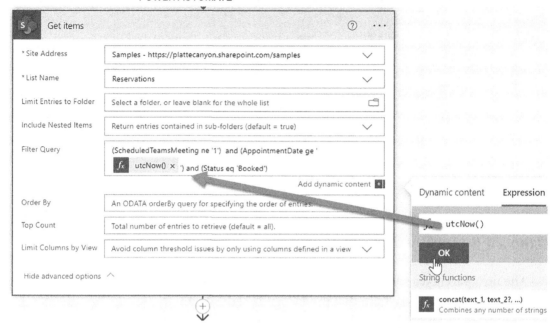

Figure 22-7. *Configuring the Filter Query in our Get items query*

This has a different syntax than what for many of us is a more familiar Standard Query Language (SQL) query, but the concepts are the same. In words, we want to find the list items that have been booked, are in the future, and have not already been scheduled as Teams meetings. Here is the text of the OData query:

```
(ScheduledTeamsMeeting ne '1') and (AppointmentDate ge '@{utcNow()}') and
(Status eq 'Booked')
```

ne means "not equals," *ge* means "greater than or equals," and *eq* means "equals." Notice also how a 1 represents *true* and a 0 represents *false*. We use the Expression window in Figure 22-7 to insert the *utcNow()* method to dynamically insert the current time in Universal Time Coordinated (UTC) format (previously known as Greenwich Mean Time). Since our *AppointmentDate* value from SharePoint includes a time zone component, Power Automate gets the math right on whether the time is in the future. We could include an OData *Order By* value, but we are going to process all the list items we get and thus the order does not matter.

We next need to loop through all the list items that are returned by the query. As shown in Figure 22-8, we do this with the *Apply to each* action and use the *values* attribute, which is the list of the SharePoint items.

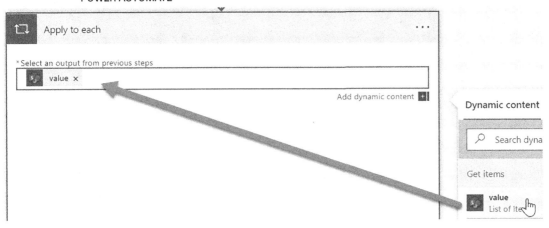

Figure 22-8. *Apply to each loop through the SharePoint list items*

The next part takes some trial and error. The *AppointmentDate* value from the list items at first looks to be right in that the format is of this form[7]:

2022-08-24T17:00:00Z

But using this value directly when we schedule the Teams meeting causes an error. Instead, we use the *Compose* action, as shown in Figure 22-9, and then use the *formatDateTime()* expression.

Figure 22-9. *Formatting the start date and time*

Getting the syntax for the *AppointmentDate* is not trivial:

---

[7] You can see the output by using the *Compose* action and putting the column(s) as the input and then looking at the value in the *Run history*.

```
formatDateTime(items('Apply_to_each')['AppointmentDate'], 'yyyy-MM-
ddTHH:mm')
```

The key part is *items('Apply_to_each')*. This will be the name of the loop and could
by 'Apply_to_each2' or a similar name. The second parameter is the date format, which
means four-digit year, two-digit month, two-digit date, time zone, two-digit hour in a
24-hour format, and two-digit minute. Looking at our Run history, the output of our
Compose action is:

```
2022-08-24T17:00
```

So what we needed to get rid of was the seconds and the Z (which means the time
zone is UTC).

We similarly need the ending date and time of our meeting. We again use the
Compose action, as shown in Figure 22-10.

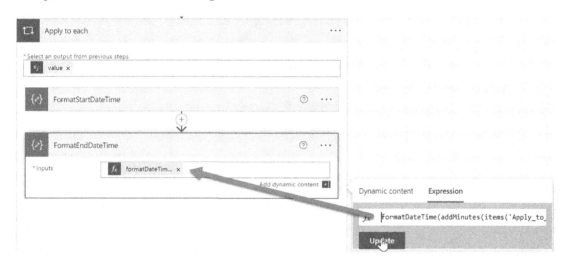

Figure 22-10. *Formatting the end date and time using the addMinutes method*

We again use the *formatDateTime()* expression but also add in the *addMinutes()*
expression to incorporate our *AppointmentLength* column:

```
formatDateTime(addMinutes(items('Apply_to_each')['AppointmentDate'],
int(items('Apply_to_each')['AppointmentLength'])), 'yyyy-MM-ddTHH:mm')
```

Notice how we have to also use the *int()* method to format the value as an integer.
That gives us a value that looks like this:

2022-08-24T17:20

We are now finally ready to schedule our meeting. We select the *Create a Teams
meeting* action and choose our primary *Calendar* from the list of available calendars.
Figure 22-11 shows how we use the *Participant Display Name* value from our SharePoint
list item in the *Subject* of the meeting.

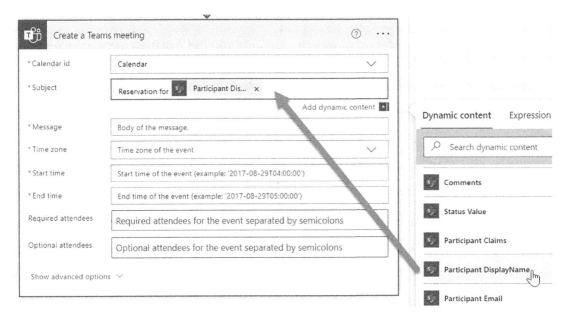

Figure 22-11. *Setting the Teams Meeting Subject*

We use a similar technique (Figure 22-12) to add the *Subject, Comments, Participant,*
and *Scheduled By* to the *Message* of the meeting.

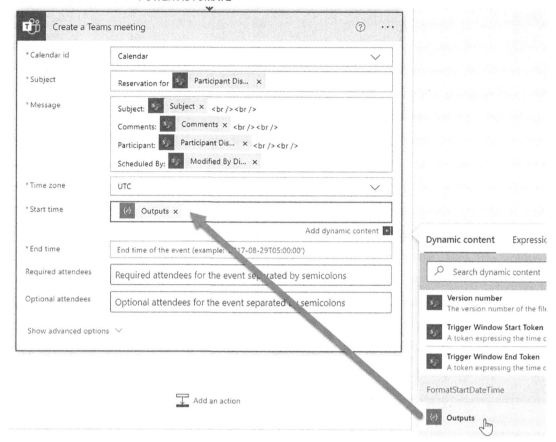

Figure 22-12. *Setting the Teams Meeting Message and Start Time*

Notice how we use the HTML Line Break (*
*) to get hard returns in the message. We use the *Outputs* from our *Compose* action (Figure 22-9) for the *Start time* and do the same for the *End time* (see Figure 22-13).

Our last scheduling task is to add our *Participant Email* as a *Required Attendee,* as shown in Figure 22-13.

Figure 22-13. *Setting the Teams Meeting Required attendee*

Now that we have scheduled the meeting, we need to make sure the next time the
flow runs that it doesn't try to schedule another one. To do that, we need to use the
SharePoint *Update item* action to set the *ScheduledTeamsMeeting* column to *Yes,* as
shown in Figure 22-14.

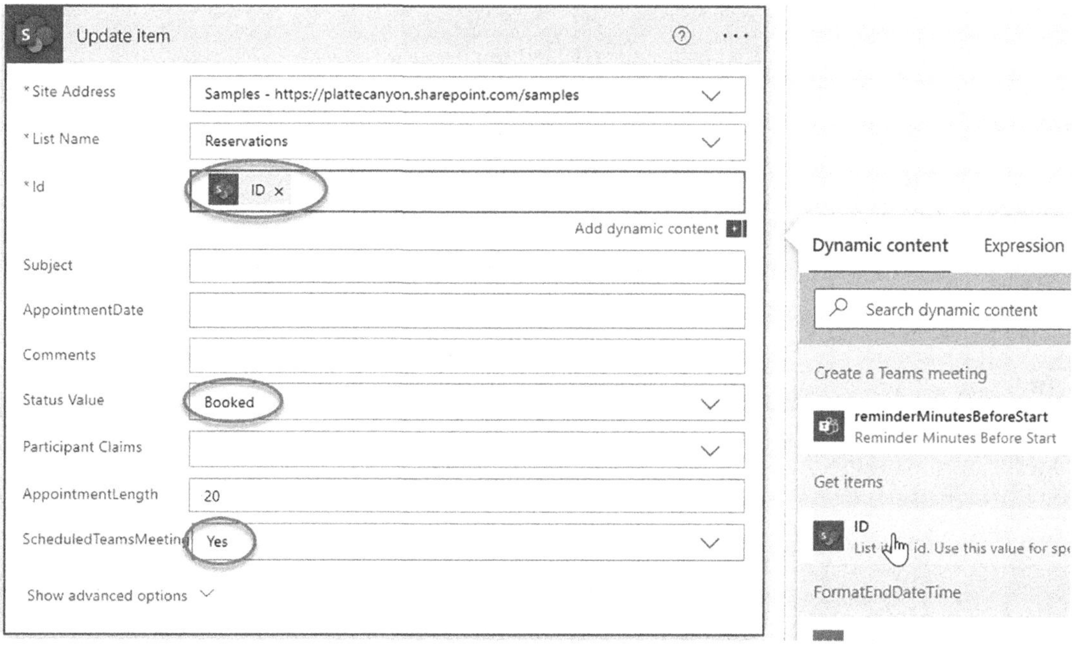

Figure 22-14. *Updating the SharePoint Item to set ScheduledTeamsMeeting to Yes*

Notice how use the *ID* from our *Get items* action (within our loop) in order to make
sure we are editing the right item. We set the *Status* to *Booked* just to be on the safe side
and then set *ScheduledTeamsMeeting* to *Yes.*

We did it! Figure 22-15 shows an example of our scheduled Teams meeting.

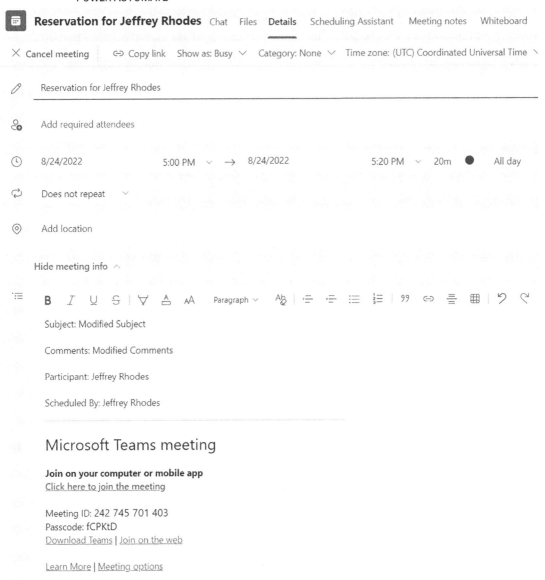

Figure 22-15. *Scheduled Teams Meeting reservation*

This solution doesn't cancel the meeting if the user cancels the reservation in our
Power App, but that would be a good enhancement. We could also easily connect Power
BI to our SharePoint list to make a dashboard showing appointments, what percentage of
available appointments were booked, and much more.

Summary

In this chapter, we connected Power Apps to SharePoint to keep track of appointment reservations. We incorporated some specialized logic to allow either the submitter or the person with the registration to edit or cancel their reservations. We then used the ability of Power Automate to do scheduled flows to automatically create Teams Meetings for the appointments. To pull this off, we learned how to do OData filter queries so that we could limit to just those appointments without a Teams Meeting as well as some gyrations around date and time formats. We then updated our SharePoint list to reflect that the meetings had been scheduled so we could avoid duplicates. In the next chapter, we will dig into Power Apps Forms control for more sophisticated adding and editing of data.

CHAPTER 23

Using the Power Apps Form Control to Create a Weekly Priorities Status Report

In this chapter, we focus on using Power Apps to add, edit, or copy status report data. Since we need to detect whether there are any changes and prompt the user, we use the built-in form control (which has an *Unsaved* property) rather than the *Patch()* method we have used in other applications. This example came from trying to update a process where each organization sent a weekly Excel spreadsheet of priorities to a person who then had to consolidate them into a single view for leadership. Our CIO saw this and asked me to come up with a better way.

Designing the SharePoint List

Since you have gotten this far, it is probably not a surprise that I chose SharePoint lists to store our data. Not only is SharePoint easy and cheap[1], but the ability for the organizer to make minor edits like fixing typos directly in SharePoint makes the solution much easier to manage. Since we are including information from different entities within the organization, we want a mechanism to control what information a particular user is allowed to view and edit. We do this with an *AuthorizedUsers* list as shown in Figure 23-1.

---

[1] There are often license considerations of going to the Dataverse or using premium connectors to connect to database instances in Azure or on-premise.

© Jeffrey M. Rhodes 2022
J. M. Rhodes, *Creating Business Applications with Microsoft 365*,
https://doi.org/10.1007/978-1-4842-8823-8_23

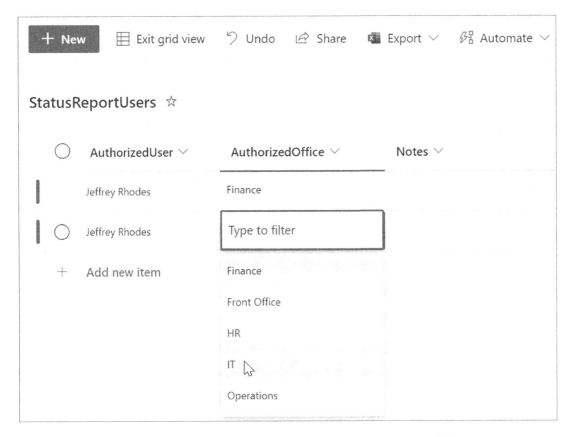

Figure 23-1. *The StatusReportUsers list controlling which office(s) a user can view or edit*

We have *AuthorizedUser* (Person), *AuthorizedOffice* (Choice), and *Notes* (Text) columns. We will compare this list to the logged-in user once we get to Power Apps.

The data is stored in a second list named *StatusReport* (Figure 23-2).

StatusReport ☆							
Title ∨	Office ∨	StatusWeekStar... ∨	Description ∨	Target Date ∨	Percentage Co... ∨	PriorityNumber ∨	Attachments ∨
Purchase Equipment	Finance	7/25/2022	Here is some description info	8/18/2022	30	3	
Test 2	Finance	8/1/2022					∥

Figure 23-2. *StatusReport SharePoint list*

In our simplified example, we have a *Title*, *Office*, *StatusWeekStartDate*, *Description*, *Target Date*, *Percentage Complete*, and *PriorityNumber*. I named the columns before I built the Power Apps solution. But if I had thought it through, I would name the

SharePoint columns to exactly match the labels I wanted in Power Apps, since editing the labels when using the Form control requires unlocking the associated data card (which we'd rather not do). It turns out that we need to unlock *StatusWeekStartDate* anyway, so I could change its display to *Week*, but I left *PriorityNumber* instead of unlocking to edit to *Priority Number*. The only surprising data type is for *StatusWeekStartDate*. The design is for that to be the Monday at the start of each week. I originally had it as a *Date* column, but working with it in Power Apps was easier changing it to a *Text* type. We still convert it back to a date when we get to Power BI.

Let's now move to Power Apps.

The Home Screen in Power Apps

We connect our two SharePoint lists as data sources in the normal way. Our next task is to come up with which offices the current user is authorized for (I decided to account for the possibility that one person might have multiple offices to view/edit). Then we need to determine the previous Monday, the current Monday, and the upcoming Monday, since my initial design was that the user could only view/edit last week's, the current week's, and next week's data. The main point of viewing the previous week's is to allow the user to copy a priority to the current week or the upcoming week. Figure 23-3 shows the opening screen with no data yet for the *office* and *week* combination.

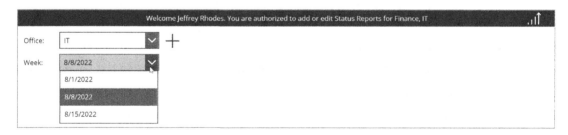

Figure 23-3. *Status Report application showing previous, current, and next weeks*

We initialize the authorized offices, weeks, and other key variables in the *OnStart* event, as shown in Listing 23-1.

Listing 23-1. OnStart to set initial variables

```
// Build collection of previous and next week for adding new entries
ClearCollect(
    colWeeksList,
    ForAll(
        Sequence(
            3,
            -1,
            1
        ) As DD,
        DateAdd(
            DateAdd(
                Today(),
                -Weekday(
                    Today(),
                    Monday
                ) + 1
            ),
            7 * DD.Value,
            Days
        )
    )
);
// Build collection of Program Offices authorized to view/edit
Clear(colAuthorizedOffices);
ForAll(
    Filter(
        StatusReportUsers,
        AuthorizedUser.Email = User().Email
    ),
    Collect(
        colAuthorizedOffices,
        {Office: AuthorizedOffice}
    )
);
```

```
Set(
    isAuthorizedUser,
    CountRows(colAuthorizedOffices) > 0
);
Set(
    varShowCopy,
    false
)
```

Coming with just the two weeks is pretty involved, but finding the code only took a short search. As we have seen previously, *ClearCollect() deletes any existing values users all the code insides its parentheses to add items to the collection.* The *ForAll()* and *Sequence()* combination is a way to loop a specified number of times, in this case, we loop three times, starting with -1, with a step of 1.[2] Note how we store the current value as *DD* so we can reference it later. The second parameter of *ForAll()* is the formula we want to run. Working from the inside, this code gives us the number (1–7) of the current date, specifying that the week starts on a Monday (the default is Sunday):

```
Weekday(
                Today(),
                Monday
          )
```

So this will be 1 if today is a Monday, 2 if it is a Tuesday, etc. Moving out a level, the *DateAdd()* function takes the first parameter, *Today()*, and adds or subtracts the second parameter's number of days:

```
            DateAdd(
                Today(),
                -Weekday(
                    Today(),
                    Monday
```

---

[2] Those of you familiar with Visual Basic syntax would write this as:

```
For index = -1 to 2 Step 1
        ' code here
Next
```

```
    ) + 1
)
```

Since there is a minus on the *Weekday()* function and then we add one, this will be
DateAdd(Today(), 0) on a Monday, *DateAdd(Today(), -1)* on a Tuesday, *DateAdd(Today(),
-2)* on a Wednesday, and so forth. So it will always return the Monday of the current week.
We move out one more level and see where the *Sequence()* value finally comes in:

```
DateAdd(
    DateAdd(
        Today(),
        -Weekday(
            Today(),
            Monday
        ) + 1
    ),
    7 * DD.Value,
    Days
)
```

DD.Value will be -1 the first time through the loop, so this will give us the previous
Monday. The next time it will be 0, so we will get the Monday of our current week. We
run it one more time to get the Monday of next week as well. If we wanted to go two
weeks out, we would just change our sequence to be *Sequence(4, -1, 1)*.

Getting our authorized offices is easier. We *Clear()* it first and then use *ForAll()* again.
Its first parameter is a table. We filter *StatusReportUsers* (see Figure 23-1) to see any
values where its *AuthorizedUser.Email* matches the current user's email. For each row in
this table, we add to the *colAuthorizedOffices* collection and store the *AuthorizedOffice*
as the *Office* column. From there, we set an *isAuthorizedUser* variable based on whether
colAuthorizedOffices has any rows.

Finally, we initialize the *varShowCopy* to be false. We will use this later to show an
interface for copying a priority report to the same or different week/office combination.

Referring to Figure 23-3, we set the *Text* of our top label to display the user and the
allowed office(s):

```
"Welcome " & User().FullName & ". You are authorized to add or edit Status
Reports for " & Left(Concat(
```

```
    colAuthorizedOffices,
    Office.Value & ", "
), Len(Concat(
    colAuthorizedOffices,
    Office.Value & ", "
)) - 2)
```

This is a little more involved than you might expect since the *Concat()* method takes all the items in the first parameter (*colAuthorizedOffices*) and applies the formula in the second parameter (*Office.Value* & " "). So that would give us a result like:

```
Finance, IT,
```

Since we don't want the trailing comma, we use the *Left()* function to return the number of characters (*Len()*) minus the two extra characters (comma and the space).

At the upper right, we have a button for displaying a filtered Power BI dashboard of our priorities. Its *OnSelect* code is:

```
If(ReportForm.Unsaved, false, Navigate(Dashboard))
```

We check the *Unsaved* property of our form so that we don't leave our screen when there are unsaved changes. If all is good, we navigate to our *Dashboard* screen.

For the *Office* drop-down box, we set its *Items* to:

```
Distinct(colAuthorizedOffices, Office.Value)
```

Distinct() is similar to *ForAll()* in that both return a table of the first parameter using the formula in the second parameter. *Distinct()* has the advantage here of not showing an office twice in case duplicate entries are made for the user.

For the *Weeks* drop-down box, we set its Items to:

```
colWeeksList
```

For both boxes, we want to make sure the first item of the gallery we use for displaying priority items has its first row selected when we change values. So we set their *OnChange* and *OnSelect* code to be:

```
If(
    CountRows(ReportsGallery.AllItems) > 0,
    Select(
```

```
    ReportsGallery,
    1
  )
)
```

We check to make sure the gallery has at least one item and, if so, select its first item.[3]

Once we add a form for adding or editing records, it will be important that we don't let the user change the Office or Week until the current record is saved or canceled. To do that, we change the drop-down boxes into *View* mode when there are unsaved changes by setting the *DisplayMode* property to:

```
If(ReportForm.Unsaved, DisplayMode.View, DisplayMode.Edit)
```

You can jump ahead to Figure 23-5 to see the boxes in *View* mode if desired.

Figure 23-4 shows the form with three priority records for the *Office* and *Week* combination.

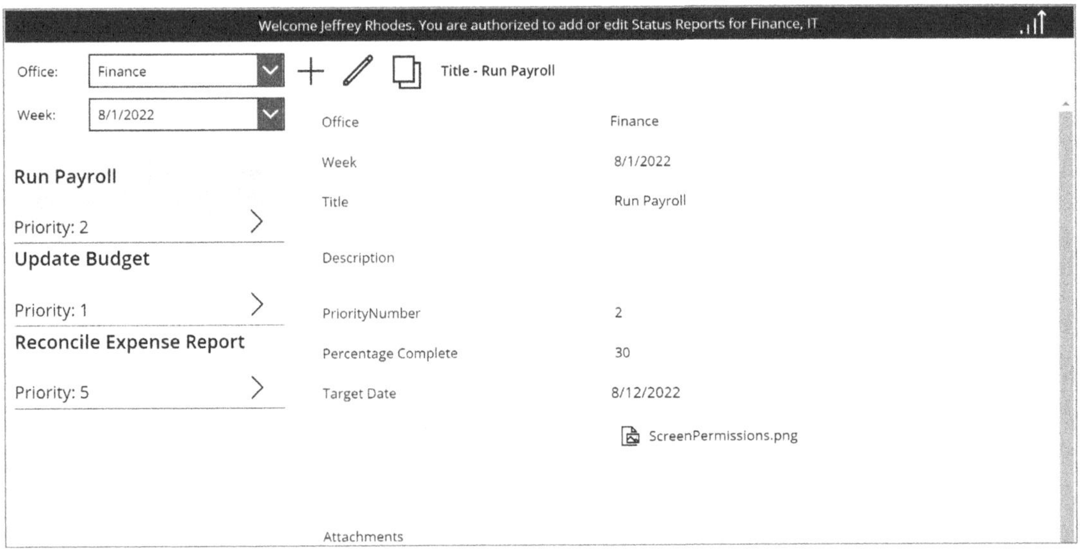

Figure 23-4. *Status Report with a priority in view mode*

---

[3] The gallery will select the first item on its own, but it WON'T call its own *OnSelect* method in that case. We need that code to run since it has quite a bit of logic in it, particularly the setting of the *varCurrentItem* variable we use in our form.

We add a gallery on the left side, a form control[4] to the right, and various button icons and a label at the top. For the *Items* of our *ReportsGallery*, it is important to sort them so the newest record is first. This helps when it comes time to add new records.

```
Sort(
    Filter(
        StatusReport,
        Office.Value = OfficeDropDown.Selected.Result,
        StatusWeekStartDate = Text(WeeksDropDown.Selected.Value)
    ),
    Modified,
    Descending
)
```

We filter our *StatusReport* list to match the *Office* and the *Week*. Since we made our *StatusWeekStartDate* column text, we convert the *WeeksDropDown.Selected.Value* date to text with the *Text()* function. We then *Sort()* it by *Modified* in *Descending* order so the newest is at the top as we want.

As in other examples, we show our selected item in yellow by setting the *TemplateFill* property to be

```
If(ThisItem.IsSelected, Yellow, RGBA(0, 0, 0, 0))
```

We use the gallery to interact with the *Form* control on the right side of Figure 23-4. To make the selection of the gallery properly match the state of the form, we set the *Default* property of the gallery to the *varGalleryDefault* variable.[5]

Due to the interaction with the form control, the gallery's OnSelect code is more complex than normal (Listing 23-2).

Listing 23-2. OnSelect code for ReportsGallery control

```
If(
    ReportForm.Unsaved,
    Notify(
```

---

[4] Either *Edit* or *Display* form type is fine as we will be setting the mode programmatically anyway.
[5] The interaction between the gallery and the form is a bit challenging to get right. I highly recommend Reza Dorrani's excellent "Power Apps Gallery Edit Form Tutorial for Beginners" video at www.youtube.com/watch?v=HHXKfB1iAH4.

```
        "You have unsaved changes. Please either save or cancel your
        changes before moving to a new item.",
        NotificationType.Warning
    );
    Set(
        varGalleryDefault,
        varCurrentItem
    ),
    Set(
        varCurrentItem,
        ThisItem
    );
    ResetForm(ReportForm);
    ViewForm(ReportForm)
)
```

Our first task is to make sure we don't change items if the user has made any changes to the record. Fortunately, the form control has an *Unsaved* property that we can check. If it is true, we use the *Notify()* method to tell the user she has unsaved changes that either need to be canceled or saved. We show it in yellow with the *Warning* parameter. We set the *varGalleryDefault* value to be our *varCurrentItem* variable.[6] This has the effect of leaving the user on the current item and not letting them leave. If the record has not changed, we set *varCurrentItem* to *ThisItem*. We then initialize the form by resetting it and putting it in view mode with the *ViewForm(ReportForm)* syntax.

Going across the top of the screen, our *New* button has this *OnSelect* code:

```
ResetForm(ReportForm);
NewForm(ReportForm);
Set(
    varGalleryDefault,
    Blank()
);
Set(
```

---

[6] *varCurrentItem* was set to the item we are on either initially (via the *Select()* call from our drop-down boxes) or when they selected this item the previous time around (e.g., before they made any changes).

```
    varGalleryDefault,
    {}
)
```

The first part is similar to the end of Listing 23-2, except we call *NewForm()* rather than *ViewForm()* so the form is ready for a new record. Since that record won't show up in the gallery until we save it, we don't want anything the gallery selected. That was the point of making its *Default* property be the *varGalleryDefault* variable. But we need to trick Power Apps by changing it to a different value (*Blank()*) before changing it to an empty record (*{}*). Figure 23-5 shows the result.

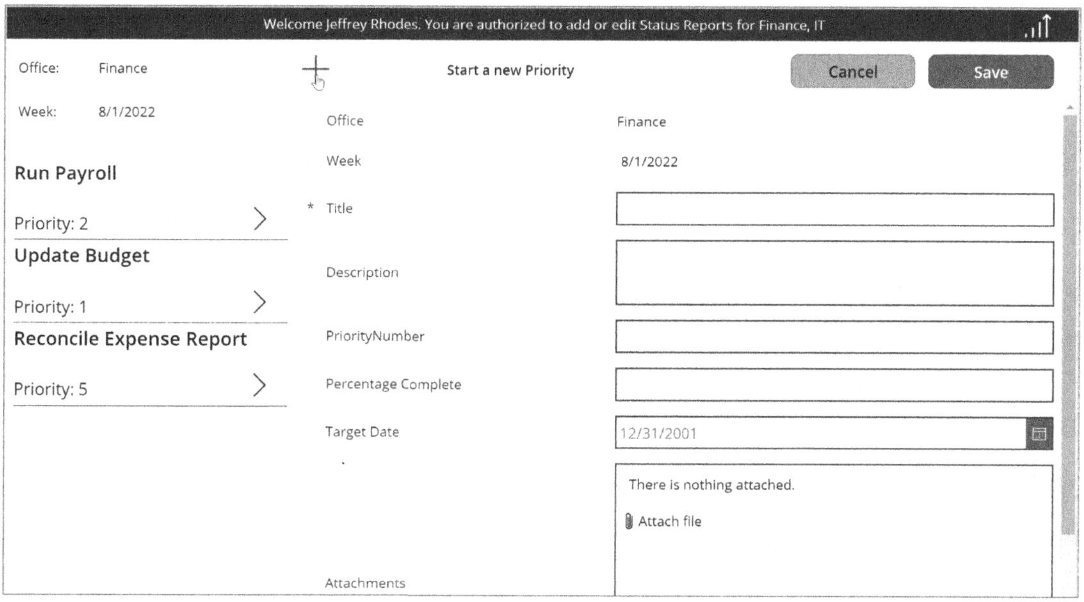

Figure 23-5. *New Status Report record*

Notice how there is no selection in the gallery, how the *Edit* and *Copy* buttons have disappeared, the text of the label says *Start a new Priority*, and how the *Cancel* and *Save* buttons have appeared. The form is editable except for *Office* and *Week*, which have taken the values of their drop-down boxes at the upper left of the form.

The *Edit* button's *Visible* property is set to:

```
(CountRows(ReportsGallery.AllItems) > 0 && !IsBlank(ReportsGallery.
Selected)) && ReportForm.Mode <> New
```

This first checks to see if the gallery has any records and if it has a selection (since we don't want to edit if there are no records or not one selected). We also check to make sure we are not in a new form (since the form is already editable). The *Edit* button's *OnSelect* is:

```
If(
    ReportForm.Unsaved,
    false,
    If(
        ReportForm.Mode = FormMode.Edit,
        ResetForm(ReportForm);
        ViewForm(ReportForm),
        ResetForm(ReportForm);
        EditForm(ReportForm)
    )
)
```

We don't do anything (return *false*) if there are currently unsaved changes in the form. Otherwise, it acts as a toggle. If the form is already editable, we change it back to view. If not, we change it to editable.

We will come back to the *Copy* button and its functionality later. For the label, we set its *Text* based on the Mode of the form:

```
If(ReportForm.Mode = FormMode.New, "Start a new Priority", "Title - " &
ReportsGallery.Selected.Title)
```

If the *Mode* is *New*, we set it to "Start a new Priority." Otherwise, we display the current record's Title.

For the Cancel button, we set is Visible to:

```
(ReportForm.DisplayMode = Edit And ReportForm.Unsaved)
```

If the form is editable[7] and there are unsaved changes, the button is visible. Its *OnSelect* code just resets the form, discarding any unsaved changes:

```
ResetForm(ReportForm)
```

---

[7] Notice that since we checked *DisplayMode* and not *Mode*, this covers both the *NewForm()* and *EditForm()* cases.

The *Save* button has similar code. Its *Visible* is:

```
ReportForm.DisplayMode = Edit
```

So any time there is a new form or the current record is being edited, the button displays. Its OnSelect code submits the form to save any changes to the record back to SharePoint.

```
SubmitForm(ReportForm)
```

Moving down to our form control, Figure 23-6 shows its key settings.

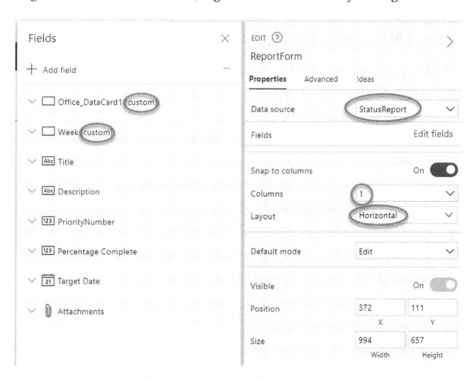

Figure 23-6. *Key settings of our form control*

We set our *Data source* to our *StatusReport* SharePoint list. The form will then automatically add controls for each column in the list. We set the layout to be a single column and *Horizontal* to maximize its readability as shown back in Figure 23-4. We don't want *Office* or *Week* to be editable since we want them to take the values from their corresponding drop-down box. So we unlock those, which is why they show *(Custom)* next to their names. This allows us to change their *DisplayMode* property from *Parent. DisplayMode* to *DisplayMode.View*. That keeps them from being editable. To have them take their values from their drop-down boxes, we change their *Default* property from *ThisItem.Office* or *ThisItem.StatusWeekStartDate* to:

```
If(ReportForm.Mode = FormMode.New, OfficeDropDown.SelectedText,
ThisItem.Office)
```

and

```
If(ReportForm.Mode = FormMode.New, Text(WeeksDropDown.Selected.Value),
ThisItem.StatusWeekStartDate)
```

If this is a new priority, we grab the value from the drop-down box. Otherwise, we stick link back to our data source. Our last change for the Week is to edit its DisplayName from *DataSourceInfo([@StatusReport],DataSourceInfo.DisplayName," StatusWeekStartDate ")* to be simply *"Week".*[8]

See Figure 23-5 for an example of all these properties in action.

For the rest of the form fields, we can choose among the available control types. Figure 23-7 shows how we set *Description* to be *multi-line*, for example.

---

[8] Since this is only possible if we unlock the card, it is best to name your SharePoint columns how you want your labels to be displayed (e.g., with spaces), as mentioned earlier.

Figure 23-7. *Editing the Description data card to be mult-line*

A key piece of functionality I wanted to add was the ability to copy a record from one office/week combination to another. A common use case would be a priority that spans multiple weeks and perhaps even gets a higher priority number as the target date approaches. Figure 23-8 shows this functionality in action.

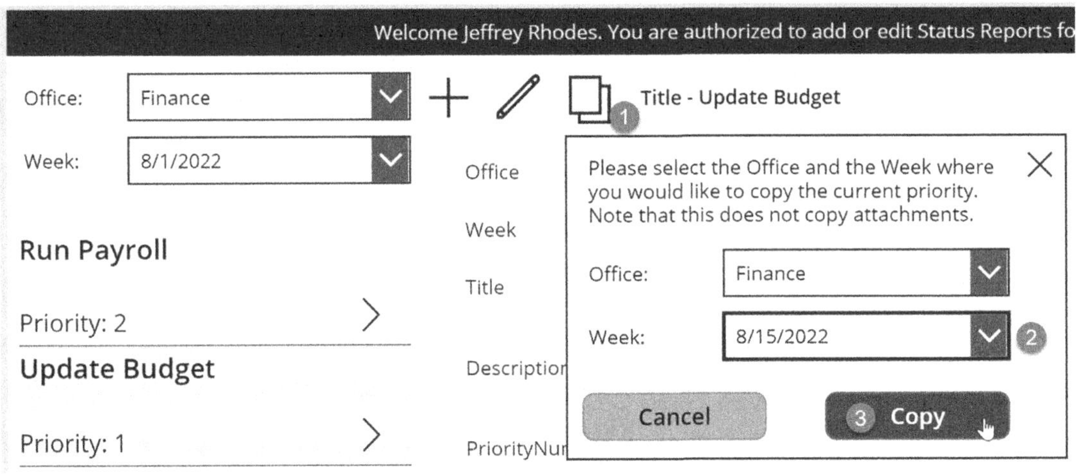

Figure 23-8. *Copying a record to a different office or week*

Our first task is to show the *Copy* button when a record is selected but not being edited.[9] For that, we set its *Visible* to:

```
(CountRows(ReportsGallery.AllItems) > 0 && !IsBlank(ReportsGallery.
Selected) && ReportForm.DisplayMode = DisplayMode.View)
```

Its *OnSelect* code is very simple, since its only job is to show our popup window:

```
Set(varShowCopy, true)
```

Our popup window consists of a *Container* control with the label, *Cancel* icon, *Office* label/drop-down box, *Week* label/drop-down box, *Cancel* button, and *Copy* button.

The container control has its *Visible* set to:

```
varShowCopy
```

You might recall back in Listing 23-1 that we set this variable to false. So the container will start hidden. Clicking the *Copy* button sets *varShowCopy* to true, showing the container and all its controls.

Both the *Close* icon and *Cancel* button have their *OnSelect* code to set the variable back to false and this hide the popup window:

```
Set(varShowCopy, false)
```

---

[9] This keeps us from copying a new record as well as the *DisplayMode* is *Edit* until the record is saved.

The *Office* and *Week* drop-down have the same *Items* properties as on the main screen, but NOT their *OnChange* and *OnSelect* code. We could do some logic to exclude the current office/week combination as the main screen, but this way they could copy a record to the same week and then edit from there if they wanted.

That leaves the *Copy* button. Listing 23-3 shows its *OnSelect* logic.

Listing 23-3. OnSelect code for the Copy button

```
Patch(
    StatusReport,
    Defaults(StatusReport),
    {
        Title: varCurrentItem.Title,
        Office: CopyOfficeDropDown.SelectedText,
        StatusWeekStartDate: Text(CopyWeeksDropDown.Selected.Value),
        Description : varCurrentItem.Description,
        'Target Date' : varCurrentItem.'Target Date',
        'Percentage Complete': varCurrentItem.'Percentage Complete',
        PriorityNumber: varCurrentItem.PriorityNumber
    }
);
Notify(
    "Copy is complete. Go to the selected office and week to view
or edit.",
    NotificationType.Success,
    2000
);
Set(
    varShowCopy,
    false
)
```

We go back to our old friend the *Patch()* function. We update our *StatusReport* data source and call the *Defaults()* method to use the default value for any columns for which we don't pass in values. We then set the value of each of our *StatusReport* columns except for *Attachments* (which can't be written via *Patch()*).[10] Notice how we used our *CopyOfficeDropDown* and *CopyWeeksDropDown* controls to get the "copy to" values for those items. For the rest, we use our *varCurrentItem* variable that holds the currently selected record.

We then use the *Notify()* method to display a "success" message for two seconds. Our last task is to hide the popup window by setting *varShowCopy* back to false.

Adding a Power BI Dashboard

Our associated Power BI report is similar to some of our past efforts. We connect to both of our lists using the 2.0 version[10] of the *SharePoint Online List* data source. We right-click the *StatusWeekStartDate* column to rename it to *Week* and change its type to *Date/Time,* as shown in Figure 23-9, so we can do some logic on which priorities to display.

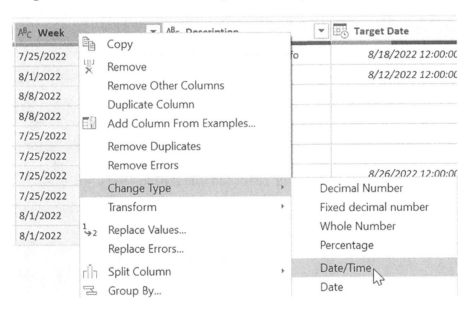

Figure 23-9. *Change type Status Week to DateTime*

---

[10] This has the current limitation of not exposing the URL of our attachments, however. If that is important, I would recommend going back to 1.0.

From there, we use some of the nice Power M functions in the Date namespace to create some custom columns that will help us filter our priority status reports. Figure 23-10 shows how we create an *IsInCurrentWeek* column:

```
Date.IsInCurrentWeek([Week])
```

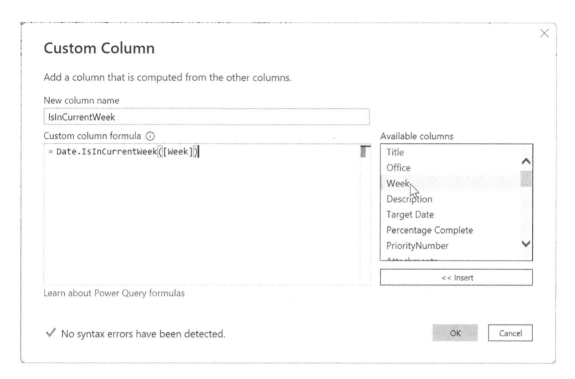

Figure 23-10. *Creating the IsInCurrentWeek column*

To give ourselves additional flexibility, we create these additional custom columns:

```
IsInFuture = [Week] > DateTime.From(DateTime.LocalNow())
```

```
IsInPastAndNotCurrentWeek = ([IsInCurrentWeek] = false) and (DateTime.
From(DateTime.LocalNow()) > [Week])
```

```
IsInPreviousMonth = Date.IsInPreviousMonth([Week])
```

```
IsInNext4Weeks = [IsInCurrentWeek] or Date.IsInNextNWeeks([Week], 4)
```

Although all of these result in either TRUE or FALSE displaying in the corresponding column, it is important to change their type to *True/False,* as otherwise there are some issues filtering on the columns, particularly after you publish to the Power BI service.

Figure 23-11 shows our visualizations. We use our *IsInNext4Weeks* column as a filter for our *Upcoming Month* page, our *IsInPastAndNotCurrentWeek* filter for the *Past* page, and the *IsInFuture* column for our *Future* page.

Figure 23-11. *Power BI Dashboard using the IsInPastAndNotCurrentWeek column*

The *All* page is to be used by Power Apps. For that, we first need to pin it to a dashboard, as shown in Figure 23-12.

Figure 23-12. *Pinning Power BI page to a Dashboard*

This gives the option to add to an existing dashboard or create a new one
(Figure 23-13).

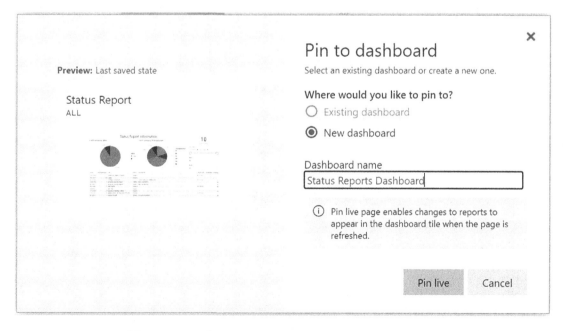

Figure 23-13. *Adding pinned page to a new dashboard*

Our last task for using our dashboard inside Power Apps is a way to filter it to match the Office(s) authorized for the user. Mohammed Adnan provides some good ideas in his "How to Pass Parameter in URL in Power BI Service" video.[11] The gist is that we need to use syntax like this:

```
<url>?filter=<tableName><columnName> eq '<value>'
```

There are some current limitations, such as neither the table name nor the column name allowing spaces, but luckily our design meets that. Our filter looks like this:

```
<url>?filter=StatusReport/Office eq 'IT'
```

After the browser URL-encodes the value, it looks like this:

```
<url>?filter=StatusReport%2FOffice%20eq%20%27IT%27
```

This is important as we need to use the URL-encoded version once we get back to Power Apps (you might skip forward to Figure 23-17 to see this). Figure 23-14 shows the filtered page. Notice how it only includes reports for the IT office.

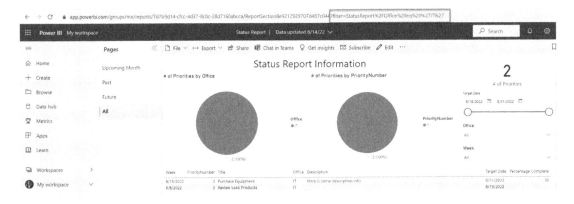

Figure 23-14. *Filtering the All page by Office*

We are now ready to return to Power Apps to complete our application.

---

[11] See www.youtube.com/watch?v=2FhaWkb9YcU.

Adding a Dashboard Screen in Power Apps

Back in Power Apps, we add a Dashboard screen and then insert a Power BI tile, as shown in Figure 23-15.

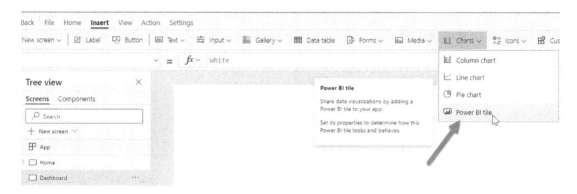

Figure 23-15.   *Adding a Power BI tile to Power Apps*

We are prompted to select our *Workspace, Dashboard,* and *Tile,* as shown in Figure 23-16.

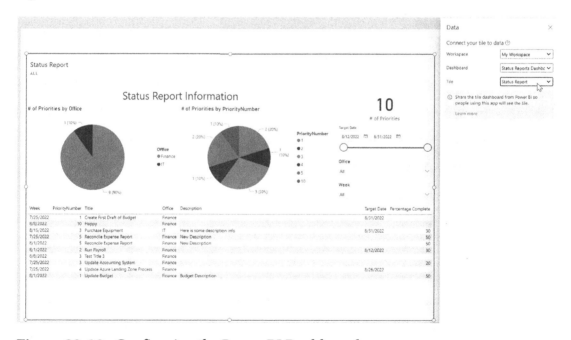

Figure 23-16.   *Configuring the Power BI Dashboard*

Notice how this currently includes all our priority reports. We add in our Office drop-down box and then edit the tile's *TileUrl* property to filter our report based on the selected office, as shown in Figure 23-17.

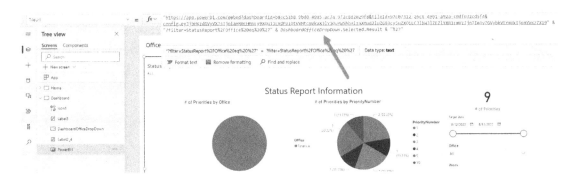

Figure 23-17. *Filtering the dashboard based on the selected Office*

Notice how we use the URL-encoded version as otherwise the filter does not work correctly. Figure 23-18 shows the final result. Notice how the Power BI dashboard matches the selected office (Finance).

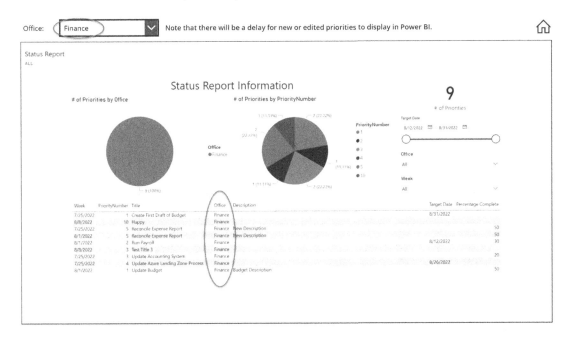

Figure 23-18. *Filtering the Power BI Dashboard*

We add a label to notify users that the dashboard will not show recent edits (since those will need to wait for the next scheduled refresh) and a *Home* button to return to the main screen. Here is its *OnSelect* code:

```
Navigate(Home)
```

Summary

In this chapter, we delved deeply into the Power Apps Form control and used it to add, edit, or copy status report data – all while prompting the user to save or cancel before proceeding if there are unsaved changes. We incorporated a significant amount of logic to make the application work as expected in regard to what item in the gallery is highlighted, limiting organization reports to authorized users, selecting from only the previous, current, and upcoming weeks, and much more. We then looked at how to visualize the data in Power BI and, very importantly in this case, filter it by organization. This allowed us to create a tile within our application and our Power BI dashboard by the selected organization. We will use a few of these techniques and many new ones in our final example in the next chapter, a scoring application and visualization.

CHAPTER 24

Creating a Scoring Application in Power Apps, SharePoint, and Power BI

In this chapter, we integrate Power Apps, SharePoint, and Power BI into a solution to solve another business problem – scoring award packages. We have a few new wrinkles related to updating multiple records (e.g., all the panelists for a particular nominee) and showing a list of all the scores for a scoring panel. In addition to reporting after the face, Power BI also helps us in real time to tell which panels have submitted scores and which might need extra assistance.

This example stems from converting an in-person process to a virtual one. Traditionally, there was a series of all-day award panels that were broken into 10+ boards consisting of three members each. Award packages were assigned to the boards for scoring. When we moved this process to Teams, the original design was a spreadsheet for each panel listing the packages, each member's score, and notes. This worked OK, but things got complicated as packages needed to move to a different board or if the membership of a board needed to change. This could happen at the last minute if members were sick, they knew the person being scored, etc. This involved going to each of the affected spreadsheets and making the changes. And when it came time to tabulating scores, the 40+ spreadsheets had to be combined and tabulated. With our new design, we can have a real-time Power BI report displaying the scores and, more importantly for the day of the event, showing which boards have submitted scores and which have not.

© Jeffrey M. Rhodes 2022
J. M. Rhodes, *Creating Business Applications with Microsoft 365*,
https://doi.org/10.1007/978-1-4842-8823-8_24

Setting Up the SharePoint List

In many of our examples, SharePoint has taken the place of a standard database. Here, however, SharePoint plays a more significant part as it is the interface for moving members and packages between boards and panels. We were able to import much of the data from another system as well. Figure 24-1 shows our *Scoring* list.

Nominee	Panelist	PanelNumber	BoardNumber	Rating1	Rating2	Comments
Bunny, Bugs	Jeffrey Rhodes	1	1	1	2	Panelist 1 Comments
Bunny, Bugs	Sue Rhodes	1	1	2	3	Panelist 2 Comments
Bunny, Bugs	James Rhodes	1	1	4	5	Panelist 3 Comments
Sam, Yosemite	Jeffrey Rhodes	1	1	5	5	
Sam, Yosemite	Sue Rhodes	1	1	4	4	
Sam, Yosemite	James Rhodes	1	1	3	3	
Duck, Daffy	Jeffrey Rhodes	1	2			
Duck, Daffy	Sue Rhodes	1	2			
Duck, Daffy	James Rhodes	1	2			

Figure 24-1. *SharePoint list with Nominee, Panelist, and other information*

The *Nominee* is a text column, showing the name associated with the award package. *Panelist* is a person column.[1] *PanelNumber*, *BoardNumber*, *Rating1*, and *Rating2* are all number columns. *Comments* is multiple lines of text. Changing a *Nominee* to a different board is a matter of choosing a different *Panelist* and updating the *PanelNumber* and *BoardNumber* values. Note that each nominee has three rows – one for each panelist in the board.

The next set of our work is in Power Apps.

---

[1] We brought in the panelists as guest members in our Microsoft 365 environment. This allowed us to make each panel a team with each board its own private channel. The package documents could then be securely shared by putting them in the private channel.

Building the Interface in Power Apps

A key to the design is that a facilitator will use the application and collect the scores and comments from each panelist.[2] So we want to select the Panel, the Board, and then each Nominee in turn. We then collect ratings and comments from each panelist. Once we save the results, we can click the Board Ratings button to display the combined ratings. We can make a screen capture of the results, put it in the breakout room chat, and have each panelist confirm their ratings. Figure 24-2 shows the application ready to enter scores for the nominee, Daffy Duck.

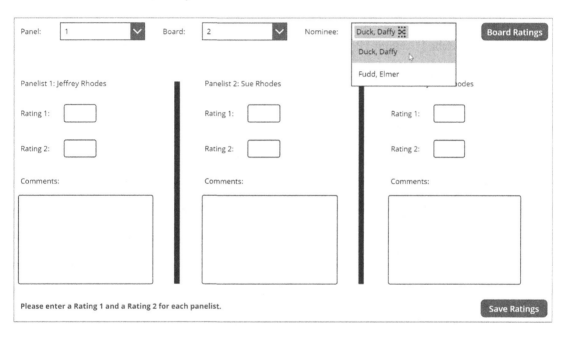

Figure 24-2. *The scoring application in Power Apps*

As is our standard practice, we initialize our variables in the App's *OnStart* event:

```
Set(varRatingRow1, Blank()); Set(varRatingRow2, Blank());
Set(varRatingRow3, Blank())
```

These variables will be used to keep track of our panelists and scores. We will set them in the following text.

---

[2] We contemplated panelists entering their own scores, but the fact that guest users are not licensed for Power Apps put the kibosh on that idea.

We want to list each of our panels in the upper-left drop-down box. Since the same panel is listed in multiple rows, using the *Distinct()* function for its *Items* property ensures that we only list each panel number once:

```
Distinct(Scoring, PanelNumber).Result
```

For the *Board* drop-down box, we want to only list boards that are in a particular panel. So we set its *Items* property to be:

```
Distinct(
    Filter(
        Scoring,
        PanelNumber = PanelBox.Selected.Result
    ),
    BoardNumber
).Result
```

We use the *Filter()* function to limit our list to only those records where the *PanelNumber* matches the panel we selected in our drop-down box.[3] From there, we again use the *Distinct()* function, which returns a one-column table named *Result*.

The Nominee combo box[4] follows this same pattern. We filter on both the Panel and Board in its Items property:

```
Distinct(
    Filter(
        Scoring,
        PanelNumber = PanelBox.Selected.Result && BoardNumber = BoardBox.
Selected.Result
    ),
    Nominee
).Result
```

---

[3] Notice that this is *Result* rather than *Value* since we are using the *Distinct()* function in its *Items* property.

[4] You might think this would also be a drop-down box, but *Person* columns work better with combo boxes, as we have seen in other chapters.

To make the names display and search correctly, we set both the *DisplayFields* and *SearchFields* properties of the combo box to be:

```
["Result"]
```

Since we only want to evaluate one nominee at a time, we set both *SelectMultiple* and *isSearchable* to *false*.

Things start getting a bit more complicated when we read in all three records at once. Listing 24-1 shows the *OnSelect* cod.

Listing 24-1. OnSelect code for the Nominee combo box

```
ClearCollect(
    colSelectedPanelRecords,
    Filter(
        Scoring,
        PanelNumber = PanelBox.Selected.Result && BoardNumber = BoardBox.
Selected.Result && Nominee = NomineeBox.Selected.Result
    )
);
Set(
    varNumItems,
    CountRows(colSelectedPanelRecords)
);
If(
    varNumItems > 0,
    Set(
        varRatingRow1,
        First(colSelectedPanelRecords)
    )
);
If(
    varNumItems > 1,
    Set(
        varRatingRow2,
        Last(
            FirstN(
```

```
                        colSelectedPanelRecords,
                        2
                )
            )
        )
    )
);
If(
    varNumItems > 2,
    Set(
        varRatingRow3,
        Last(
            FirstN(
                colSelectedPanelRecords,
                3
            )
        )
    )
);
```

We want to create a collection that holds the three records we want. We use *ClearCollect()* since we want to start over with panel, board, and nominee combination. We use a similar filter as before, but now add in the *Nominee*. So we are getting all the records for this panel, board, and nominee.

We'd like to create a separate variable for the records associated with each of our panelists. We need to work a little since Power Apps collections can't be accessed by item (0, 1, 2, etc.). We first set *varNumItems* to the count of our collection (we expect this to be 3). We then do some error checking and set *varRatingRow1* to the *First()* row of our collection as long as our count is greater than zero. Similarly, we make sure there is more than one row and then get that second row using this syntax:

```
If(
    varNumItems > 1,
    Set(
        varRatingRow2,
        Last(
            FirstN(
```

```
        colSelectedPanelRecords,
        2
      )
    )
  )
);
```

The key to this logic is the *FirstN()* function. It grabs the number of rows specified by the second parameter, 2 in this case. We then grab the *Last()* of these rows, which will be the second row.

We use this same logic to get the third row, just changing our parameter to *FirstN()* to 3.

Note that if we have a mistake in our SharePoint list and have more than three panelists assigned to this board, it will just skip those.

Moving to our panelist ratings, we can group the controls or place them in a container. We use our variables in their Visible properties. For the first panelist, we have:

```
!IsBlank(varRatingRow1)
```

So only if *varRatingRow1* is not blank will we show the corresponding ratings.

We set our label text to show the name of the corresponding panelist:

```
"Panelist 1: " & varRatingRow1.Panelist.DisplayName
```

We also use the *varRatingRow1*, *varRatingRow2*, and *varRatingRow3* variables in associating the Rating 1, Rating 2, and Comments text boxes with the corresponding list columns. Here is the *Default* for the *Panelist1_Rating1* box:

```
varRatingRow1.Rating1
```

We also set it to only accept a number. We could do some logic to make sure it is between 1 and 5, but since we have facilitators to enter the data, we don't go to that extra effort.

We want to show our *Please enter a Rating 1 and a Rating 2 for each panelist* label until there is a rating for each of the three panelists. We set its *Visible* property to:

```
(!IsBlank(varRatingRow1) && (Panelist1_Rating1.Text = "" || Panelist1_
Rating2.Text = "")) || (!IsBlank(varRatingRow2) && (Panelist2_Rating1.
Text = "" || Panelist2_Rating2.Text = "")) || (!IsBlank(varRatingRow3) &&
(Panelist3_Rating1.Text = "" || Panelist3_Rating2.Text = ""))
```

For each panelist, we only want to show the label once we have picked a nominee and thus initialized our variable (*varRatingRow1* for panelist 1). Then we show the label if *Rating 1* is blank or if *Rating 2* is blank.

We then use the visibility of this *ErrorLabel* in our *Save Ratings* button. Listing 24-2 shows its *OnSelect* code.

Listing 24-2. OnSelect code for the Save Rating button

```
If(
    ErrorLabel.Visible,
    false,
    If(
        !IsBlank(varRatingRow1),
        Patch(
            Scoring,
            varRatingRow1,
            {
                Rating1: Value(Panelist1_Rating1.Text),
                Rating2: Value(Panelist1_Rating2.Text),
                Comments: Panelist1_Comments.Text
            }
        )
    )
);
If(
    ErrorLabel.Visible,
    false,
    If(
        !IsBlank(varRatingRow2),
        Patch(
            Scoring,
            varRatingRow2,
            {
                Rating1: Value(Panelist2_Rating1.Text),
                Rating2: Value(Panelist2_Rating2.Text),
                Comments: Panelist2_Comments.Text
```

```
            }
        )
    )
);
If(
    ErrorLabel.Visible,
    false,
    If(
        !IsBlank(varRatingRow3),
        Patch(
            Scoring,
            varRatingRow3,
            {
                Rating1: Value(Panelist3_Rating1.Text),
                Rating2: Value(Panelist3_Rating2.Text),
                Comments: Panelist3_Comments.Text
            }
        )
    )
);
If(
    ErrorLabel.Visible,
    false,
    Notify(
        "This information has been saved.",
        NotificationType.Success
    )
)
)
```

This code is a bit longer since we want to *Patch()* all three records at once. We first check to see if our *ErrorLabel* is visible. If so, we don't have ratings for each and return *false*. We then check to make sure that our variable (*varRatingRow1* for the first panelist) is not blank. If not, we jump into *Patch()*. Our first parameter is our data source (*Scoring*). The second parameter is the record we are patching. We often use the *LookUp()* function to find the right one, but in this case we already have the variable we need: *varRatingRow1*, *varRatingRow2*, or *varRatingRow3*. From there, we just update *Rating1*, *Rating2*, and *Comments* to be the corresponding info from the form. Note how we use the *Value()* function to convert the *Text* of our rating boxes to a number.

Once we have done this for each of our three panelists, we use the *Notify()* function to tell the user the data has been saved. Figure 24-3 shows this notification.

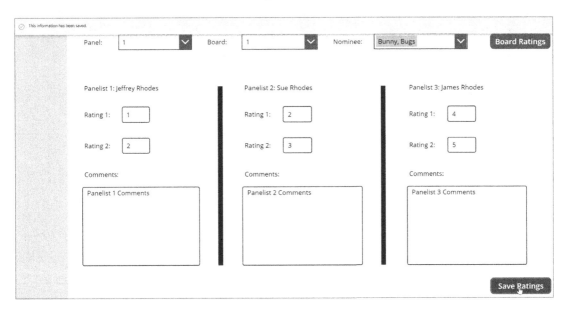

***Figure 24-3.** Notification of the successful saving of the board ratings*

Our last task is to display the ratings for all nominees. While this could be done in Power BI, the fact that there is a delay in the refreshing of reports doesn't make this the best choice. Instead, we want to stick directly with Power Apps.

We wait to show the *Board Ratings* button until we have a panel, board, and nominee combination have thus set *varRatingRow1* and the other variables. Its *Visible* is:

```
!IsBlank(varRatingRow1)
```

Listing 24-3 shows it *OnSelect* code.

***Listing 24-3.** OnSelect code for the Board Ratings button*

```
ClearCollect(
    colPanelRatings,
    ForAll(
        Filter(
```

```
            Scoring,
            PanelNumber = PanelBox.Selected.Result && BoardNumber =
BoardBox.Selected.Result
        ),
        {
            Nominee: Nominee,
            Panelist: Panelist,
            Rating1: Rating1,
            Rating2: Rating2,
            AverageRating: (Rating1 + Rating2) / 2,
            Comments: Comments
        }
    )
);
Navigate(DisplayResultsScreen)
```

We create a new collection, *colPanelRatings*, to store our ratings for the entire board. Since we want to loop through all the records (3 per nominee), we use *ForAll()*. As we have seen before, its first parameter is our data source. We use the same filter we used for our *Nominee* combo box:

```
        Filter(
            Scoring,
            PanelNumber = PanelBox.Selected.Result && BoardNumber =
BoardBox.Selected.Result
        ),
```

For each record, we run our "formula," which is the second parameter of *ForAll()*. We just add the columns we want. For those that already exist in our SharePoint list, we use the same names for simplicity: *Nominee, Panelist, Rating1, Rating2*, and *Comments*. But we don't have to include them all and can add additional ones as we want. Since we want *AverageRating*, we include that and do the math: *(Rating1 + Rating2) / 2*.

We then navigate to our *DisplayResultsScreen*, shown in Figure 24-4.

Nominee	Panelist	Rating1	Rating2	AverageRating	Comments
Bunny, Bugs	Jeffrey Rhodes	1	2	1.5	Panelist 1 Comments
Bunny, Bugs	Sue Rhodes	2	3	2.5	Panelist 2 Comments
Bunny, Bugs	James Rhodes	4	5	4.5	Panelist 3 Comments
Sam, Yosemite	Jeffrey Rhodes	5	5	5	
Sam, Yosemite	Sue Rhodes	4	4	4	
Sam, Yosemite	James Rhodes	3	3	3	

Figure 24-4. *Board ratings in the DisplayResultsScreen*

The most important part of the screen is the *Data Table* control. Much like the *Form* control we saw previously, you connect it to the data source (in this case the *colPanelRatings* collection we created in Listing 24-3). You can then add or edit fields to determine what will be shown in each column. This is shown in Figure 24-5.

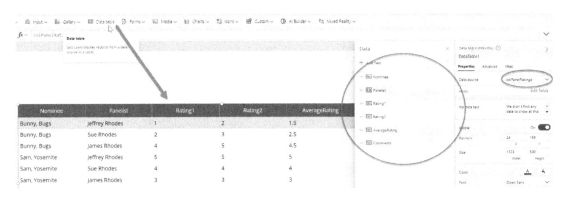

Figure 24-5. *Configuring the Data Table control*

When you first do this, the Panelist shows up as *[object Object]*. That is because it is a Person object, and we haven't told it which of its properties to display. As shown in Figure 24-6, we select the column and change its *Text* property to include the *DisplayName*:

```
ThisItem.Panelist.DisplayName
```

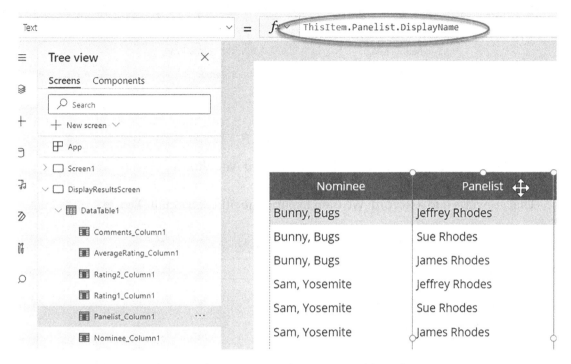

Figure 24-6. *Using the DisplayName in the Data Table column*

The last piece is our *Home* button. We set its *OnSelect* code to return to our entry screen so the facilitator can collect more scores:

```
Navigate(Screen1)
```

Let's jump over to Power BI to see what kind of insights we can gain.

Adding a Power BI Dashboard

We again connect to our list using the 2.0 version of the *SharePoint Online List* data source. Since *Panelist* is a person column in SharePoint, we *Expand to New Rows,* as shown in Figure 24-7.

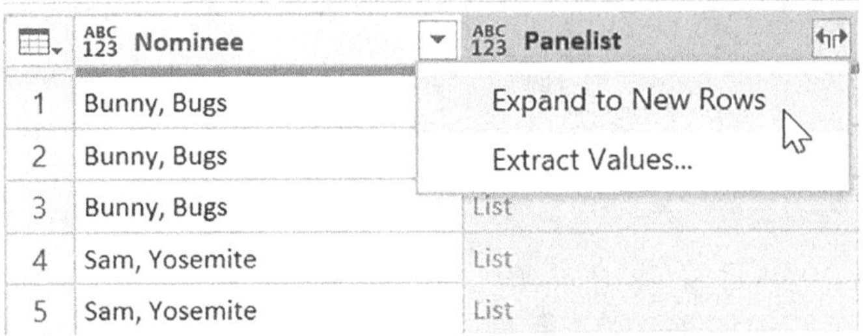

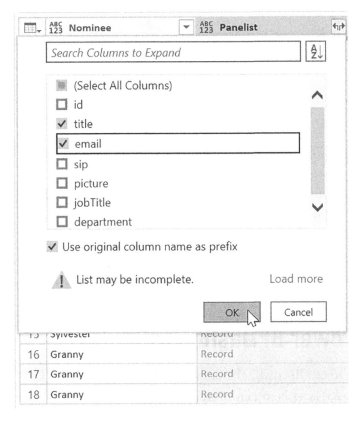

Figure 24-7. *Expanding the Panelist Column to New Rows*

That converts it to a Record. We then expand the title and email (Figure 24-8).

Figure 24-8. *Loading the title and email from the Panelist records*

We rename *title* to *Participant* and *email* to *Participant Email*.

We then create an *Average Score* custom column using the same math we used in Power Apps (Figure 24-9).

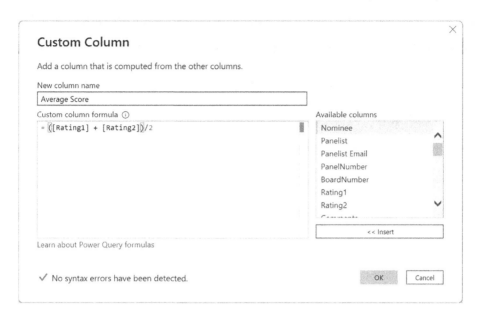

Figure 24-9. *Average Score custom column*

We change the type of the column to *Decimal Number,* as shown in Figure 24-10, since we decimal points will be important.

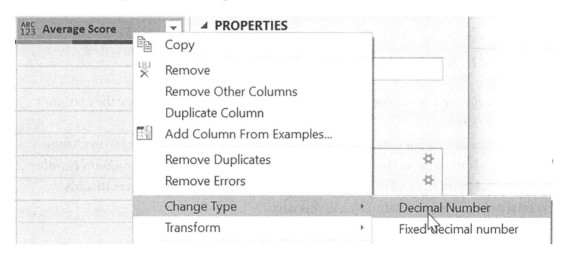

Figure 24-10. *Changing the Column Type to Decimal Number*

Since one of our key reasons for creating the visualizations is to tell in real-time[5] what boards have yet to be scored, we create a special *IsMissingScore* custom column (Figure 24-11).

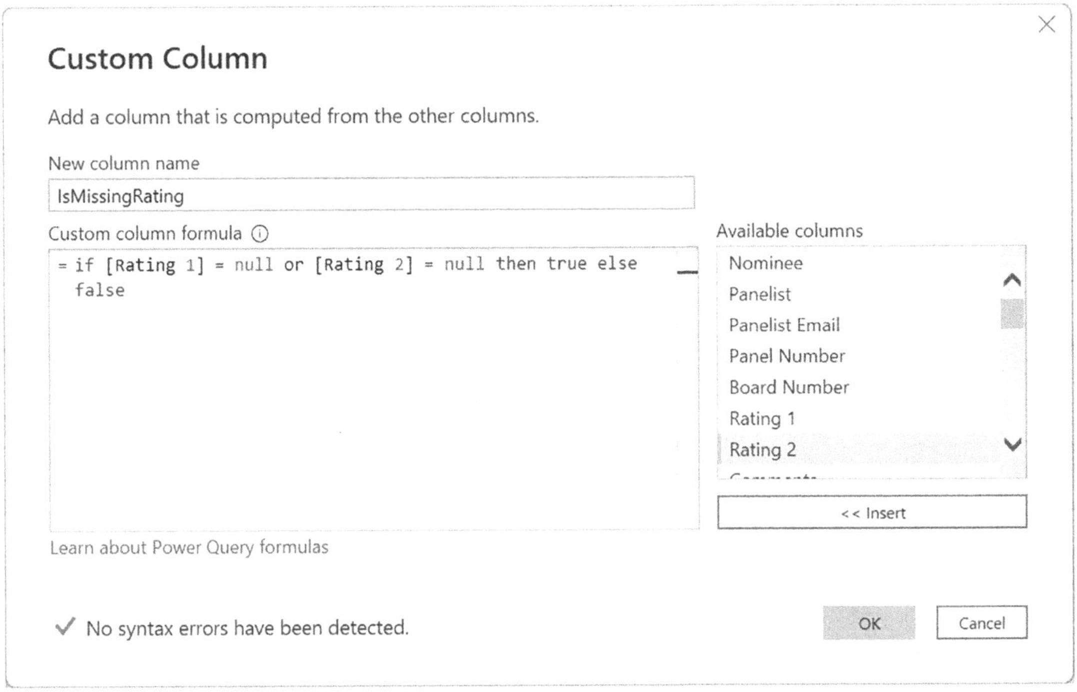

Custom Column

Add a column that is computed from the other columns.

New column name

IsMissingRating

Custom column formula ⓘ

```
= if [Rating 1] = null or [Rating 2] = null then true else
  false
```

Available columns

Nominee
Panelist
Panelist Email
Panel Number
Board Number
Rating 1
Rating 2

<< Insert

Learn about Power Query formulas

✓ No syntax errors have been detected.   OK   Cancel

Figure 24-11.   IsMissingScore custom column

If either *Rating 1* or *Rating 2* is null, we set it to true. We then change the column's type to *True/False*.

This takes care of our data transformations. We next go to the Data tab to change the display of our data. As shown in Figure 24-12, we set *Panel Number, Board Number, Rating 1*, and *Rating 2* to all display as *Whole numbers*. Otherwise, Power BI adds decimal points, which is distracting in this case.

---

[5] We don't want to rely on scheduled refreshes when we are tracking the boards in real-time. Instead, the user can manually refresh the data set periodically or even view the report in Power BI Desktop and refresh there.

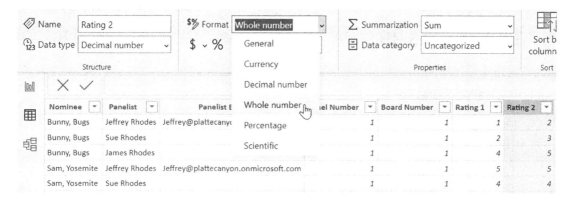

Figure 24-12. *Changing Panel Number, Board Number, Rating 1, and Rating 2 to Whole number formatting*

It will be useful to have average score data per nominee, board, panel, and overall. That's where the ability of measures to evaluate to the context of the current data is so important. Figure 24-13 shows how we create the *Average Rating 1* measure.

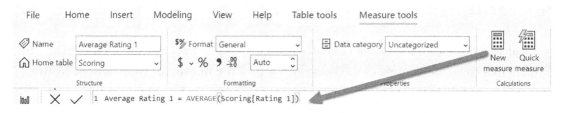

Figure 24-13. *Creating an Average Score Measure*

We similarly create measures for *Average Rating 2* and *Overall Average*:

```
Average Rating 1 = AVERAGE(Scoring[Rating 1])
```

```
Average Rating 2 = AVERAGE(Scoring[Rating 2])
```

```
Overall Average = AVERAGE(Scoring[Average Score])
```

Figure 24-14 shows these measures in action as well as slicers for *Missing Rating, Nominee, Panelist,* and *Panel Number/Board Number*. The Missing Rating slicer uses the *IsMissingRating* column discussed earlier.

Figure 24-14. *Scoring Reports - All Records*

It also includes a bar chart of *Overall Average by Nominee* as well as a table of all our data. In this case, the context of the measures are all the nominees with ratings. Notice how this currently includes all of our priority reports. Notice how the values change when we select *Panel 1 – Board 1* in Figure 24-15.

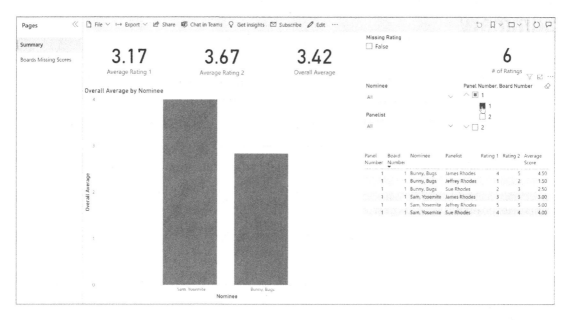

Figure 24-15. *Scoring Report for one panel showing context of measures changing*

This makes it very easy to compare our averages as we drill down and slice our data.

Even though we can limit to *Missing Data* on our current page, that information is so important we add it as a page-level filter on its own page. That allows us to have a single spot for seeing our unscored panels (Figure 24-16).

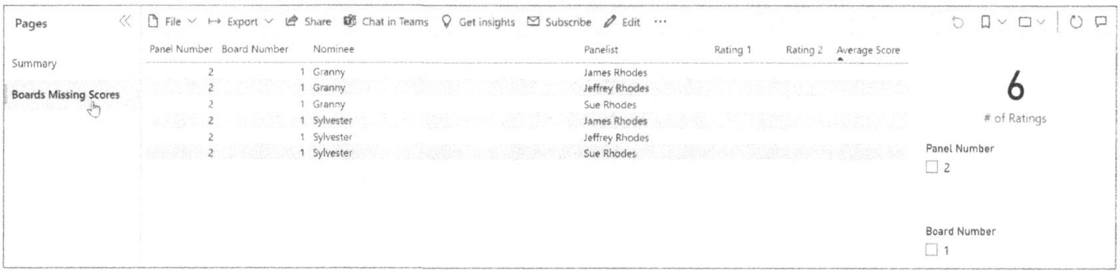

Figure 24-16. *Boards Missing Scores visualization*

Summary

In this chapter, we learned techniques like filtering our drop-down and combo boxes (for Boards, Panels, and Nominees), creating variables and collections to add and edit scores/comments for three panelists at once, patching this data back to SharePoint, and aggregating all the scores for the nominees and panelists in a particular panel and showing in a data table. On the Power BI side, we saw how to create a custom column for the average score for each nominee by panelist and then create measures to calculate averages *across* panelists and nominees. We demonstrated how the context of the measures adjusted based on the slicers and drill-down selections. We also examined how to monitor the boards in real time by creating an *IsMissingScore* custom column and a corresponding *Boards Missing Scores* page-level filter.

Conclusion

Thanks for joining me on this journey. Hopefully, I have shared my passion for using these Microsoft 365 tools for creating business applications that improve processes, boost productivity, reduce errors, automate tasks, and make work more fun. I look forward to hearing about the awesome applications you build for your organizations.

Index

A

Adaptive Card JSON, 211, 213

Adaptive cards, 208, 210, 211, 214, 215

AddColumns() method, 221

AdditionalGuidance, 202, 210

AllData column, 280, 281, 284

AttachmentsControl, 233, 235

AttachmentsGallery, 225–227, 233, 235

Automated cloud flow, 298

    add list, 307

    Apply to each, 39

    approvals, 34, 35

    ApprovalStatus variable, 42, 43

    approval values, 35, 36

    approved email, 40, 41

    condition and compose, 302

    configure, 298

    control/condition, 37, 38

    copy, 299

    creation, 32, 33

    custom flow, 299

    file name/content, 308

    Form Id, 300

    JSON output, 303

    looping, 305

    Office 365 Outlook, 39, 40

    parse JSON, 304

    path/name, 306

    populated approval request, 36, 37

    rejected email, 40, 42

    Responses Approver response, 38

    SharePoint, 301

    SharePoint list item, 43, 44

    testing

        approval form, 45, 46

        debugging/logic path, 48, 49

        email, 46–48

        notification, 44, 45

    triggering, 33, 34

B

BorderColor property, 101, 232

Built-in SharePoint, 101, 265

C

Cascading Style Sheet (CSS), 8

Christmas.jpg, 235, 241

Class sign-up solution

    Delete Registration Screen, 168

    delete screen

        gallery's Items property, 168

        IsSelected property, 169

        OnSelect code, 169

        Remove() method, 170

        Visible property, 169

    home screen

        colUserTraining, 161

        delegation warnings, 160

        Delete Existing Registration, 158, 159

    new screen

        Already Registered label, 164

© Jeffrey M. Rhodes 2022

J. M. Rhodes, *Creating Business Applications with Microsoft 365*,

https://doi.org/10.1007/978-1-4842-8823-8

S

Printed in the United States
by Baker & Taylor Publisher Services